W9-AYZ-831

THE DECLINE OF HELL

THE DECLINE
OF HELL

*Seventeenth-Century Discussions
of Eternal Torment*

by
D. P. WALKER

The University of Chicago Press

Library of Congress Catalog Card Number: 64-19849

THE UNIVERSITY OF CHICAGO PRESS, CHICAGO 37, U.S.A.
ROUTLEDGE & KEGAN PAUL LTD, LONDON, E.C.4, ENGLAND.
THE UNIVERSITY OF TORONTO PRESS, TORONTO 5, CANADA.

© *1964 by D. P. Walker.   Published 1964.*
Composed and printed in England.

CONTENTS

CONTENTS

ACKNOWLEDGEMENTS

I WISH to express my thanks to scholars and friends who have helped me in the writing of this book. Dr Gotthold Müller of Tübingen has very generously given me bibliographical information of the greatest value. Professor Ernst Benz, Professor De Sola Pinto and Dr W. H. Barber have also given me valuable help. Gerard Van Het Reve, M.O.D.B., was kind enough to read through and criticize the manuscript of this book. Finally, I am most grateful to my colleagues at the Warburg Institute for their help and encouragement, and especially to Professor Bing and Miss Frances Yates for their valuable criticism.

D. P. WALKER

October, 1963.

Part One

GENERAL

Chapter I

INTRODUCTION

(i) SECRECY AND DISHONESTY

It is but too visible, that since men have learnt to wear off the Apprehension of Eternal Punishment, the Progress of Impiety and Immorality among us has been very considerable . . . Unusual crimes have appeared; Uncommon heights of Wickedness have been attained . . .

THIS passage occurs in a sermon preached before the University of Oxford on Sunday, March 21st, 1741 by William Dodwell.[1] This clergyman may have been unduly pessimistic, but it is true that by the fourth decade of the 18th century the doctrine of eternal torment for the damned was being challenged openly, though seldom, and that in the 17th century a few attacks on it, mostly anonymous, had appeared. This is not true of the preceding centuries. In the early 3rd century A.D. Origen, in his *De Principiis*,[2] put forward a scheme for the ultimate salvation of everyone. This eminent Greek Father was, of course, condemned as heretical.[3] His doctrine was revived in the 9th

[1] William Dodwell, *The Eternity of future Punishment asserted and vindicated. In answer to Mr Whiston's late Treatise on that Subject. In Two Sermons . . .*, Oxford, 1743, p. 85.
[2] V. infra, pp. 12 seq.
[3] V. infra, p. 21.

3

century by Scotus Erigena, whose writings were also condemned.[1] But it is not until the mid 17th century that one finds explicit attacks on the orthodox doctrine of hell.

Now, considered from moral, logical, and metaphysical points of view, the orthodox hell has its strong and its weak points, which will be examined in the next two chapters. Most people today would, I think, agree that the weak points outweigh the strong. We are thus justified in asking: why did the doctrine of hell remain almost unchallenged for so long a time, and why did it begin to lose its hold in the 17th century?

In this book I shall suggest several answers to both questions. The most obvious answer to the first question is the very strong scriptural authority for the doctrine.[2] But a more fundamental reason for the long triumph of hell was the firm and almost universal belief in its value as a deterrent in this life. It was thought that, if the fear of eternal punishment were removed, most people would behave without any moral restraint whatever and that society would collapse into an anarchical orgy. The association between atheism, which of course includes disbelief in hell, and immoral behaviour was so strong that it was usual to infer that any thoroughly depraved person must be an atheist.[3] This is one reason why atheists and Socinians, who were supposed to believe in the annihilation of the wicked, were generally considered outside the bounds of even the broadest religious tolerance; since they were socially dangerous, it was the business of the state to eliminate them. Conversely, it was claimed that only criminals and debauchees could have any motive for questioning the doctrine; Dom Sinsart, for example, in his *Defense du Dogme Catholique sur l'Eternité des Peines* (1748), writes:[4]

[1] Though Scotus asserted an Origenist restoration of all things, and reduced the torments of hell to those of a bad conscience, he allowed the latter to be eternal, v. M. Cappuyns, *Jean Scot Erigène*, Louvain and Paris, 1933, pp. 247, 365, 374-7.
[2] Cf. infra, p. 19.
[3] Cf. D. P. Walker, 'Ways of dealing with Atheists', *Bibliothèque d'Humanisme et Renaissance*, 1955, T. XVII, p. 256.
[4] Strasbourg, 1748, pp. vii–viii: 'Je ne balance pas à dire que le systême qui borne les peines de l'autre vie, n'a été enfanté que par des cœurs vicieux & corrompus. En effet quel interêt auroit un bon Chrétien à tordre l'Ecriture pour la détourner du sens qu'elle offre naturellement? . . . Une bonne conscience n'a aucun interêt à inventer des chicanes sur une chose qui ne la touche point. C'est donc au crime & au crime obstiné, que cette opinion doit le jour . . .'

4

I do not hesitate to say that the system which limits the punishments of the afterlife has been conceived only by vicious and corrupt hearts. Indeed what motive would a good Christian have in distorting Scripture so as to divert it from the meaning it naturally presents ? . . . A good conscience has no motive for inventing quibbles about a matter which does not concern it. It is, therefore, to crime, to stubborn crime, that this opinion owes its existence.

This is the reason why nearly all discussions of hell until well into the 18th century are veiled by a mist of secrecy and dishonesty.

The peculiar dangers attached to any discussion of the eternity of hell were such that they produced a theory of double truth: there is a private, esoteric doctrine, which must be confined to a few intellectuals, because its effect on the mass of people will be morally and socially disastrous, and a public, exoteric doctrine, which these same intellectuals must preach, although they do not believe it. The second kind of truth is not, of course, a truth at all, but a useful, pragmatically justifiable lie. This secrecy was already being advocated by Origen, who, when discussing hell in his *Contra Celsum*, forbore to go beyond the mere statement that it was a place of punishment, because,[1]

to ascend beyond this is not expedient, for the sake of those who are with difficulty restrained, even by fear of eternal punishment, from plunging into any degree of wickedness, and into the flood of evils which result from sin.

Thus people who had doubts about the eternity of hell, or who had come to disbelieve in it, refrained from publishing their doubts not only because of the personal risk involved, but also because of genuine moral scruples. In the 17th century disbelief in eternal torment seldom reached the level of a firm conviction, but at most was a conjecture, which one might wish to be true; it is therefore understandable that one should hesitate to plunge the world into moral anarchy for the sake of only conjectural truth. This being so, it may seem surprising that we should have any evidence for the esoteric doctrine at all; for

[1] Origen, *Contra Celsum*, VI, xxvi, cf. V, xv (Migne, *Patr. Gr.*, T. 11, col. 1332, 1203; *The Writings of Origen*, trans. F. Crombie, (Anti-Nicene Christian Library), Edinburgh, 1872, Vol. II, pp. 364, 283).

it is obviously foolish to publish an esoteric truth, if one wishes people to go on believing the exoteric doctrine. In fact, the evidence we have is from posthumous and anonymous publications, manuscripts and hearsay. The one exception to this statement is the writings of certain chiliasts;[1] why this was so we shall see later.

Examples of the secrecy and dishonesty which surrounded the subject of hell will appear throughout this book. There is one surprising example of someone publicly preaching both an exoteric and an esoteric doctrine. Tillotson, in a famous sermon preached before the Queen in 1690,[2] a few months before he became Archbishop of Canterbury, argued that, although the Scriptures plainly threaten the wicked with eternal punishment, God would not be breaking His word, if He did not carry out this threat; for the failure to execute a threat of vengeance is not considered morally wrong, as is the failure to fulfill a promise of reward. But at the same time he strongly urged that it would be unwise to disbelieve in the eternity of hell and pernicious to preach this disbelief.

The double doctrine is seen even more clearly in Thomas Burnet's *De Statu Mortuorum*.[3] Burnet is more firmly opposed to the eternity of hell, and argues against it at great length. But he too cannot reach absolute certainty on the point, and very strongly advises that only the traditional doctrine should be divulged to the common people. Indeed Burnet sees a tradition of esoteric and exoteric truth from Scripture and the Fathers onwards, and terms such as 'veritas arcana', as opposed to 'veritas vulgaris', run like a refrain through his book.

That some religious or philosophical truths should be confined to an intellectual aristocracy and veiled from the vulgar is an ancient and respectable theory and practice, both before and after Christianity. But this case is different and more dangerous. For with regard to hell the public, exoteric doctrine is not merely a veiled, parabolic form of the esoteric truth; it is another, directly contradictory truth, or lie. Poets and religious

---

[1] And a few works which appeared during the Commonwealth (v. infra, pp. 93, 104).
[2] John Tillotson, *A Sermon Preach'd before the Queen at White-Hall, March 7th, 1689–90* (on Matt. XXV, 46), London, 1690.
[3] Cf. infra, Ch. IX.

writers who concealed their meaning in symbols, fables and allegories could not be accused of lying, and they could and did appeal to the example of Christ preaching in parables, that seeing they might not see and hearing they might not understand. But any preacher threatening his congregation with an eternity of torment, in which he does not believe himself, is quite plainly a liar. Moreover this particular kind of double doctrine involves not only the preacher in lying but God as well, as Tillotson's suggestion does. For the threats in the Scriptures are quite clear. Even if one argues, as Burnet and others did with some success, that the word used for 'eternal', αἰώνιος, in Matthew XXV and other crucial texts, need not mean more than age-long, the veracity of God is still impugned, since the Holy Ghost would not have caused such an ambiguous word to be used, if the misunderstanding were not intended, nor would He have allowed the misunderstanding to continue in all Christian churches for over a thousand years.

Now to concede that the Scriptures contain useful lies, or deliberately deceptive ambiguities, is to undermine the basis of revealed truth; a revealed useful lie is not a revealed truth. It is moreover to follow in the footsteps of Spinoza, who in his *Tractatus Theologico-politicus* (1670) presented the Bible as consisting almost wholly of lies useful to the vulgar; the few useful truths it contains are superfluous for intellectuals in whom the natural light of reason shines clearly. The influence of this work of Spinoza's on French clandestine anti-Christian literature of the 18th century was enormous.[1] The double doctrine of hell is the thin end of a very large wedge.

It is interesting that Luther, in discussing eternal damnation, realized the supreme importance of preserving the veracity of God. In a letter, written and published in 1522,[2] he deals with the question: whether anyone who has died without faith can be saved; the answer to which is of course: No. He begins by admitting that to human reason God's judgments seem harsh and unjust, and recalling that this has led Origen and people of

[1] See Ira O. Wade, *The Clandestine Organization and Diffusion of Philosophic Ideas in France from 1700 to 1750*, Princeton, 1938, p. 269.
[2] Luther, *Werke*, Kritische Gesamtausgabe, Weimar, 1907, Bd. 10², pp. 322 seq.

7

his own day to propose universal salvation. But, he says, in answering this question,[1]

> one must separate widely our way of thinking from God's truth, and take care that we do not make God a liar, but far rather allow that all men, angels and devils will be damned than that God should not be truthful in His words.

He then goes on to advise that this matter should not be discussed with intelligent intellectuals whose faith being young and weak is probably unable to stand the shock, but only with simple, deeply pious people whose faith being firmly established is able easily to pluck out the eye of natural reason. This version of the usual secrecy about hell differs from later esotericism in two ways. First, it is the simple-minded, not the intellectuals, who are the initiates to whom the truth is to be revealed. Secondly, eternal damnation is this esoteric truth, to be confined to initiates, instead of being the exoteric doctrine which is to be publicly preached.

(ii) GROUPS OF WRITERS

Those who doubted or denied the doctrine of eternal torment belonged to various religious traditions. Although these will be treated in more detail in the Second Part of this book, it may help the reader of the First Part if I give here a brief description of them.

The Socinians' main heresy was Arianism, that is, the denial that the Son is consubstantial with the Father; but they were also accused of disbelief in the eternity of hell, and at least some of them did believe in the eventual annihilation of the wicked. They flourished during the late 16th and early 17th century in Poland, where, until the 1640's, they were officially tolerated. After this date they were dispersed throughout Europe. They published very little against the orthodox doctrine of hell. Indeed, the chief importance of the Socinians for our purposes is a negative one: because of their Arianism and their radically

---

[1] Luther, ibid., p. 322: 'Aber hyrauff zu anttwortten, musz man unszer duncken und Gottis warheyt gar weyt sundern und yhe darob halten, das wyr Gott nicht lügen straffen, sondern viel eher zu lassen, das alle menschen, engel unnd teuffel verloren werden, denn das Gott nicht sollt warhafftig seyn ynn seynen wortten.'

rationalist theology, religious tolerance stopped short of them even in Protestant countries, and the association with them of the denial of eternal torment made Protestants reluctant to attack the orthodox hell lest they be accused of Socinianism.

The English Arians, though their christology was similar, were distinct in outlook and origin from the Socinians; but they too disbelieved in the eternity of hell. Most of them, such as Newton, Locke and Samuel Clarke, did not publish their heterodox views, and we know about them only from manuscript sources and reliable hearsay. William Whiston alone, Newton's successor as Professor of Mathematics at Cambridge, publicly defended both his Arianism and his denial of eternal torment. He was also an enthusiastic chiliast.

The group of thinkers known as the Cambridge Platonists reacted sharply against the Calvinist predestinationism in which they had been brought up by developing an extremely liberal theology, heavily Neoplatonic and concentrated on moral values. The most famous of these, Benjamin Whichcote, Ralph Cudworth,[1] and Henry More, did not deny the eternity of hell, though their religious outlook pointed in this direction; but several thinkers closely associated with them did attack this doctrine. Among these were two friends, Peter Sterry and Jeremiah White, who wrote outstanding works in favour of universal salvation, and who, unlike the other Cambridge Platonists, remained predestinationists. A group of Henry More's friends believed, like him, in preexistence of the soul, and, unlike him, in universal salvation: Lady Anne Conway, Francis Mercurius Van Helmont, Joseph Glanvill, and George

---

[1] MS. Add. 4983 in the British Museum consists of interesting notes on eternal torment and arguments against it. It is one of a series (Add. 4978–87), once in the possession of Lady Masham, Cudworth's daughter. Some of these are in Cudworth's hand, but not Add. 4983, and some correspond to Birch's description of Cudworth's MSS. in his *Life* of Cudworth, but not Add. 4983. The series is attributed to Cudworth in Ayscough's catalogue (1783), an attribution accepted by J. A. Passmore in his *Ralph Cudworth, An Interpretation*, Cambridge, 1951. Professor Passmore has recently informed me that he is now doubtful about this attribution. The Keeper of Manuscripts at the British Museum, Mr T. C. Skeat, kindly allowed me to look at descriptions of these MSS. made about fifty years ago, with a view to publishing a new catalogue. The description of Add. 4983 is: 'not in Cudworth's hand, but mostly in one that occurs occasionally, apparently as that of an editor, in the five preceding volumes.' Since there is as yet no hard evidence on the authorship of this MS., I shall not discuss it.

Rust, who was probably the author of the anonymous *Letter of Resolution concerning Origen* (1661). Finally there are two thinkers less closely associated with the Cambridge Platonists: Thomas Burnet, whose treatise on the afterlife has already been mentioned, and Shaftesbury, whose *Characteristics* contain an attack on the moral basis of heaven and hell.

Towards the end of the 17th century the subject of hell and its eternity played an important, though not predominant part in French religious polemics. The chief protagonists were the following. Pierre Bayle, usually in the disguise of a strict Calvinist, refuted, tirelessly and efficiently, theologians of every opinion, but especially his personal enemy Pierre Jurieu, the self-appointed leader of the Protestants exiled by the revocation of the Edict of Nantes (1685), who was an orthodox, if imprudent Calvinist. Other victims of Bayle were two rationalist theologians, Saurin and Jaquelot, and Jean Le Clerc, head of the Remonstrant or Arminian[1] Seminary in Amsterdam. Of these only Le Clerc was, perhaps, a believer in universal salvation. The Arminians, like the Cambridge Platonists, had reacted against the moral harshness of Calvinist predestination, and their theology too was liberal, but more Erasmian than Neoplatonic. Except for Le Clerc, and Episcopius, the founder of their seminary, they did not cast doubts on eternal torment.

In his *Dictionnaire Historique et Critique* (1697) Bayle included articles in which he proposed objections, claimed to be insuperable, that a Manichaean might bring against any system based on a good and omnipotent God. These started a long controversy, in which the question of eternal torment was discussed. Le Clerc answered the objections by suggesting a 'reformed' version of Origenist universal salvation. The debate culminated in Leibniz's *Théodicée* (1710). Malebranche may be regarded as taking part in it, since his system of theodicy was much discussed and is very similar to that of Leibniz.

The Philadelphians were a small chiliastic society led by a blind widow, Mrs Jane Lead, who had learnt her mysticism from Dr John Pordage, a follower of Jakob Boehme. In 1694

---

[1] These two names designate the same group of people. Arminius was Professor of Theology at Leiden from 1603 to 1609. His followers in 1610 made a public protest against the doctrine of strict predestination; hence the name 'Remonstrant'. They were condemned at the Synod of Dordrecht (1618–19).

she published a small treatise, *Enochian Walks with God,* in which the doctrine of universal salvation was propounded. In the same year she was joined by a young clergyman, Richard Roach, who carried on the movement after her death in 1704. In 1712 Roach published Jeremiah White's treatise, *The Restoration of All Things,* accompanying it with a long preface.

From 1694 onwards Mrs Lead's works were regularly translated into German and published at Amsterdam, at the expense of a statesman at the Prussian court, Freiherr von Knyphausen, who was also the patron of a Pietist and chiliast theologian, Johann Wilhelm Petersen. Through Knyphausen, Petersen and his wife were sent the manuscript of one of Mrs Lead's works, containing an exposition of the doctrine of universal salvation. They were soon converted to it, and from 1700 onwards made active propaganda for it. In 1702 the English sent a proselytizing missionary to Germany; but, as in England, their movement had little success. The Petersens, on the other hand, made many converts, and their movement continued to grow after their death.

(iii) THE EARLY FATHERS

An aspect of the Renaissance which has hitherto been somewhat neglected is the revival of interest in the early, pre-Nicene Fathers of the Church. It is relevant to our subject in several ways, the most obvious of which is that it directed attention towards Origen's doctrine of universal salvation.

The revival of interest in Origen is part of a general renaissance of the early Fathers; nevertheless the case of Origen, compared with other early Fathers, such as Justin, Irenaeus, Lactantius, or Clement of Alexandria, is exceptional.[1] Even in Christian antiquity Origen's position was oddly uncertain and showed striking contrasts. On the one hand, his reputation and

---

[1] On Origen see: *Dictionnaire de Théologie Catholique,* ed. Vacant and Mangenot, Paris, 1931, T. 11, Ière Partie, art. Origène (by G. Bardy), art. Origénisme (by G. Fritz); J. Daniélou, *Origen,* tr. W. Mitchell, London and New York, 1955.

On the revival of Origenism see: Edgar Wind, 'The Revival of Origen', in *Studies in Art and Literature for Belle da Costa Greene,* ed. Dorothy Miner, Princeton U.P., 1954; D. P. Walker, 'Origène en France', in *Courants Religieux et Humanisme à la fin du xvᵉ et au début du xviᵉ siècle* (Colloque de Strasbourg, 1957), Paris, 1959.

INTRODUCTION

influence as a theologian, especially as an exegete, was enormous; on the other, he was condemned as heretical by the Council of Alexandria in 400 and by the Fifth Oecumenical Council at Constantinople in 553.[1] St Jerome praises him warmly and fully acknowledges his debt towards him; but Jerome, from 495 onwards, in the course of his controversy with Rufinus, the defender and translator of Origen, violently attacks the errors of his former master and treats him as an heresiarch. In consequence of this curious combination of great fame as a theologian and of ill fame as an officially condemned heretic, a source of Arianism, Pelagianism, and fantastic eschatology, a large part of his works has been preserved, he continued to be read and cited, though with caution, and his most daring and unorthodox work, the De Principiis (περὶ ἀρχῶν), has survived, but only in Rufinus's Latin translation.[2]

The whole of Origen's eschatology is based on two principles:[3] first, the justice and goodness of an omnipotent Creator; secondly, the absolute free will of every rational being (man, animated star, angel, demon). It is by extending the scope of free will beyond all bounds that he solves the problem of the existence of evil, and that he safeguards the justice and goodness of God. All differences of nature between individual men, and between the various orders of rational beings, are explained as resulting from the exercise of free will by the creature in question. Since many of the most important of these differences are congenital, it is necessary to suppose preexistence of the soul. God loved Jacob and hated Esau even before they were born; in order not to attribute capricious injustice to God, one must assume, not only that He foresaw the former's virtues and the latter's defects, but also that Jacob and Esau deserved their congenital characters for the good or bad actions, freely chosen, which they did in a former life. This former life

[1] V. infra, p. 21.
[2] See Origen, *Werke*, ed. Koetschau, Leipzig, 1913, Bd. V, pp. cxviii seq.
[3] The fullest exposition of Origen's eschatology is in Book III of his *De Principiis*. Rufinus's translation, which tones down Origen's bolder speculations, can in many places be checked against St Jerome's translation, fragments of which are preserved in a letter to Avitus (see Origin, *Werke*, ed. cit., Bd. V, pp. lxxxviii seq.). On the logical unity of Origen's system, see Daniélou, op. cit., pp. 206 seq.

occurred not in this age, bounded by the creation and the Last
Judgment, but in earlier age. There is a series of such ages, each
with its creation and Last Judgment. The series has no beginning, because God would not be omnipotent, if He had no
creatures on which to exert His power, and it continues indefinitely into the future. At the end of each age, after the
torments of hell, which are purely curative, and the joys of
heaven, which may lead certain souls into pride or negligence,
the middling souls, who still need the test and purgation of an
earthly life, are reborn into a situation appropriate to their
deserts. The very good souls remain or become angels; the very
bad ones demons. Thus, in the course of these successive ages,
the same soul can go up or down the whole hierarchy of rational
creatures, from the most miserable order of demons to the
highest order of angels. This series of ages will perhaps come to
an end when all souls, not excepting Lucifer's, have cleansed
themselves of sin, and freely united themselves with God; this
will be the Restoration of All Things, ἡ ἀποκατάστασις πάντων.[1]

The impact of Origen, when his works were first printed in
the late 15th and early 16th centuries, produced the same mixture of passionate defence and attack as in antiquity. At this
period his eschatology was too wildly unorthodox to exert much
influence.[2] But there were two aspects of his thought which
could be absorbed by some 16th-century theologians: his insistence on free will, and his wish to keep God clear of injustice
and cruelty. Erasmus, though quite aware of Origen's unorthodoxies, had the greatest admiration for him. He used Origen's
exegesis on Romans IX to combat Luther's harsh predestinationism, and he was preparing an edition of Origen's works
when he died.[3] Through Erasmus Origen became one strand in
the liberal Arminian tradition which led to Le Clerc, the editor
of Erasmus, and his Origenist answer to Bayle's Manichaean
attacks on the Christian God.

One of Pico's 900 *Conclusiones* which was condemned as
heretical was: 'It is more reasonable to believe that Origen is saved

[1] Acts III, 21.
[2] Matteo Palmieri, however, the author of the *Città di Vita*, did accept the
Origenist theory that good human souls after death become angels (see Walker,
'Origène en France', p. 105).
[3] See Walker, ibid., pp. 113 seq.

than damned.'[1] In his *Apologia* for the condemned conclusions
he devoted a long section to the defence of this proposition,
in which he discussed Origen's writings. His main argument
is that of earlier defenders of Origen. The unorthodoxy of
certain passages, especially in the *De Principiis*, is admitted,
but it is denied that these are authentic; they have been altered
or interpolated by envious enemies, or by heretics wishing to
use Origen's great authority. In view of the great logical
coherence of Origen's philosophy, this argument is not very
convincing. Another of Pico's arguments, also traditional, is
stronger. He points out that Origen presents most of his heterodox theories as pure speculations, which he often explicitly
submits to the present or future decisions of the Church; he
writes *inquisitivè*, as opposed to *dogmaticè* or *adhesivè*. The
strongest perhaps is an historical argument: Pico excuses
Origen's speculations on the grounds of the late formation of
certain dogmas. In discussing, for example, the Origenist doctrine of the creation of souls *ab aeterno*, he writes:[2]

> Origen in his time was not obliged explicitly to believe con-
> cerning the soul everything that we are obliged to believe now;
> for these beliefs are neither evident from Scripture, nor at this
> time were they determined by the Church, as they later were.

This historical argument is also Erasmus's main line of defending Origen.

All these arguments were used by Jacques Merlin, who in
1512 produced the first edition of Origen's complete works, in
Latin, and who in the 1520's had a long dispute with the
Syndic of the Sorbonne, Noël Beda, on the subject of Origen.[3]
They continue to be used into the 17th century. For the debate
about Origen's salvation or damnation went on, and of course

[1] Giovanni Pico, *Opera Omnia*, Basileae, n.d., (1572), T. I, p. 95 (Conclusiones
in theologia numero xxix secundum opinionem propriam à communi modo
dicendi theologorum satis diversam, N° 29): 'Rationabilius est credere Origenem
esse salvum quàm credere ipsum esse damnatum.' N° 20 of these conclusions,
also condemned, is: 'peccato mortali finiti temporis, non debetur poena infinita
secundum tempus, sed finita tantum' (Pico, ibid., p. 94); but in his *Apologia*
(ibid., p. 152) Pico indignantly denied that he intended thereby to 'negare
poenam aeternam damnatorum'.
[2] Pico, ibid., p. 210: 'Origenes non omnia tenebatur suo tempore explicitè de
anima credere, quae nos nunc tenemur, quia nec in scriptura habebantur
manifesta, nec per Ecclesiam ut postea fuit, tunc fuerat determinatum.'
[3] Cf. Walker, 'Origène en France', pp. 107 seq.

14

always involved the question of his heretical writings. The history of the debate in the 16th century was summed up in an oddly frivolous manner by a French Jesuit, Etienne Binet, in his *Du Salut d'Origene* (1629). He ranges Baronius and Bellarmine, who are 'en cholere contre le pauvre Origene', against Pico and Genebrard, who are 'resolus de le sauver'.[1]

It will be noted that none of these arguments attempts to defend Origen's opinions, but only the man; indeed they all make or imply the admission that his writings are full of errors and heresies. It is not until the *Letter of Resolution Concerning Origen* of 1661 that one finds a defence of the opinions themselves; this work, and subsequent ones favourable to Origenism, will be dealt with later. Origen's eschatology might have been more easily accepted, if it had not involved metempsychosis through a series of ages and universal salvation, rather than the annihilation of the wicked. The former had no scriptural basis. The latter was particularly shocking to later Fathers because, as Jerome pointed out, it meant that eventually Satan might be of equal status with Gabriel, demons with the Apostles, and prostitutes with the Virgin Mary.[2]

The theological tradition mainly responsible for the general revival of the early Fathers goes back to the platonizing syncretists of the 15th century, such as Ficino and Bessarion, who found in these Fathers the model of a method by which ancient pagan philosophy, especially Platonic and Neoplatonic, might be integrated into Christianity. The method is that of the *prisca theologia*, i.e. the assumption of a pagan tradition of religious truth which derived from Moses.[3] With a few notable exceptions, these theologians, from the Florentine to the Cambridge Platonists, were acutely aware of the danger of being contaminated by the errors of these Fathers, and succeeded in remaining within the bounds of orthodoxy. Nor did they emphasize these Patristic variations on fundamental points of dogma. They were more concerned with conciliating divergent opinions and finding underlying truths, than with pointing out

[1] Etienne Binet, *Du Salut d'Origène*, Paris, 1629, Dedication.

[2] Jerome, *Comm. in Jonam*; Migne. *Patr. Lat.*, T. 25, col. 1142.

[3] Cf. D. P. Walker, 'Orpheus the Theologian and Renaissance Platonists', in *Journal of the Warburg and Courtauld Institutes*, 1953, Vol. XVI, p. 100; 'The Prisca Theologia in France', ibid., 1954, Vol. XVII, p. 204.

variations of doctrine and heretical views. Nevertheless the dangers remained, especially to Protestant theology. For the Platonic tradition entered Protestant theology with apologists such as Duplessis Mornay, and there merged with Arminian rational and liberal theology, which derived ultimately from Erasmus, who also had done much to revive the early Fathers.

This Platonic tradition was inherently dangerous to Protestant theology for the following reason. The Reformation had denied the Catholic tradition of doctrinal infallibility, and had claimed to go back to the original sources of revelation. But with regard to several dogmas, such as the Trinity and original sin, it went back in fact no further than St Augustine. The Platonists, by directing attention to the pre-Augustinian Fathers, led to the question: why stop at Augustine? To which there is no good answer. Even for the most rational theology, the belief in a revelation must entail a strong primitivist drive—the earlier the purer, the nearer the divine source, unless, like some Catholics, one supposes a progressive revelation guaranteed by infallible conciliar or papal decisions. Thus sooner or later some of the Christians who had rejected the Catholic tradition were bound to question the validity of doctrines which had either not existed in primitive Christianity or only in various and unorthodox forms. This is certainly a major cause of the prevalence of crypto-Arianism among intelligent Englishmen of the later 17th and early 18th centuries.[1] The crypto-Arians who resulted, such as Newton or Whiston, differed from the Socinians in that they were, however rationalist their approach, primarily trying to reach primitive Christian doctrine; whereas the Socinians were attempting the impossible task of a purely, radically rationalist interpretation of the Scriptures, impossible because, if it succeeded, it would make the revelation superfluous. Nevertheless, the early Fathers stand behind the Socinians too, in so far as the 16th-century Polish Arians were influenced by Michel Servet,[2] whose main authorities are the less orthodox Fathers, especially Irenaeus.[3]

[1] Cf. H. McLachlan, *The Religious Opinions of Milton, Locke and Newton*, Manchester, 1941; *Socinianism in 17th-century England*, Oxford, 1951.

[2] See Earl Morse Wilbur, *A History of Unitarianism Socinianism and its Antecedents*, Cambridge, Mass., 1946, pp. 214 seq.; Stanislas Kot, *Socinianism in Poland*, tr. Wilbur, Boston, 1957, pp. xii seq.

[3] See Walker, '*Prisca Theologia* in France', pp. 248 seq.

Interest in the early Fathers was encouraged in the 17th century not only by Platonic syncretism, but also by two other trends, which are especially important with regard to French thinkers: the use of these Fathers in Protestant-Catholic polemics, which will be dealt with in a later chapter,[1] and the rise among French Catholics of critical historical scholarship applied to the primitive church and its theology.[2]

One of the most widely read transmitters of early patristic theology was the great Jesuit scholar Denis Pétau, whose *Theologica Dogmata* presents, systematically and copiously, the early history of each dogma he examines. His work was not completed, but among the fields he covered are the Trinity and hell. Of the latter his account is firmly and serenely orthodox.[3] Though he gives a full exposition of the views of Origen and other possibly unsound Fathers, he is easily able to show that the Church as a whole has never wavered in her belief in eternal torment. But with regard to the Trinity his honest scholarship led him to give a full account of the diverse unorthodox christologies of the early Fathers; and this was, rightly, thought to be extremely dangerous. He was even accused of being a crypto-Socinian, and was obliged to add a long preface, in which he argued that these apparent unorthodoxies were only a matter of expression, of unfortunate philosophical (usually Platonic) terminology.[4] But the evidence in the book itself continued to be printed and read.

When Pierre-Daniel Huet, later Bishop of Avranches and co-tutor with Bossuet to the Dauphin, first went to Paris as a young man in 1651, he met Pétau and became friends with him. He read the *Theologica Dogmata* with passionate interest, and found his faith severely shaken. Although in his *Memoirs* he states that later, 'my mind being illuminated by brighter rays from Heaven, the clouds were dispelled, and my faith struck firmer and deeper roots', this experience certainly made a

[1] V. infra, p. 179.
[2] Cf. Paul Hazard, *La Crise de la Conscience Européenne*, Paris, 1935, pp. 184 seq., 211, on Richard Simon and Elie Dupin.
[3] Denis Pétau, *Theologicorum Dogmatum Tomus Tertius* . . ., Paris, 1644, III, v–viii, pp. 193 seq.
[4] See Bayle, *Dict. Hist. & Crit.*, art. Pétau, note (B); against the view that Pétau was obliged to add the preface, see *Dict. de Théol. Cath.*, T. XII¹, art. Pétau, by P. Galtier, cols. 1327 seq.

lasting impression on him. At the same time he became a close friend of Gabriel Naudé, who may well have been the starting-point of Huet's strong inclination towards philosophical scepticism.[1] These two interests persisted through his other very diverse activities, which included experimental science and writing novels. His last book was an ultra-sceptical treatise,[2] and his greatest work of scholarship was his *Origeniana* (1668),[3] which still remains the fullest account of Origen's life, writings, opinions and subsequent reputation. Origen's works had been easily available since the early 16th century, and his scheme for universal salvation was already widely known; but Huet provided also full and accurate information about other over-merciful Fathers and about the reactions to Origen's eschatology from antiquity onwards, including the Middle Ages. Huet was in correspondence with Le Clerc, who took his side in a controversy with Boileau about Longinus, and may well be one of the main sources of Le Clerc's knowledge of Origenism.[4]

[1] *Memoirs of The Life of Peter Daniel Huet, Bishop of Avranches*: written by himself; and translated . . . by John Aikin, London, 1810, pp. 53–62.

[2] *Traité Philosophique de la faiblesse de l'esprit humain*, Amsterdam. 1722.

[3] In his *Origenis Commentaria in sacram Scripturam graece-latine . . .*, Paris, 1668; also in Migne, *Patr. Gr.*, T. 17, cols. 633 seq. On Huet, cf. A Dupront, *Pierre-Daniel Huet et l'Exégèse Comparatiste au XVIIe siècle*, Paris, 1930.

[4] See Huet, *Memoirs*, pp. 223, 379. Le Clerc also edited Pétau's *Theologica Dogmata* in 1700 (see Annie Barnes, *Jean Le Clerc (1657-1736) et la République des Lettres*, Paris, 1938, p. 149).

Chapter II

STRENGTHS OF THE DOCTRINE
OF HELL

(i) AUTHORITIES: SCRIPTURE. FATHERS. COUNCILS.
PROTESTANT CONFESSIONS

THE scriptural authority for the doctrine of eternal torment is extremely strong. As Dom Sinsart wrote:[1]

It was not possible that such an important article of religion as that of the punishments in the afterlife should be hidden, so to speak, in a corner. The Gospels are full of it.

There are two crucial texts for the eternity of hell: Christ's eschatological discourse in Matthew XXV, and the lake of fire and brimstone in Revelations XIV and XX. With regard to the former it could be argued that the 'everlasting fire' and 'everlasting punishment' (τὸ πῦρ τὸ αἰώνιον, κόλασις αἰώνιος), to which Christ says He will send the wicked at the Last Judgment, did not necessarily mean that their torments would be eternal, since the word αἰώνιος or its Hebrew equivalent is often used elsewhere in the Bible in contexts where it cannot

---

[1] Sinsart, *Defense*, p. 52: 'Il n'étoit pas possible qu'un article aussi important de la Religion, que l'est celui des peines de l'autre vie, ne se trouvât, pour ainsi dire, que dans un coin. L'Evangile en est plein.' Cf. C. Spicq, 'La Révélation de l'enfer dans la Sainte Ecriture', in M. Carrouges, C. Spicq, o.p., G. Bardy, C. V. Héris, o.p., B. Dorival, J. Guitton, *L'Enfer*, (Collection *Foi Vivante*), Paris, 1950, pp. 89 seq.

STRENGTHS OF THE DOCTRINE OF HELL

mean an infinite period of time, as for example in Jude 6, where it is applied to the fire which destroyed Sodom and Gomorrah. But this interpretation is highly improbable, since Christ is clearly drawing a parallel between the eternity of bliss awaiting the sheep and the eternity of misery awaiting the goats. It can only stand if one also denies eternal life to the saved; only the ruthlessly honest and literal-minded Whiston dared to take this step.[1] The texts from Revelations are also difficult to explain away philologically; for here the phrase used is 'for ages of ages' (εἰς τοὺς αἰῶνας τῶν αἰώνων). A German defender of hell, Friedrich Lampe, noted that this phrase does not occur in ordinary Greek;[2]

> Hence it is abundantly clear that the Holy Ghost intended *this*, that he might express eternity more nervously than it had formerly been done in human language, and remove all possible evasions which the genius of the language seemed otherwise to admit.

It is however possible, particularly for chiliasts, to use these texts from Revelations against the eternity of hell, as we shall see.[3]

We must bear in mind the exceptional importance of Scripture at this period. It was the only authority accepted by all churches and sects, and thus in polemics and apologetics tended to carry more weight than any other.

In spite of Origen, and a few doubtful texts from less eminent Greek Fathers, the weight of patristic authority is heavily on the side of eternal torment.[4] The solidity of the tradition in favour of eternal torment was such that Pétau felt it necessary to apologize for even troubling to discuss the question:[5]

---

[1] V. infra, p. 99.

[2] F. A. Lampe, *Theological Dissertations concerning the Endless Duration of Punishment*, transl. Joseph Robertson, Edinburgh, 1796, p. 9 (original edition: *Dissertationes duae de Poenarum Aeternitate*, Bremae, 1728).

[3] V. infra, p. 143.

[4] See G. Bardy, 'Les Pères de l'Eglise en face des problèmes posés par l'enfer', in *L'Enfer*, pp. 222 seq. Gregory of Nyssa was quite clearly in favour of universal salvation (see Bardy, ibid., pp. 232–3).

[5] Pétau, *Theol. Dogm.*, 1644, T. III, p. 199: 'Nihil est Christianorum tam doctorum, quàm indoctorum sensibus insitum magis, quàm daemonum, ac damnatorum hominum, perinde atque immortales ipsi sunt, sic aeternas esse poenas, ac nullo unquam tempore desituros. Itaque supervacanea cuipiam, aut etiam ludicra videbitur ista quaestio, quam ea de re instituimus.'

Nothing is more firmly rooted in the minds of Christians, both learnèd and uneducated, than that the torments of demons, and of damned men, since these too are immortal, will be eternal and will never end. This question we are discussing will therefore seem to some to be superfluous and even ridiculous.

It should however be remembered that the condemnations of Origen are quite late, and it is evident from Augustine's discussion of the matter in the *City of God* that 'merciful doctors' were still prevalent and vocal in the early 5th century.[1] But, as we have seen, there was a strong tendency among the orthodox, both Catholic and Protestant, not to go back further than Augustine. The first condemnation of Origen's doctrine of universal salvation was by a Council held at Alexandria in 400. After that there are no official condemnations until Justinian's edict against Origen, signed at the Council of Constantinople in 543. The ninth anathema of this edict reads:[2]

> whoever says or thinks that the punishment of demons and the wicked will not be eternal, that it will have an end and that there will then be an ἀποκατάστασις of demons and the wicked, let him be anathema.

This Council was probably the author of fifteen anathemata, in which Origen's Restoration of All Things is condemned. These were published with the acts of the Fifth Oecumenical Council of Constantinople in 553; but it is doubtful whether they were included in the general condemnation of Origen by this Council.[3]

These official condemnations settled the question for the Catholics of our period.[4] For Protestants the situation was a little more open, since no articles or confessions of faith had for them the infallibility of conciliar or papal decisions. Nevertheless the clergy had to subscribe to such articles, and some of

---

[1] Augustine, *Civitas Dei*, XXI, c. xvii, xxiii, xxiv.

[2] Denzinger-Bannwart, *Enchiridion Symbolorum*, No. 211.

[3] See *Dict. de Théol. Cath.*, T. XI[2], art. Origénisme, cols. 1571, 1576, 1580–7.

[4] The *Catechismus Romanus* (1564), ordered by the Council of Trent, also contains very emphatic assertions of eternal torment (see Percy Dearmer, *The Legend of Hell*, London, 1929, pp. 24–5). For other decisions binding on Catholics, see C. V. Héris, 'Le Dogme de l'Enfer et la Théologie', in *L'Enfer*, pp. 246–8.

them contained an explicit assertion of the eternity of hell. Article XVII of the Augsburg Confession (1530) reads:[1]

> Christ . . . will give pious men eternal life and perpetual joy, but He will condemn impious men and devils to torture without end (ut sine fine crucientur). They condemn the Anabaptists, who hold that there will be an end to the punishments of the damned and of devils (hominibus damnatis & diabolis finem poenarum futurum esse).

Petersen, who, before his conversion to Origenism, had signed this Confession, argued that Luther's original German version used only the scriptural terms 'ewige Strafe' and 'ewige Pein', which, like αἰώνιος in the New Testament, could be interpreted as meaning only age-long, whereas Melanchthon's Latin version unjustifiably altered these to the unambiguous 'without end'.[2] But this argument is very feeble, since Petersen himself admits that the intention of the original signatories to the Confession was to affirm the eternity of hell. It was also unfortunate for the opponents of eternal torment that their doctrine was here associated with the Anabaptists, who, ever since the communistic régime at Münster in 1534 with its appalling excesses,[3] had an even worse reputation than the Socinians. The practical importance of this article of the Confession of Augsburg can be seen from a decree issued in 1707 by the Imperial Councillor at Nürnberg, which Petersen quotes. This decree, aimed at suppressing modern errors of doctrine among the clergy, recalls Article XVII, in which eternal torment is affirmed 'in dry and unambiguous words . . . the Latin sine fine expressing the sense of the German ewig quite clearly', and commands that the orthodox doctrine be publicly proved by Scripture, and the weakness of the opposing doctrine demonstrated, 'in order that there may be so much the less possibility of any objections being brought against this clear truth'.[4]

The Thirty-nine Articles of the Church of England do not contain any affirmation of the eternity of hell, whereas the

[1] *Die Augsburgische Konfession,* ed. H. H. Wendt, Halle, 1927, p. 66.
[2] J. W. Petersen, Μυστηριον 'Αποκαταστασεως παντων, . . . Tomus Secundus, Pamphilia, 1703, Vorrede, pp. (28)–(31).
[3] See Norman Cohn, *The Pursuit of the Millennium,* London, 1957, pp. 295 seq.
[4] Petersen, op. cit., T. III, pp. 127–9.

Forty-second Article of those issued under Edward VI in 1552 is:[1]

> All men shall not bee saved at the length. Thei also are worthie of condemnation who indeavour at this time to restore the dangerouse opinion that all menne, be thei never so ungodlie, shall at length bee saved, when they have suffered pain for their sinnes a certaine time appointed by God's justice.

It is possible to use these facts in support of Origenism. Rust, for example, in his *Letter of Resolution concerning Origen* (1661) writes:[2]

> I would fain know why she [sc. the Church of England] who in her 39 *Articles* does so punctually follow the Articles agreed upon in King Edward's Days, or with little Variation, should wholly *Omit* that *Article* which Condemns the *Restorers* of this Opinion, if she had thought it ought to have been condemned.

(ii) STATIC AND DYNAMIC HELLS

A still more powerful support for hell than this massive scriptural, patristic, and conciliar authority is one that I have already mentioned: the value of hell as a deterrent in this life. It is mainly the wish to preserve the maximum moral intensity of this deterrent that accounts for an apparently unnecessary characteristic of the strictly orthodox afterlife, namely, that there is a complete moral freezing at death; neither the damned nor the saved can acquire merit or demerit. As Thomas Aquinas explains, the damned do continue to commit evil acts, particularly by way of blasphemy; but these acts are due to the obstinate perversity of their will, which is part of their punishment, and do not therefore constitute a demerit ('mala in damnatis non sunt demeritoria, sed pertinent ad damnationis poenam').[3] It is only by making this earthly life the unique period of trial that the greatest possible moral weight can be thrown on our

---

[1] Quoted by Frederic W. Farrar, *Eternal Hope*, London, 1877, p. 85; cf. D. Cajus Fabricius, *Die Kirche von England* . . . (Corpus Confessionum, Abt. 17, Bd. I), Berlin and Leipzig, 1937, p. 401.

[2] George Rust, *A Letter of Resolution concerning Origen and the chief of his opinions*, London, 1661 (Fascimile ed. by M. H. Nicholson, Columbia, 1933), p. 133. On the attribution of this letter, v. infra, p. 125.

[3] Thomas Aquinas, *Summa Theologica*, 2ᵃ 2ᵃᵉ, q. 13, a. 4; Suppl. q. 98, a. 6.

present actions and the greatest force be given to the fear of hell. If there were to be other periods of probation, we might decide to fail the present test by enjoying a riotously debauched life and to make an effort later to pass some future examination. As Matthew Horbery, one of Whiston's opponents, puts it:[1]

> The great Argument for *working out our Salvation* in the present Life, *while it is called today*, is, *because the Night cometh, when no Man can work*. But if Men are once taught to believe that there will be *another Day*, that will answer their purpose as well; it is natural to think, that they will be too apt to trust to that Resource, and so live and die without Repentance. I don't say that this Conduct would be reasonable, but that it is likely to be Fact, considering how strongly Men are attach'd to their old and favourite Sins

and in his next chapter:

> it should seem that it is the Eternity of the Punishment, which gives it its chief Weight and Edge, and makes it pierce deepest into the Hearts of Sinners. It is the Notion that *That* miserable State will admit of neither Remedy, nor End, that alarms their Fears, that restrains their Wickedness within some bounds, and is most likely after all to make them repent of it. It seems natural to think that it must be so in Reason, and it evidently appears to be so in Fact.

According to the orthodox doctrine of a morally static afterlife, the damned are eternally punished only for sins committed in this life. In hell, since as a punishment their will has been made immutably evil, their blasphemies and hatred of God are not, strictly speaking, sins, because they do not proceed from free will, and cannot therefore justly be punished. This aspect of the orthodox hell was by no means undisputed, because one of the easiest and most obvious justifications of eternal torment is to suppose that the damned continue freely to sin and therefore continue to be justly punished.

This argument is used by Leibniz in his *Théodicée*. Though he is aware that it is condemned by most theologians, he hopes that the inability of the damned to acquire demerit need not be considered an article of faith, and refers to Fecht's *De Statu*

---

[1] Matthew Horbery, *An Enquiry into the Scripture-Doctrine Concerning the Duration of Future Punishment*, London, 1744, pp. 294–5, 305.

Damnatorum (1683), a treatise devoted to proving the contrary opinion.[1] But this way of justifying the eternity of hell involves insuperable difficulties. Leibniz also quotes from Jurieu's *Traité de l'Unité de l'Eglise* (1688) the statement:[2]

> Reason tells us that a creature which cannot stop being criminal cannot stop being miserable also.

But he does not quote Bayle's refutation of it: one must suppose, either that it is absolutely necessary that the damned should continue to sin, or that it is not so; if the latter, then at any moment God could convert or destroy them; if the former, then[3]

> As soon as creatures could not stop being criminal, they would stop being so, just as a madman and a maniac cease to sin once they are unable to avoid what they do or say.

Leibniz does attempt to answer this refutation, by means of the sophistry usually employed for reconciling free will and efficacious grace:[4]

> In a man who sins, even when he is damned, there is always a freedom which makes him guilty, and a potentiality, but a remote one, of self-reform, though this potentiality is never actualized.

These deviations from the orthodox doctrine of a morally static afterlife, beside the great disadvantage of diminishing the moral weight on this life as a unique period of trial, also bring with them the danger of giving support to schemes for universal salvation. In nearly all theological systems the ability to sin presupposes some measure of free will and hence the possibility

[1] Leibniz, *Essais de Théodicée sur la Bonté de Dieu, La Liberté de l'Homme, et l'Origine du Mal*, Amsterdam, 1734, Pt. II, p. 149 (first ed. Amsterdam, 1710). Joannes Fechtius, *De Statu Damnatorum, quod actiones ipsorum, in primis malas, concernit, Tractatio Scholastica*, Spirae, 1683.

[2] Leibniz, ibid., p. 150: 'la Raison nous dit, qu'une créature qui ne peut cesser d'être criminelle ne peut aussi cesser d'être misérable.'

[3] Pierre Bayle, *Oeuvres Diverses*, T. III, La Haye, 1727, p. 879 (*Réponse aux Questions d'un Provincial*, 1706): 'dès là que les Créatures ne pourroient cesser d'être criminelles, elles cesseroient de l'être, comme un frénétique & un maniaque cessent de pécher dès qu'ils sont dans l'impossibilité d'éviter ce qu'ils font & ce qu'ils disent.'

[4] Leibniz, ibid., p. 151: 'il y a toujours dans l'homme qui peche, lors même qu'il est damné, une liberté qui le rend coupable, & une puissance, mais éloignée, de se relever, quoiqu'elle ne vienne jamais à l'acte.'

of repentance; one could argue as we shall see, that conditions in hell would be peculiarly favourable to repentance and that God would be bound to save a truly contrite sinner.[1] It is true that according to the orthodox doctrine the damned are said to repent of their misdeeds, but only in the very restricted sense that they regret them because of the punishment they have brought.[2] Thus we may say that the doctrine of hell is at its strongest in its orthodox, morally static form.

(iii) HELL AND THE MYSTERIES

Another source of strength for hell is its close connection with other doctrines, especially mysteries, of Christianity. It has a special relation to the orthodox doctrine of the Redemption.

Both with the Socinians and the English Arians a doctrine of the Trinity in which Christ is not very God of very God is accompanied by doubts about, or the denial of, the eternity of hell. There is a logical connection between these two heresies, as William Dodwell, in refuting the English Arian, Whiston, pointed out.[3] In the orthodox doctrine of the Redemption, the expiation by the crucifixion is considered infinite because it was a God who suffered and died; infinite expiation was necessary to atone for the infinite offence of man's sin; the infinite offence of man's sin is shown by its deserving eternal punishment. If, as in the Arian doctrine, Christ was not fully God, then His expiation, if there was an expiation (which the Socinians denied), was not infinite, and there is no necessary reason to suppose that the offence of man's sin is infinite and deserves eternal punishment. This is not of course a proof that hell is not eternal, but it does remove one of the most serious obstacles to such a proof. Moreover, the orthodox doctrine of the Redemption presupposes the validity of retributive justice.[4] Since God demanded the vicarious punishment of His Son to expiate the sins of man, *a fortiori* non-vicarious retributive punishment, of sinning men, is just. The acceptance of the validity of retributive punish-

---

[1] V. infra, pp. 164 seq.
[2] Thomas Aquinas, *Summ. Th.*, Suppl., q. 98, a. 2.
[3] W. Dodwell, op. cit., pp. 6–8.
[4] Retributive or vindictive justice is a species of the genus distributive justice, i.e. the right distribution of rewards and punishments.

ment does not necessarily justify eternal torment; but the denial of it makes any justification extremely difficult, as we shall see, if not impossible.

The Redemption, original sin, retributive justice, and expiation by suffering—this complex of interrelated doctrines and ideas rests on an archaic and infantile moral assumption, namely that the bad consequences of an act can be annulled or compensated for by the suffering of the doer, or vicariously by someone else's suffering. If therefore anyone attacks the doctrine of hell by denying this assumption, one can justifiably accuse him of also attacking these other fundamental Christian doctrines and conceptions.

Thomas Hobbes, in accordance with his strictly practical morals, did explicitly deny this assumption, and assert that all punishment must be curative or deterrent, that is, useful.[1] But Hobbes was too radically original and unchristian a thinker for most theologians and philosophers to take his views into serious account, with the exception of such very liberal Protestants as Bayle, Leibniz and Petersen.

Peter Sterry and Jeremiah White, who both disbelieved in the eternity of hell, rejected the concept of retributive justice because it was incompatible with their kind of God, in Whom the attribute of goodness or love had absolute priority over all other attributes.[2] Another eminent chaplain of Cromwell's, John Owen, published a *Diatriba de Justitia Divina*,[3] in which he showed that retributive justice is inseparable from the orthodox doctrine of the Redemption. This treatise, though primarily against the Socinians, was probably also directed against Sterry and White, or other puritan Platonists holding this heterodox conception of the divine attributes; it is difficult to imagine how they could effectively have answered it.

There is also a more general kind of connexion between hell and other mysteries. They can both be defended from the same fideist position, that is, one admits that the doctrine is inaccessible, or even contrary, to human reason, and claims that, precisely because of this, it must be accepted by faith alone. This is

[1] Thomas Hobbes, *Leviathan*, ed. M. Oakeshott, Oxford, 1946, pp. 100, 203-4.
[2] V. infra, pp. 110 seq.
[3] John Owen, *Diatriba de Justitia Divina seu Justitiae Vindicatricis Vindicia* . . ., Oxoniae, 1653.

the position that Bayle sometimes takes up, who usually compares the irrationality of the mysteries to philosophical antinomies arising from the concept of infinity, such as those involved in the divisibility of matter.[1] Leaving on one side the question of how orthodox this extreme fideist position is, one can say that it is both difficult to attack and extremely flexible, in that it could be used to defend almost any old set of beliefs. It is particularly strong when used to defend a revealed religion because, if all the doctrines of such a religion were accessible to human reason, the revelation was plainly unnecessary. As Jurieu frequently pointed out, Socinians and rationalist Protestants, by explaining away or rejecting the mysteries, leave themselves with nothing but a deistic philosophy.[2] But the fideist defence applied to hell involves a kind of trick.

There are two distinct ways in which one can say that a doctrine or opinion is contrary to, or above human reason: one may mean, on the one hand, that it is illogical, self-contradictory, unintelligible or incompatible with well established scientific fact, or, on the other, that it is morally unacceptable, that it will not fit with basic moral principles or values. The Trinity or transubstantiation are irrational in the first way; predestination, original sin and hell, in the second. The former kind of doctrine is morally neutral, but intellectually mysterious; the latter is perfectly clear and intelligible, but in conflict with some people's moral principles. Bayle's fideist defence therefore, based on a sceptical demonstration of the impotence of human reason and the analogy with metaphysical antinomies, is valid for the former type of mystery, but irrelevant to the latter. By ignoring the distinction between these two kinds of mystery, one may persuade an unsuspicious reader that a fideistic defence of the Trinity is also valid for eternal torment. Bayle of course uses this defence only when wearing his Calvinist mask;[3] elsewhere he attacks the immoral mysteries by means of analogies which show that they do offend against most people's moral

---

[1] E.g. Bayle, *Oeuvres Div.*, T. III, 1727, pp. 771, 864, cf. pp. 778, 992; *Dict. Hist. & Crit.*, art. Zénon, rem. (G).

[2] Jurieu, *Le Tableau du Socinianisme*, La Haye, 1690, pp. 86–90.

[3] Bayle was quite aware of the distinction between the two kinds of mystery, see *Dict. Hist. & Crit.*, Eclaircissement II (ed. Amsterdam and Leide, 1730, IV, 625).

principles.[1] An honest defence of the real or apparent immorality of such mysteries is likely to lead to dangerous results, as we shall see, and constitutes rather a weakness than a strength of hell.[2]

(iv) THE ABOMINABLE FANCY

Finally there is an aspect of the traditional doctrine of hell which was once a strength, since it linked it with the doctrine of eternal beatitude, but which is seldom mentioned in the 17th and 18th centuries and which had perhaps by that time become a weakness: that part of the happiness of the blessèd consists in contemplating the torments of the damned. This sight gives them joy because it is a manifestation of God's justice and hatred of sin, but chiefly because it provides a contrast which heightens their awareness of their own bliss. This is a logical development of the orthodox afterlife, since the blessèd, knowing God directly, face to face, are bound to find satisfaction in all His acts. It also has considerable scriptural authority: the wicked shall be tormented with fire and brimstone in the presence of the angels and of the Lamb (Rev. XIV, 9–11); since Dives could see Lazarus, there is every reason to suppose that Lazarus could see Dives (Luke XVI); the worshippers of the Lord shall go forth, and look upon the carcases of the men that have transgressed against Him: for their worm shall not die, neither shall their fire be quenched (Isaiah LXVI, 22–4).[3] It has moreover the support of the greatest Father and the greatest Doctor of the Church, St Augustine[4] and St Thomas Aquinas,[5] and of the Master of Sentences, Peter of Lombardy.[6]

It is therefore odd that this aspect of hell should become almost obsolete by the late 17th century,[7] especially since it

[1] V. infra, pp. 195 seq.
[2] V. infra, p. 54.
[3] Cf. Ernst Benz, 'Der Mensch und die Sympathie aller Dinge am Ende der Zeiten (nach Jakob Boehme und seiner Schule)', in *Eranos-Jahrbuch*, 1955, Bd. xxiv, pp. 137 seq.
[4] Augustine, *Civ. Dei*, XX, xxi, xxii. It appears also in Tertullian and St Cyprian (see G. Bardy, op. cit., in *L'Enfer*, pp. 152–3).
[5] Thomas Aquinas, *Summ. Th.*, Suppl., q. 94, art. i.
[6] Petrus Lomb., *Sent.*, IV, dist. 50, 7 (Migne, *Patr. Lat.*, T. 192, col. 962).
[7] It was still current in the late 16th century, cf. e.g. St Robert Bellarmine, *De Aeterna Felicitate Sanctorum*, IV, ii (Bellarmine, *Opera Omnia*, Neapoli, 1872, T. 8, p. 303): 'Nec sine laetitia voluptate videbimus scelera et tormenta perditorum; in quibus sanctitas piorum et justitia Dei, mirifice collucebunt.'

provided an adequate answer to one of the main objections to eternal torment, namely, its uselessness after the Last Judgment. The reason for its obsolescence is, I think, a general change in the attitude to other people's suffering, a change which was only just beginning at this period and which today is still not completed. What I am suggesting is not that there has been any change in our immediate, instinctive feelings of pity for, or enjoyment in the suffering of others, but that our evaluation of these feelings has changed. Closely connected with this is a change, also only incipient, in the conception of justice: a tendency to minimize, or even occasionally to reject, retributive or vindictive justice. The two are closely connected because, as long as we accept the validity of retributive justice, we must also approve of other people's suffering when it is deserved, and we may well regard any pity for them as moral weakness—there is indeed no good reason why we should not frankly enjoy that suffering. Retributive justice, as we have seen, was too deeply rooted in Christian doctrine for any but the boldest thinkers to attack it, but the above aspect of hell could quite easily be dispensed with.

Like all such major evolutions of basic values, this change remained in its early stages largely unconscious; Bayle writes, not I think ironically:[1]

> There is even something ('je ne sai quoi') which shocks our reason in the hypothesis that the Saints of Paradise gain part of their happiness from knowing that other men are being tormented and will be eternally.

Although the frank, untroubled, innocent enjoyment in the suffering of enemies or of the wicked has gone (there is 'je ne sai quoi' wrong with it), the evolution has not advanced as far as a positive dislike of other people's pain; provided that the suffering, however violent and protracted, is justly inflicted, it is calmly, indifferently accepted. Bayle, in a passage quoted by Leibniz, where he examines various analogies to the torments of hell, states that, if an executioner deliberately prolonged a

[1] Bayle, *Oeuvres Div.*, T. III, p. 863: 'Il y a même je ne sai quoi qui choque notre raison dans l'hypothese que les Saints du Paradis tirent en partie leur félicité de ce qu'ils savent que d'autres hommes sont tourmentez & le seront éternellement.'

decapitation, the spectators would revolt at such cruelty; but he adds this note:[1]

> Note that this should not be taken in a strictly universal sense. There are cases in which the people approve of certain criminals being slowly burnt to death.

and he cites examples, such as the heretics burnt in Paris after the placards against the mass of 1534 and the execution of Ravaillac. If eternal torment can be shown to be just, hell still stands firm.[2] The enjoyment taken by the blessèd in the torments of the damned is quietly dropped, but we are still far from the time when Dean Farrar could, in the pulpit, call it 'an abominable fancy'.[3]

In how rudimentary a stage this evolution was can be seen from a variant of the abominable fancy proposed by William King. Having abandoned the orthodox morally static afterlife, and believing in utter freedom of will, King is left with the blessèd constantly liable to sin. This provides a splendid justification for hell; the torments of the damned are a continual reminder of exactly what the wages of sin is:[4]

> The goodness as well as the happiness of the blessed will be confirmed and advanced by reflections naturally arising from their view of the misery which some shall undergo: (which seems to be a good reason for the creation of those beings who shall be finally miserable, and for the continuation of them in their miserable existence).

As can be seen from this passage, King's blessèd are pleased as well as edified by the spectacle of hell, and he goes on to discuss this point:

> And though in one respect a view of the misery which the damned undergo might seem to detract from the happiness of

[1] Bayle, *Oeuvres Div.*, T. III, p. 878; Leibniz, *Théodicée*, ed. cit., Pt. II, pp. 31–2: 'Notez qu'on ne doit pas entendre ceci dans l'Universalité à la rigueur. Il y a des cas où le peuple approuve qu'on fasse mourir à petit feu certains criminels."

[2] Cf. J. Brandon, τὸ πῦρ τὸ αἰώνιον: *or, Everlasting Fire no Fancy*, London, 1678, p. 110: 'though a punishment be never so great and grievous, yet if it be such as the person punished doth deserve for his offence, it is not cruelty but justice. That wretched Villain Ravilliack . . . was . . . tormented to death in a fearful manner, yet I believe there were few honest men that ever accused his Judge of cruelty . . .'

[3] F. W. Farrar, *Eternal Hope* (five sermons preached in Westminster Abbey in 1877), London, 1878, p. 66.

[4] William King, *An Essay on the Origin of Evil*, 5th ed., London, 1781, pp. 393–5 (1st ed. *De Origine Mali*, 1702).

the blessed, through pity and commiseration: yet there is another, a nearer, and much more affecting consideration, viz. that all this is the misery which they themselves were often exposed to, and were in imminent danger of incurring; in this view, why may not the sense of their own escape so far over-come the sense of another's ruin, as to extinguish the pain that usually attends the idea of it, and even render it productive of some real happiness?

There is here already the assumption that justly inflicted pain will produce in the beholder pity rather than enjoyment;[1] but the pity is so feeble that it is entirely swamped by the keen satisfaction of the blessèd in the contrast of their own bliss with the misery of the damned.

It is rare even for opponents of eternal torment to mention the abominable fancy; but Thomas Burnet does refer to it, and is angry enough to be ironical:[2]

> Consider a little, if you please, unmerciful Doctor,[3] what a theatre of providence this is: by far the greatest part of the human race burning in the flames for ever and ever. Oh what a spectacle on the stage, worthy of an audience of God and angels! And then to delight the ear, while this unhappy crowd fills heaven and earth with wailing and howling, you have a truly divine harmony.

[1] Pity for the damned is usually excluded by even very liberal theologians. John Norris, for example, in his *The Theory and Regulation of Love. A Moral Essay . . . To which are added Letters Philosophical and Moral between the Author and Dr Henry More*, Oxford, 1688 (dedicated to Lady Masham, Cudworth's daughter), pp. 119–20, argues that no charity should be felt towards the damned because, first, it would be useless, since they cannot be helped, and secondly: 'For our will would not be then conformable to Gods, but directly opposite to it, and besides we should disapprove, at least tacitly and interpretatively, the *Justice* of his waies, by thus loving them whom he *extremely* hates, and Blessing them whom he curses and abandons for ever.' Cf. Benz, op. cit., p. 138.

[2] Thomas Burnet, *De Statu Mortuorum & Resurgentium Tractatus*, London, 1733 (1st ed.: 1720), p. 307: 'Respice paulisper, si placet, Doctor immisericors, quale Theatrum Providentiae: multo majorem partem humani generis aestuantem inter flammas per aeterna saecula. O digna Deo & Angelis spectatoribus scena! Dein ad demulcendum aures, dum plangoribus & ululatu Coelum Terramque replet haec infelix turba, harmoniam habes planè divinam.'

[3] I.e. Tertullian (see his *De Spectaculis*, c. xxx, Migne, *Patr. Lat.*, T. 1. cols, 735–6).

Chapter III

WEAKNESSES OF THE
DOCTRINE OF HELL

(i) SCRIPTURE

ALTHOUGH the scriptural authority for hell is so strong, stronger perhaps than for any other fundamental doctrine, there are some texts that can be used to attack it; but they do not amount to a serious weakness. They consist chiefly of passages in the New Testament where it is said that God wishes the salvation of all men and that Christ is the Saviour of all men.[1] These passages are also in conflict with the Catholic and Protestant doctrines of predestination, and there were therefore already traditional methods of explaining them away by the time that they were used by advocates of universal salvation. It was claimed that 'all' referred to salvation being open to all nations, and not merely to the Jews; or recourse was had to the Thomist distinction between the antecedent and consequent wills of God. Though the latter argument, used by Leibniz,[2] is an uncon-

---

[1] I Timothy II, 4, IV, 10; Romans XI, 32; I Corinthians XV, 22, 28. To these can be added some Psalms (LXXVII, 7–9; CIII, 8–9), which can be interpreted in a merciful sense (cf. Augustine, *Civ. Dei*, XXI, xvii–xviii), and the texts on Christ preaching to the dead (I Peter III, 19–20, IV, 6), used by advocates of universal salvation as evidence for a dynamic afterlife.

[2] Leibniz, *Théodicée*, ed. cit., Pt. I, 89; Pt. II, 117, 270.

vincing sophistry, the former is difficult to reject if one places these passages in their context. It was, nevertheless, awkward for the defenders of hell to be obliged to argue, at one and the same time, that eternal punishment in the Scriptures meant just what it said, but that the salvation of all men did not.[1]

There are also texts where the wicked are threatened with death; these were used by Arians in support of their belief in the eventual annihilation of the wicked.[2] But they were still left with the threats of eternal punishment in Matthew XXV and elsewhere.

Finally, there is the awkward problem raised by the parable of Dives and Lazarus.[3] If this parable is taken as a representation of the afterlife, which it appears to be, then Dives's charitable concern for the fate of his five brothers is difficult to fit into the orthodox conception of the damned as immutably evil. Bonaventura, and after him Thomas Aquinas, suggest that Dives would have liked everyone to be damned, but that, knowing this would not happen, he preferred that his brothers should be saved rather than anyone else. We may accept Leibniz's verdict on this explanation: 'Il n'y a pas trop de solidité dans cette réponse.'[4]

There is another, potentially dangerous weakness in hell's scriptural basis: mainly owing to the evolution of Christian eschatology in the first centuries of our era, the orthodox afterlife has come out in an untidy, evidently botched form. Polemics about hell were liable to lead to an examination of the scriptural authority for orthodox eschatology, and to a realization of how far it had evolved from that of the New Testament.

Whether one accepts Schweitzer's interpretation of the New Testament or not,[5] it must be admitted that most, though not all, of the texts later taken to be descriptive of the afterlife of each human soul at death can as easily, or more easily, be taken to refer to the state of things after the Second Coming, to the fate of the elect and the reprobate in the New Age which the

[1] Cf. e.g. Sinsart, op. cit., pp. 137–70; Abraham Ruchat, *Examen de l'Origenisme*, Lausanne, 1733, pp. 82–124.

[2] E.g. Locke (v. infra, p. 94).

[3] Luke XVI.

[4] Leibniz, *Théodicée*, ed. cit., Pt. III, p. 154.

[5] Albert Schweitzer, *The Quest of the Historical Jesus*, transl. W. Montgomery, London, 1910 (*Von Reimarus zu Wrede*, 1906).

Messiah is bringing about.[1] As long as the Parousia was thought of as imminent, the intermediate state of the few Christians who died before it occurred was not of great moment. They could be supposed to be sleeping or just waiting until the resurrection; this was the prevalent opinion until as late as the 5th century.[2] When the Second Coming receded into a remote future, there was a natural wish not to postpone indefinitely the reward of the saved and the punishment of the damned;[3] hence the doctrine of the immediate judgment of each soul at death. But, since the Second Coming could not be entirely eliminated, the Last Judgment still remained, by now a superfluous ceremony for all but the tiny minority of men alive at the Last Day.

This confusion is further complicated by the two resurrections in Revelations XX, the first for the just at the beginning of the millennium, the second for everyone else at the end of it; which also involves two judgments. This passage was ignored by orthodox Christians, perhaps fortunately, since otherwise there would have been three judgments. But chiliasts, such as Whiston and Petersen, whose attention was concentrated on Revelations, believed in these two resurrections and in the sleep, or waiting state, of the dead until them.

(ii) NUMBER OF DAMNED. INFANT DAMNATION

Most of the graver weaknesses of hell are connected with theodicy. One aspect of the traditional hell which many people began, from the 17th century onwards, to consider as a weakness was the very high proportion of damned to saved. This had once been a strength; there is, after all, no great point in being one of the elect, if almost everyone else is chosen too, and indeed the very term 'elect' implies a minority (one does not pick out a larger class from a smaller). Moreover the small

---

[1] See Martin Werner, *Die Entstehung des christlichen Dogmas*, Bern-Leipzig. 1941, pp. 667 seq.

[2] See *Dict. de Th. Cath.*, T. V, Ière Partie, art. Enfer, cols. 49 seq.; G. Bardy, op. cit., in *L'Enfer*, pp. 175 seq.

[3] Jurieu (*Le Tableau du Socinianisme*, p. 78) gives the following reasons against the dead sleeping until the resurrection: 'par là les méchants espereront avoir du relasche durant plusieurs siecles; c'est beaucoup pour eux . . . D'autre part un fidele qui a porté les fatigues de la penitence, qui a travaillé à mortifier sa chair, qui a renoncé au monde & à ses plaisirs . . . n'est-il pas bien aise de trouver sa récompense toute preste en sortant de la vie presente ?'.

number of the saved is strongly asserted in the Gospels: 'strait is the gate and narrow is the way' (Matt. VII, 14; Luke XIII, 24), and 'many are called, but few are chosen' (Matt. XX, 16, XXII, 14). But once attention was turned to the great problems of theodicy, this enormous majority of the damned was inevitably felt to be a nuisance. It was assumed that a satisfactory theodicy would be achieved, if it could be shown that the total amount of good in the universe exceeded the bad. In this case God was considered justified in carrying out the creation. Some quantity of evil was excusable because of the inevitable imperfection of anything created. But if the universe, let alone its admitted present defects, is to contain for all eternity a heavy preponderance of evil both physical and moral, that is, the great mass of the wicked and tormented damned compared with a handful of happy saints, then it is difficult to explain why a good God created it. As Leibniz wrote:[1]

> It seems strange that, even in the great future of eternity, evil must win against good, under the supreme authority of Him who is the sovereign good; for there will be many called and few chosen or saved.

Few writers, however, dared to deny outright that most adult human beings will be damned, though Leibniz does recall the crypto-Anabaptist Curione's *De Amplitudine beati regni Dei* (1554), which argued in favour of God having a larger kingdom than Satan,[2] and Horbery tried feebly to explain away the Gospel texts just quoted.[3] But there were other methods of reducing the relative size of Satan's kingdom without contradicting the Gospels. Leibniz, as so often, has recourse to an infinite universe which may contain an infinity of virtuous and happy souls, compared with which the misery and wickedness

[1] Leibniz, *Théodicée*, ed. cit., Pt. I, p. 82: 'Il paroit étrange que même dans le grand avenir de l'éternité, le mal doive avoir l'avantage sur le bien, sous l'autorité suprême de celui qui est le souverain bien: puisqu'il y aura beaucoup d'appellés, & peu d'élus ou de sauvés.'

[2] Leibniz, *Théodicée*, ed. cit., Pt. I, p. 86. Celio Secondo Curione, *De Amplitudine beati Regni Dei Dialogi, sive Libri duo*, n.p., 1554 (other eds.: Goudae, 1614; Francofurti, 1617); Bayle (*Dict. Hist. & Crit.*, art. Curion, rem (B)) commented on Curione's doctrine: 'Il y a lieu d'être surpris qu'il osât prêcher cet Evangile au milieu des Suisses; car une telle doctrine est fort suspecte aux véritables Réformez, & je ne pense pas qu'aucun Professeur la pût soutenir aujourd'hui en Hollande impunément.'

[3] Horbery, op. cit., pp. 17–18, 197, 203–4.

of damned men will appear 'presque comme rien'.[1] But, as Burnet points out, these innumerable other worlds may also contain a majority of damned.[2] Leibniz also suggests another way out, even if the number of damned in the whole universe exceeds that of the saved: the degree of virtue and bliss in the few saved may be so much greater than the degree of sin and misery in the many damned that the former outweighs the latter; for the saved may make indefinite progress towards good, which is infinite, whereas the damned can only become as wicked as the Devil, who is finite.[3] But this ingenious solution involves the unorthodox conception of a morally dynamic afterlife.

A safer solution of this difficulty is to take into account not only the adult dead, but also children who die in infancy. Since infant mortality has until recently been extremely high, it is reasonable to suppose that dead babies constitute at least 50% of the total population of the dead. As Horbery says, 'one half of our species die, perhaps, before they have actually committed any Sin to *deserve the Damnation of Hell*'.[4] If then, as Bernard, one of Bayle's victims, argued,[5] these infants are saved and at least some adult Christians, the population of heaven will be greater than that of hell, though consisting largely of babies. But, as Bayle pointed out, for orthodox Protestants and Catholics all these infants are not saved, but only the baptized ones, who are obviously a very small minority. Bayle also argued that it was inconsistent of the Protestants and Catholics to accept each other's baptism, since they mutually damned each other as adults.[6] In fact, however, they did do so, and Catholics by Bayle's time did not, in spite of St Augustine, damn unbaptized infants, but put them in Limbo, where, though deprived of the beatific vision, they are not tormented.[7] It is therefore possible for Catholics to claim that these should be counted as belonging to God's rather than Satan's kingdom, and that

[1] Leibniz, ibid.

[2] Burnet, *De Statu Mortuorum*, ed. of 1733, p. 308.

[3] Leibniz, ibid., Pt. III, pp. 264–5. Lady Conway (v. infra, p. 140) used the same argument in favour of universal salvation.

[4] Horbery, op. cit., p. 207.

[5] Bayle, *Oeuvres Diverses*, T. III, p. 1077.

[6] Bayle, ibid.: 'Je trouve là des inconséquences prodigieuses. Il faudroit ou dire moins de mal des Hérétiques, ou reconnoître nul le Batême qu'ils conferent'.

[7] But cf. infra, p. 61, note (1).

God's kingdom is thus greater than Satan's. This argument is still current today.[1]

Moreover many Protestants were becoming anxious to drop the torment of infants altogether, even if unbaptized. As Leibniz said:[2]

> Among the dogmas of St Augustine's disciples, the damnation of unregenerated infants is not to my taste . . .

It is indeed a matter of taste, and, as we have already noted, taste with regard to the suffering of others was perhaps slowly beginning to change. Even Jurieu, a staunch defender of hell in general, was violently opposed to sending infants there. Nicole, a Jansenist and hence in favour of the Augustinian torment of unbaptized infants, wrote:[3]

> This doctrine is so odious to Mr Jurieu that, when it comes into his mind, he cannot control himself and he cannot talk of it without a fit of convulsions.

He then pointed out that Jurieu was quite inconsistent in accepting the doctrines of original sin and eternal torment, 'which are, as it were, the triumph of God's authority over human reason',[4] and in rejecting infant damnation, which follows directly from them. Bayle, who delighted in exposing the inconsistencies of rationalist theology and who anyway hated Jurieu with good reason, reproduced this argument of Nicole and also Jurieu's reply,[5] which evades it: human reason must not presume to judge the cruelty of any doctrine contained in the Scriptures ('when God speaks, reason must hold her peace'[6]), but it is 'a great crime to burden God's conduct with odious things

---

[1] See *Dict. de Th. Cath.*, T. IV² (1924), art. Elus (Nombre des), by A. Michel, cols. 2355, 2374–5.

[2] Leibniz, *Théodicée*, ed. cit., Pt. III, pp. 161–2: 'Dans les dogmes mêmes des Disciples de Saint Augustin, je ne saurois goûter la damnation des enfans non regenerés'; cf. ibid., Pt. I, pp. 79, 131–149.

[3] Nicole, *De L'Unité de l'Eglise*, Paris, 1687, pp. 325 seq., quoted by Bayle, *Oeuvres Diverses*, T. III, pp. 873–4: 'Cette doctrine est si odieuse à Mr Jurieu que quand elle se présente à son esprit, il ne se possède plus & il n'en sauroit parler qu'avec transport & avec des especes de convulsions.'

[4] 'Qui sont comme le triomphe de l'autorité de Dieu sur la raison humaine.'

[5] Bayle, ibid., p. 875.

[6] 'Où Dieu parle, il faut que la raison se taise.'

which are capable of giving an unfortunate idea of it',[1] and which have no scriptural proof; if there were scriptural proof, Jurieu would accept 'this odious dogma'.

The high proportion of adult damned to saved, though felt as a disadvantage by thinkers concerned with theodicy, was still accepted by most writers on the subject, by some almost with enthusiasm. Tobias Swinden, in his *Enquiry into the Nature and Place of Hell* (1714), dedicated very obsequiously to the Bishop of Rochester, does indeed admit that 'it is a sad and dismal Contemplation'; but, having quoted Matthew VII, 13–14 ('strait is the gate'), he goes on:[2]

> the subject of it, although melancholick and sad, is yet beyond a possibility of Contradiction

and then, quite angrily:

> It is a poor, mean and narrow Conception both of the Numbers of the Damned, and of the Dimensions of Hell, which Drexelius hath laid down . . .

namely, 100,000,000,000 damned in a hell one German mile square. But Swinden, whose treatise was translated into French and published by the minister of the English church in Amsterdam in 1728, and was quoted at great length in the article 'Enfer' of the *Encyclopédie*,[3] had a special motive for insisting on the large number of the damned: the main thesis of his book is that the sun is the site of hell. His chief objection to its traditional place, inside the earth, is that this could not contain the enormous number of damned souls and their resurrected bodies, whereas the sun is many, perhaps a million times greater than the earth. Moreover the sun is evidently fiery and permanently so, while in the centre of the earth there could not be enough combustible matter to provide eternal flames, nor could

---

[1] 'un grand crime de charger la conduite de Dieu de choses odieuses qui sont capables d'en donner une idée fâcheuse.'

[2] Tobias Swinden, *An Enquiry into the Nature and Place of Hell*, London: 1727, pp. 74–6 (1st ed. 1714).

[3] Swinden, *Recherches sur la Nature du Feu de l'Enfer, et du lieu où il est situé*, trans. J. Bion, Amsterdam, 1728 (reed. 1733, 1757); Diderot, D'Alembert, etc., *Encyclopédie*, Paris, 1755, T. 5, art. Enfer, pp. 667–8. There was also a German translation of Swinden, which ran into four editions (1728, 1731, 1738, 1755).

it burn without air. Swinden's scheme has the advantage of preserving the mediaeval picture of the universe in a Copernican age: hell is still at the centre, the lowest point, the furthest from the outer heavens where the blessèd and the angels reside; and he illustrates this with the familiar diagram of concentric circles.

(iii) HELL AS A DETERRENT

Hell's greatest strength, its deterrent effect in this life, also has its weak points, and is moreover closely linked to a grave weakness: the uselessness of hell after the end of the world.

There are several ways in which the effectiveness of hell as a moral deterrent can be questioned or disproved. A purely empirical disproof was attempted by Bayle in his *Pensées sur la Comète* and in several articles in his dictionary.[1] In the former work he does not discuss the connection between atheists' behaviour and their disbelief in rewards and punishments after death, and in the dictionary he avoids as far as possible going beyond matters of historical fact. But in the *Réponse aux Questions d'un Provincial* (1706), when justifying his defence of atheists' morality in the *Comète*, he does mention what must have been uppermost in his and his readers' minds: that on *a priori* grounds atheists ought to be immoral, because they have no fear of hell.[2] Bayle, apart from the motives of practical prudence which prevented anyone discussing hell honestly, had good reasons for keeping his demonstration on a strictly empirical and historical level: he genuinely believed that people's conduct was only indirectly and very variously conditioned by their beliefs and principles, and that therefore *a priori* deductions about atheists' behaviour were likely to be mistaken. His demonstration, confined to the few cases of self-confessed atheists or of sects, such as the Saducees, who did not believe in an afterlife, was necessarily incomplete, but, as far as it could go, it was honest and convincing; and today, with our greater but still rudimentary knowledge of the extreme complexity of

---

[1] *Lettre . . . où il est prouvé . . . que les Cometes ne sont point le présage d'aucun malheur . . .*, Cologne, 1682 (later eds.: *Pensées Diverses sur la Comète*); *Dict.*, Eclairc. I (ed. 1730, IV, 619).

[2] Bayle, *Oeuvres Div.*, T. III, p. 949. Bayle himself sometimes argued on these lines, e.g. *Dict.*, art. Socin, rem. (I).

human motivation, it seems clear that he was on the right lines
—the effectiveness of savage deterrents, in this life or the next,
could be, and has been, only disproved by experience.[1]

A still more radical method of attacking the value of hell as a
moral deterrent is to admit its possible efficacy in preventing
wicked actions, but to deny that the resultant behaviour can
properly be called good or virtuous. This is, at our period, an
extremely rare line of attack, because it is so obviously incompatible with most kinds of Christian ethic. Although others,
notably Aristotle and Spinoza, had denied any moral value to
actions performed through fear, the only thinker I know of to
apply this principle to the doctrine of hell, and to heaven considered as a reward, was Shaftesbury, whose views will be discussed later.[2]

There is yet another way of arguing against the efficacy of hell
as a deterrent: on psychological grounds. This kind of argument
is used by Marie Huber in her *Sentiments différents de quelques
Théologiens sur l'état des âmes séparées des corps* (1731).[3] She
suggests that the excessiveness of eternal torment makes it an
ineffective deterrent. Although Christians imagine they believe
in hell,[4]

> everyone is persuaded that he himself is not of the number of
> the wicked, whose Portion shall be in the Lake of Fire and
> Brimstone.

That is to say, few if any men do in fact feel the degree of guilt
that would merit an infinite punishment; they therefore ignore
the threat altogether—

> the fear of a violent Distemper of twenty or thirty years con-
> tinuance, would make a deeper Impression on them.

[1] J. G. Walch, in his *Historische und Theologische Einleitung in die Religions-
Streitigkeiten der Evangelisch-Lutherischen Kirchen* (2nd ed., Jena, 1733–9, III,
529), defends eternal torment by the analogy of draconian punishments in this
life: men are now fully aware of the gallows and the wheel, but there are still
robbers and murderers—how much more crime there would be, if these punishments were made milder.

[2] V. infra, Ch. X.

[3] Published anonymously. I quote from the English translation: *The World
Unmask'd . . . To which is added, The State of Souls separated from their Bodies
. . .*, London, 1736. On Marie Huber see Gustave-A. Metzger, *Marie Huber
(1695–1753) Sa Vie, ses Oeuvres, sa Théologie*, Genève, 1887.

[4] M. Huber, op. cit., pp. 290 seq.

She is arguing, not only that eternal hell is a disproportionate punishment for any finite life however wicked (an ancient objection to which we shall return), but also that men are so psychologically constituted that they do not in fact fear threats of disproportionate punishment because, they are unable to believe in them:[1]

> Let a Schoolmaster tell his Scholar that his Father will hang him, if he doth not study; he laughs at the menace . . .

In addition to this psychological argument, which could only be proved or disproved empirically, Marie Huber, like Petersen, also attacks the deterrent value of hell from a standpoint similar to Shaftesbury's. Even if it is granted that hell may be an effective deterrent for some people, it cannot lead to a satisfactory religious conversion and a truly virtuous life, because such converts are 'only actuated by servile Fear'—satisfied if they avoid major sins,[2]

> they are content with the lowest place in Paradise; and provided they do but escape Hell, they aspire at nothing more.

(iv) VINDICTIVE JUSTICE AND FREE WILL

Hell as a deterrent is closely linked to the problem of the uselessness of hell after the Last Day, because, with the orthodox morally static afterlife, its deterrent function ceases abruptly, and it is difficult to conceive of any other function except that of giving pleasure to the blessèd, an idea which was becoming distasteful and hence obsolescent. The effort to solve this problem produced, as we have seen, the unorthodox theory of a morally dynamic afterlife, in which the continued sinning of the damned, continually punished, serves by example to preserve the saved in their state of virtue. This theory has the grave weakness of opening wide the door to the doctrine of universal salvation; how can we ensure that the damned will go on sinning, and what is to happen if they don't?

The orthodox way of dealing with the future uselessness of hell is, of course, to admit it, but to claim that nevertheless eternal torment is right and good because it is justified or

[1] Ibid., p. 404.
[2] Ibid., p. 293.

required by the principle of vindictive justice. But even if the validity of this principle is conceded, the defender of hell still has to show that eternal torment is a just punishment for wicked men, i.e. that it is proportionate to the iniquity of their sins. The usual way of doing this, which Bayle calls 'la règle ordinaire des Théologiens', was to argue[1]

> that demerit increases in proportion to the dignity of the person offended; from which they conclude that sin deserves infinite punishments, since it offends an infinite Being, but that, since these punishments cannot be infinite in degree, they must be so in duration

or, as Malebranche more vividly puts it:[2]

> The offence increases in proportion to the majesty offended. It is just to condemn an insolent subject who has insulted his Prince to be a galley-slave for life. Compare and judge whether God, without belying what He is, can be satisfied with a transitory vengeance.

It is an attack on this argument that constitutes the main substance of one of the few published Socinian writings against eternal torment, Ernst Soner's *Theological and Philosophical Demonstration that the eternal torments of the wicked do not show God's justice, but His injustice.*[3] His method of refutation is a *reductio ad absurdum*. If every sin deserves infinite punishment, infinite in intensity and duration, then it is evidently impossible for each sin to be properly avenged, since any one sin of a damned man will fill his eternal life with infinite suffering and leave no room for any more punishment of his other sins. Moreover, the orthodox doctrine of hell asserts the gradation of torments in proportion to the gravity of the sins; this is impossible if all sins deserve and receive infinite punishment. It might be objected that these difficulties could be avoided by supposing

---

[1] Bayle, *Oeuvres Div.*, T. IV, p. 31 (*Entretiens de Maxime et Themiste*, 1707), 'que le démérite croît à proportion de la dignité de la personne offensée, d'où ils concluent que le péché mérite des peines infinies, puisqu'il ofense un Etre infini, mais que ces peines ne pouvant être infinies en degrez le doivent être en durée.'

[2] Quoted by Sinsart, op. cit., pp. 154–5: 'L'offense croît à proportion de la majesté offensée. Il est juste de condamner aux galères perpétuelles un sujet insolent qui auroit outragé son Prince. Comparez & jugez si Dieu, sans démentir ce qu'il est, doit se contenter d'une vengeance passagère.'

[3] *Demonstratio Theologica, & Philosophica, quod aeterna impiorum supplicia non arguant Dei justitiam, sed injustitiam.* V. infra, pp. 84 seq.

'an infinite pain of the teeth, another of the ears, a third of the eyes, &c.', by the addition and subtraction of which different sins could be punished and the torments gradated. Soner answers this by maintaining that no pain is infinite if any other pain can be added to it. He also uses the orthodox doctrine of the Redemption for his *reductio ad absurdum* by denying that Christ's suffering was infinite in intensity or duration—he ignores the usual argument that Christ's divinity gave an infinite value to His expiation; moreover, if each human sin requires infinite punishment, Christ's death could have expiated only one.

Similar *reductiones ad absurdum* appear in later attacks on hell. Burnet, for example, states that the principle of the infinite guilt of sin due to the infinite God offended[1]

> will confound all the Proportions of vindictive Justice, and render all Sins equal,

and Jeremiah White and George Rust use the same argument, the former also pointing out that Christ's suffering was not infinite in duration.[2] It is, however, unlikely that these derive from Soner, whose book was not easily available; for there are other possible sources, among which is Thomas Aquinas's *Summa Theologica*.[3] Thomas uses in one place[4] the principle of the infinite guilt of sin due to the infinite God offended, in order to justify the eternity of hell, but elsewhere he rejects it on the same grounds as Soner, Burnet, etc., namely, because it makes all sins equal. Thomas's own justification of eternal torment is more subtle and satisfactory. Since the torments of hell are infinite in duration but finite in intensity (though much more intense than any pain in this life), the sin must be both infinite and finite; it is infinite in that it is a turning away from God, but finite in that it is a turning toward a creature. But this justification is not used by the writers we are considering.

These arguments about the proportion of sin to punishment

---

[1] Burnet, *Of the State of the Dead*, transl. Earbery, 2nd ed., London, 1728, pp. 84–5.

[2] White, *The Restoration of All Things*, London, 1712, pp. 45–7. Rust, *A Letter of Resolution*, 1661, p. 75.

[3] Thomas Aquinas, *Sum. Th.*, 1ª 2ᵃᵉ q. 87, a. 4.

[4] Ibid., Suppl., q. 99, a. 1.

presuppose the validity of vindictive justice. Though this principle had great strength from its close connection with the doctrine of the Redemption, as we have seen, it was occasionally attacked directly, and still more often by implication. The defences of it are few and feeble; which shows that it was at least beginning to be a serious weakness of hell.

The discussion of this principle is likely to involve the question of free will, because the most obvious, though perhaps not the soundest, justification of vindictive justice is based on the conception of an absolutely free will. William King, for example, gives as the great disadvantage of denying absolute free will that then[1]

> Malefactors are punished not because they deserve punishment, but because it is expedient, and laws are used to restrain vices, as physic to remove diseases . . .

In King's view a malefactor does deserve punishment because his crime is the result of a free choice, conditioned by no causes external or internal, or because, allowing for habit, his crime goes back through a series of evil actions to a free choice; one can therefore claim not only that he is a wicked man, but also that he alone is responsible for making himself wicked. Another frequent form of this argument uses the apodosis only of a conditional sentence; Horbery, justifying hell, writes:[2]

> Men shall be punished only for the Sins *which they might have avoided* [my italics].

Here the implied protasis of the italicized apodosis is presumably: 'if they had not been wicked men, which they became by their own absolutely free choice.'

This justification of vindictive justice does at least have the advantage that it apparently avoids making God punish a sin of which He Himself is the ultimate author. By supposing that the vessel of dishonour has deformed itself, one certainly makes the potter seem less unreasonable in being angry with the pot instead of with Himself. But, leaving aside the philosophical and theological difficulties of this kind of free will, we may note that it is still not explained what good is achieved by inflicting on the self-made malefactor a purely vindictive punishment,

[1] King, op. cit., pp. 193–4.
[2] Horbery, op. cit., p. 187.

45

that is, a punishment neither curative nor deterrent. Indeed King seems to be aware of this gap; for, although in the above passage he clearly accepts vindictive justice, he is elsewhere at pains to prevent God's inflicting any purely vindictive punishment. It is to avoid this that he adopts the obsolescent theory that the blessèd enjoy, and profit from the torments of the damned;[1] from which it follows that 'there is no necessity . . . to attribute eternal punishment to the divine *vengeance*'.[2]

The philosophical difficulties of this conception of free will, the *libertas indifferentiae*, are so enormous that only rather naïf thinkers, such as King, or occasionally dishonest ones, such as Descartes,[3] or thinkers that were both, such as Le Clerc, accepted it. Absolute free will is, as Leibniz called it,[4] a chimaera because it is an immediately self-contradictory concept. If the free will by which a man performs any action is free, not merely from specific constraints, external or internal, but from all determining causes, then his action must be a random one; but wholly random, haphazard actions are not called acts of will, free or otherwise, and, since they can only be performed by people who are unaware of what they are doing or are mad, they are rather the opposite of voluntary acts. Alternatively, man must be the absolute first cause of his actions, in which case we are involved in a polytheism so vast as to be unintelligible. The theological difficulties are equally insuperable. Absolute free will is in direct contradiction with the omnipotence of God, accepted by all Christians, and with the doctrine of predestination and grace, accepted, in some form, by all Catholics and, at this period, by a majority of Protestants. It is possible to attempt to reconcile absolute free will with sublapsarian predestination by making Adam's decision to eat the apple the last act of free will ever performed. But this solution still infringes God's omnipotence, and involves its users in defending the difficult doctrine of original sin, a task which was usually avoided by constructors of theodicies and defenders of hell.

Even if all these defects are overlooked, absolute free will is

[1] V. supra, p. 31.
[2] King, op. cit., p. 415.
[3] See Boorsch, *Etat présent des études sur Descartes*, Paris, 1937, pp. 128, 144.
[4] Leibniz, *Théodicée*, ed. cit., Pt. I, pp. 54, 98 seq., Pt. II, pp. 295, 308 seq., 321.

of no real use in justifying hell or in theodicy in general. First, as Bayle pointed out, the absolute freedom to sin or not to sin has had 'very odd results, which God had foreseen',[1] namely, that all men do in fact sin, and most of them to the point of damnation; whereas it would be just as compatible with absolute free will that only a few should sin or none at all, or one could argue, as More did in defending original sin,[2] that by the law of averages there should be 50% of saints and 50% of sinners. Secondly, as Bayle also demonstrated again and again, this chimaera does not exculpate God from being ultimately responsible for the sins He punishes, unless one takes from Him His omniscience as well as His omnipotence, which only the Socinians dared to do. For if, before the creation, He foresaw that most men would abuse their free will and commit sins, He could have refrained from creating them, in which case there would have been no sins to punish.

Peter Sterry had argued against free will on the same lines. He compares his own view that man, because of the inevitably imperfect nature of all creatures, must necessarily fall into sin and damnation unless supported by God's grace, which He refuses to most men, with the view that most men, endowed with absolute freedom of choice, do in fact choose sin and damnation. He makes the comparison by means of a Bayle-like story:[3]

> There are two Fathers, with their two little Children; one Father setteth his Child down so, that he may run into a pleasant Field, or a devouring Flood. He for-seeth that he will certainly run, not into the Field, but into the Flood, he suffers him to run and perish in the Flood, when he may as easily prevent him, by laying his hand upon him, or taking him into his arms. The other Father holdeth his Child fast and safe in his arms for a while over the cruel Flood, then he casteth him not in, but he taketh away his arms, and leaves him by his own weight necessarily to drop into the Flood and perish there.

---

[1] Bayle, *Oeuvres Div.*, T. III. p. 1002: 'des suites fort étranges, que Dieu avoit prévues'.

[2] More, *Annotations*, p. 8, to Glanvill and Rust, *Two Choice and Useful Treatises: the one Lux Orientalis ... The Other A Discourse of Truth ...*, London, 1682.

[3] Sterry, *A Discourse of the Freedom of the Will*, London, 1675, p. 149.

Sterry then asks:

> I appeal to every equal and impartial Judge, whether both these Fathers seem not both guilty or innocent? . . . Is not the two-fold Plea of both these Wills [sc. free and predestined] of equal force against the Justice and Goodness of God?

We may say, then, that absolute free will was a weak and ineffective way of showing the validity of vindictive justice or of justifying eternal torment. This nonsense-concept has, however, shown great vitality and is still flourishing today. It was perhaps more generally current in the 17th and 18th centuries than an examination of professional theologians and philosophers would suggest. For here again we meet a double doctrine. It was sometimes thought, not without reason, that the doctrine of predestination, imperfectly and only partially understood, might produce a morally pernicious fatalism among ordinary people; it was wiser therefore, as Jurieu said, letting the cat out of the bag as usual, to 'dogmatiser comme St Augustin, & prêcher comme Pélage'.[1] It is quite likely that then, as now, a very large number of Christians believed, in a vague way, in absolute free will and thought that it justified vindictive punishment and eternal torment.

(v) VINDICTIVE JUSTICE AND PREDESTINATION

It is possible to defend the principle of vindictive justice without having recourse to the chimerical free will. But such defences are rare, partly because this principle is so deeply embedded in Christianity that its validity is usually assumed without discussion, as by Malebranche,[2] and partly because an explicit defence of it is liable to involve an analysis that would lay bare its emotional origin, namely, the satisfaction of vengeful anger.[3]

If vindictive justice is used to justify hell, as it often was, its emotional origin is especially worrying, because in this case it is God's vengeful anger that is being satisfied by the torments

---

[1] See Leibniz, *Théodicée*, ed. cit., Pt. II, p. 148; Bossuet, *Oeuvres Complètes*, ed. F. Lachat, Paris, 1863, T. XV, p. 264.

[2] V. infra, p. 207.

[3] V. infra, p. 209.

of the damned. It is, of course, not proper to ascribe any emotions or passions to God. Even His love is only an anthropomorphic description of His will to benefit, help or save; similarly His anger is only His will to punish or destroy—though no one, I think, has ever explained why 'will' is not a grossly anthropomorphic term. But this is not much help; unless God's will to benefit or His will to punish vindictively has some real analogy with human love or anger, they are totally unintelligible caprices or arbitrary decrees, in which case it is impossible to think about them or discuss them. In fact, the reality of this analogy has been accepted by all theologians except those who demand a complete separation of divine from human values, a fundamentally perilous step, as we shall see.[1]

The divine anger, then, involved in vindictive justice was beginning to be a weak spot in the defences of hell, and it was attacked by the few whole-hearted adversaries of eternal torment with great fierceness. The predestinationist God was particularly vulnerable to such attacks, since He appeared to be deceitful as well as angry: He gives commands to men whom, by His eternal decree of reprobation, He forces to disobey, and also, by the preaching of the Gospel, offers them salvation from which He has already decided to exclude them. Shaftesbury, for example, makes the following attack on this God and His moral influence:[2]

If there be a religion which teaches the adoration and love of a God whose character is to be captious and of high resentment, subject to wrath and anger, furious, revengeful, and revenging himself, when offended, on others than those who gave the offence; and if there be added to the character of this God a fraudulent disposition, encouraging deceit and treachery among men, favourable to a few, though for slight causes, and cruel to the rest, 'tis evident that such a religion as this being strongly enforced must of necessity raise even an approbation and respect towards the vices of this kind, and breed a suitable disposition, a capricious, partial, revengeful and deceitful temper.

The moral turpitude of this God is made much more striking by the doctrine of hell; He who has gone through this pointless

[1] V. infra, section (vii).
[2] Shaftesbury, *Characteristics*, ed. J. M. Robertson, London, 1900, Vol. I, p. 263 (first ed. 1711).

49

comedy with the reprobate will then punish them eternally for their disobedience and rejection of salvation—*horribile decretum* indeed.[1] If, on the other hand, all the reprobate will eventually be saved, after purgatorial torment, this God appears considerably less cruel and deceitful, though still mysteriously capricious. Jeremiah White, who did believe in absolute predestination, is especially pleased with this result of his scheme for universal salvation;[2] and Petersen repeatedly points out that the acceptance of universal salvation will make unnecessary all the endless disputes about grace, free will and predestination.[3] There was perhaps a general tendency on this account for morally sensitive predestinationists to wish to be rid of the doctrine of hell;[4] and this may be one of the reasons why the doctrine began to be questioned when it did—soon after Calvin and Luther had established predestination in an uncompromising form, and at the same time as the Jansenists were trying to do so in France.

The discussion of vindictive justice in the context of hell was, I think, important beyond the bounds of theology. In all human punishment there are three possible motives or intentions: curative, deterrent, and retributive or vindictive. In most actual punishments all three may be, and usually are present, though the first, of course, is absent in all capital punishment. In considering human justice it is, in consequence, difficult to disentangle and evaluate the intentions behind punishments and easy to pass over or assume the most questionable motive, retribution, without seriously examining it. But in considering hell after the Last Day attention is inevitably focussed solely and therefore clearly on the retributive aspect of punishment,

---

[1] Calvin, *Institutio Religionis Christianae*, ed. of 1559, III, xxiii, 7.

[2] V. infra, p. 108.

[3] Petersen, *Mysterion*, T. I, Vorrede, p. (xvii), Gespräch I, pp. 137–40; T. II, Auffgelöste Dubia, p. 63.

[4] Cf. Burnet, *De Statu Mortuorum*, ed. of 1733, p. 308: 'Denique quibus displicent absoluta reprobationis decreta, quòd naturae & attributis divinis repugnare videantur, iis non minùs displicere debent aeternae malorum poenae, quum iisdem attributis non minùs repugnent. Et ex alterâ parte, qui haec decreta recipiunt, eorum interest aeternas poenas respuere, quâ ratione levantur sui oneris parte gravissimâ. Cum non tanti sit praeordinari aut condemnari aliquem ad poenas desituras; sed ad poenas aeternas & intolerabiles, *Hic stimulus est, hic aculeus severitatis.*'

since, in the orthodox afterlife, there is no other. This is probably one reason why Hobbes, for example, who was certainly not a soft or sentimental thinker, came to reject vindictive justice; for he was very much preoccupied with hell, as is witnessed by the extraordinary eschatology suggested in the *Leviathan* and retracted, in favour of annihilation of the wicked, in his *Answer* to Bramhall.[1]

The attacks on the vindictive and deceitful God of the predestinationists naturally produced counter-attacks. The Calvinists, whether genuine, like Jurieu, or pretending, like Bayle, demonstrated that the Arminian, Jesuit, or even Socinian God, in spite of free will, mitigated or rejected predestination and original sin, reduction of the relative number of the damned, and so forth, was, if thoroughly analysed, equally cruel and perhaps more deceitful.[2] In both cases, whether by a decree of reprobation, or by permitting the misuse of free will, God is ultimately responsible for the sins He punishes with eternal torment. Is there any way of avoiding this blasphemous conclusion?

(vi) LIMITATIONS OF GOD'S OMNIPOTENCE

One way of saving the goodness of God is at the expense of His omnipotence, that is, by supposing there to be obstacles which His goodness cannot completely overcome. These obstacles, as Bayle points out,[3] may be of two kinds: external or internal. The former kind, which is flagrantly unorthodox, is supposed by Manichaeans, for whom the obstacle is the bad God, or by any system which posits an independently existing matter resistant to God's will, or by extreme free will systems (Hobbes calls them Manichaean);[4] these we will leave on one side for the moment. The internal kind of obstacle is less obviously unorthodox, since it does not involve the limitation of God's omnipotence by any independently existing entity; it may therefore be compatible with Christian monotheism. One form of this

---

[1] Hobbes, *Leviathan*, ed. cit., pp. 299–300, 404 seq., 411 seq.; Hobbes, *An Answer to a book published by Dr. Bramhall*, in *The English Works of Thomas Hobbes*, London, 1840, Vol. IV, p. 359.

[2] V. infra, Ch. XI.

[3] Bayle, *Oeuvres Div.*, T. III, p. 812.

[4] Hobbes, *English Works*, 1840, Vol. IV, pp. 390, 399.

internal limitation, traditionally used in defences of hell, arises from a conflict between the attributes of God, all of which, it is assumed, must be manifested in His acts.

God's goodness or mercy demands that all men be saved (I Tim. II, 4). But the manifestation of His justice or of His hatred of sin requires that at least some men should sin so that they may be justly punished. Since it is impossible that all men should be saved and some damned, His antecedent will to save all men, as Thomas Aquinas explains,[1] is modified by the demands of His justice and produces His consequent will, which effects a compromise between the two conflicting attributes: He will save the elect, thus manifesting His mercy, and damn the reprobate, thus manifesting His justice. Bayle, and after him Leibniz, quote these words of Théodore de Bèze, spoken at the Colloquy of Montbelliard in 1586:[2]

> God has created the world for His glory; His glory is not known, unless His mercy and His justice are declared: to this end He has, as an act of sheer grace, destined some men to eternal life, and some, by just judgment, to eternal damnation. Mercy presupposes misery, justice presupposes guilt.

Even if the premises of this argument are admitted, there are some weak spots in it. First, it does not account for the great majority of damned to saved, still a generally accepted fact, since a majority of saved to damned would also have manifested both attributes. Secondly, it does not explain why all men have been involved in sin, since quite a few would have been enough to give examples of divine punishment. This second objection could however be answered by arguing that God's mercy is shown more vividly by His saving some undeserving sinners than by saving wholly virtuous men, who might be thought to deserve salvation; it could also be answered by the *felix culpa* argument, which we shall meet in Malebranche and Leibniz.[3]

---

[1] Thomas Aquinas, *Sum. Th.*, I, q. xix, a. 6.

[2] Bayle, *Oeuvres Div.*, T. III, p. 814; Leibniz, *Théodicée*, ed. cit., Pt. II, p. 126: 'Dieu a créé le Monde à sa gloire; sa gloire n'est connue si sa misericorde & sa justice n'est déclarée: pour ceste cause il a declaré aucuns certains hommes de pure grace à vie éternelle, & aucuns par juste jugement à damnation éternelle. La misericorde présuppose la misere, la justice présuppose la coulpe.'

[3] V. infra, pp. 204, 212.

One can also attack the premisses of the argument. Jurieu had stated it thus:[1]

> If God had not allowed sin to come into existence, how could His supreme hatred of sin have been manifested? But that supreme sanctity of God by which He hates sin is, among the virtues of God that are to be manifested, by far the greatest. Therefore, in order that it could be manifested, sin had to be allowed.

Bayle refuted this by arguing that the manifestation is superfluous, because hatred of sin, i.e. justice, is contained in our idea of God and therefore known to us without practical demonstration, and that hatred of sin is better manifested by preventing it than by punishing it—an argument also used by Leibniz.[2] But the second half of this refutation is of doubtful validity if the attribute of justice is taken to be retributive justice, as it was by the theologians using this argument. Retributive justice implies the existence of some wrong act to be avenged; it can only be manifested by punishing sin, not by preventing it. The only way of successfully refuting the basis of this argument is to deny that God's justice is vindictive, as did Sterry and White, and make this attribute subordinate to that of goodness, so that a conflict between attributes cannot arise.

Internal conflicts which limit God's omnipotence, but of a different kind from that just discussed, form the basis of Malebranche's and Leibniz's theodicies, which will be dealt with later.[3]

(vii) SEPARATION OF DIVINE AND HUMAN VALUES. MANICHAENISM

In attempting his largely negative theodicy Leibniz's most important aim was to prevent the separation of divine from human moral values:[4]

---

[1] Jurieu, *De Pace inter Protestantes ineunda Consultatio*, Ultrajecti, 1688, p. 188, quoted by Bayle, *Oeuvres Div.*, T. III, p. 862: 'Si deus peccatum fieri non permiserit, quomodo summum ipsius in peccatum odium manifestari potuerit? At illa summa Dei sanctitas quâ horret peccatum, est inter virtutes Dei manifestandas longè maxima. Ergò ut posset manifestari, debuit peccatum permitti.'

[2] Bayle, ibid., and *Dict. Hist. & Crit.*, ed. cit., art. Pauliciens, rem. (E), p. 627; Leibniz, *Théodicée*, ed. cit., Pt. II, p. 127.

[3] V. infra, Ch. XII.

[4] Leibniz, ibid., Pt. I, p. 75: 'Notre but est d'éloigner les Hommes des fausses idées qui leur représentent Dieu comme un Prince absolu, usant d'un pouvoir despotique, peu propre à être aimé, & peu digne d'être aimé.'

Our aim is to lead men away from false ideas which make God appear to them as an absolute monarch, exerting despotic power, unsuited to be loved, and unworthy to be loved.

He rightly saw that this was one of the most dangerous points in Bayle's Manichaean objections to a good and omnipotent God, a point which Bayle emphasized by asserting, in his Calvinist rôle, that the only way to refute a Manichaean was *not* to admit[1]

as the measure of God's goodness and sanctity the ideas which we have of goodness and sanctity in general.

This separation is disastrous in several respects, as Bayle himself showed at length when refuting William King.[2] As regards human morals: at best it reduces religiously based morality to servile obedience to rules which may at any moment be changed by some new divine decree; at worst it may lead men into positive wickedness through imitation of God's arbitrary exercise of power, His Justice becoming, as Leibniz remarks, merely that of Thrasymachus in the First Book of Plato's *Republic*—the advantage of the stronger (τὸ τοῦ κρείττονος συμφέρον).[3]

It is no way out of these dangers to assert, as Luther and the Calvinists did, that, although God's justice or goodness are not the same as ours, and consist merely in the arbitrary exercise of His will, God is nevertheless just and good. These epithets, used in such a way, lose all meaning, and are merely a device for avoiding obvious blasphemy. Shaftesbury demonstrates this clearly:[4]

For whoever thinks there is a God, and pretends formally to believe that he is just and good, must suppose that there is

[1] Bayle, *Oeuvres Div.*, T. III, p. 997: 'pour la regle de la bonté & de la sainteté de Dieu les idées que nous avons de la bonté & de la sainteté en général.' Cf. ibid., T. IV, p. 24, the atheists' syllogism:
'Si le Dieu des Chretiens est faux, il n'y a point de Dieu. Or le Dieu des Chretiens est faux, si sa conduite n'est pas conforme aux notions communes de la bonté, de la sainteté & de la justice.
Donc si la conduite du Dieu des Chretiens n'est pas conforme à ces notions-là il n'y a point de Dieu.'
Bayle would deal with this by denying the second proposition.
[2] Bayle, *Oeuvres Div.*, T. III, p. 675.
[3] Leibniz, *Théodicée*, ed. cit., Pt. I, pp. xxii seq.; Plato, *Republic*, Bk. I, 338 C.
[4] Shaftesbury, *Characteristics*, ed. cit., Vol. I, p. 264.

independently such a thing as justice and injustice, truth and falsehood, right and wrong, according to which he pronounces that God is just, righteous, and true. If the mere will, decree, or law of God be said absolutely to constitute right and wrong, then are these latter words of no significancy at all . . . Thus if one person were decreed to suffer for another's fault, the sentence would be just and equitable. And thus, in the same manner, if arbitrarily and without reason some beings were destined to endure perpetual ill, and others are constantly to enjoy good, this also would pass under the same denomination. But to say of anything that it is just or unjust on such a foundation as this is to say nothing, or to speak without a meaning.

As regards religion, this separation, far from refuting Manichaean objections, as Bayle maliciously suggested, leads straight to a pessimistic Manichaeanism in which the bad deity has gained the upper hand. For the only conceivable way in which God's justice and goodness can be wholly different from ours is by being what we should call injustice and cruelty. Leibniz says hopefully:[1]

> But such strange principles, so little suited to make men good and charitable by the imitation of God, will soon be abandoned, when it is fully realized that a God who took pleasure in the misfortune of others would be indistinguishable from the evil Principle of the Manichaeans, supposing that this Principle had become the sole master of the universe.

The only way to prevent this disastrous separation, which leads to something worse than atheism, namely devil-worship, is to make the ideas of goodness, justice, etc., anterior to, and independent of God's decrees, as we have seen Shaftesbury doing, so that it is true to say that God wills what is just because it is just, and false to say that what God wills is just merely because He has willed it. The establishment of this priority of moral ideas over the divine will was, as Ernst Cassirer has shown,[2] the great aim of the Cambridge Platonists, who were

[1] Leibniz, ibid., Pt. I, p. xxii (cf. p. 32): 'Mais on abandonnera bientôt des maximes si étranges, & si peu propres à rendre les hommes bons & charitables par l'imitation de Dieu; lorsqu'on aura bien considéré qu'un Dieu qui se plairoit au mal d'autrui, ne sauroit être distingué du mauvais Principe des Manichéens, supposé que ce Principe fût devenu seul Maître de l'Univers.'
[2] Cassirer, *The Platonic Renaissance in England*, transl. J. P. Pettegrove, London, 1953.

asserting it against the Calvinism in which most of them had been brought up; it is the explicit and sole aim of the *Discourse of Truth* of George Rust, the defender of Origen.[1] Cassirer sees the main source of the separation of divine from human moral ideas in St Augustine's voluntaristic conception of God, which was revived by Luther, Calvin, and Jansen. The assertion or denial of this separation is the kernel of all debates about free will, grace and predestination from Erasmus's *De Libero Arbitrio*[2] to Leibniz's *Théodicée*. But it is, I think, only in the later part of this period that, thanks largely to Bayle, the consequences of this separation for religion, as distinct from the consequences for human morals, became evident—that the terrible shape of the Manichaean evil God began to loom up at the side of the God of Augustine and his followers.[3]

But this shape was there from the beginning. St Augustine had been a Manichaean, and there are good grounds for supposing that Manichaean doctrine continued to influence him strongly even after his conversion.[4] If one passes from Manichaean dualism to Christian monotheism, what happens to the evil principle? One solution is to adopt the Platonic negative conception of evil as sheer privation, lack of being, inevitably present to a gradually greater degree as the scale of created entities extends further from its divine source. Augustine does indeed expound this solution, which was one of the causes of his conversion;[5] but, apart from other difficulties, it is in flagrant contradiction with any Christian conception of sin, and especially with his own doctrine of original sin. Sin must be something positive in that it is to be punished or expiated, and it must therefore have a positive cause. It is no real solution to put the cause in Adam's fall, since this would make Adam the evil principle and lead back to Manichaeanism. It is inevitable that the two Manichaean principles should coalesce into

---

[1] V. infra, pp. 124–5, 134 seq.

[2] Published in 1524; cf. Walker, 'Origène en France', pp. 115 seq.

[3] Attacks on the Calvinist God as a cruel devil begin of course well before Bayle, cf. e.g. infra, Ch. VIII, section (v).

[4] See R. Reitzenstein, 'Augustin als antiker und als mittelalterlicher Mensch', in *Vorträge der Bibliothek Warburg*, 1922–3, I. Teil, Leipzig-Berlin, 1924, pp. 40 seq.

[5] Augustine, *Confessions*, VII, xi seq.

one, that the Christian God who punishes Christian sin should be both God and Devil.

This inclusion of the principle of evil in God is a danger that threatens any kind of Christianity, as Bayle, together with Calvinist and Jansenist polemicists, showed.[1] But the danger is much more apparent in strictly Augustinian theologies, because they deny that God's justice is our justice, and it did lead, as we shall see, to Calvinists and Jansenists being accused of devil-worship. From the time that Luther insisted that 'I will harden Pharaoh's heart' means what it says, such theologians have been said by their adversaries to make God the author of sin, and according to Bayle,[2]

> Orthodox terminology does not vary on this point; from time immemorial this usage has been established: that to be a Manichaean, and to make God the author of sin, are two expressions which mean the same thing.

Even Leibniz, whose main aim was to prevent this coalescence of the good and bad Gods, and who also adopted a Platonic conception of evil as privation, cannot avoid nevertheless putting evil into God, combining in Him the two principles of a dualistic system. Now the Platonic system, though it calls evil non-being, is really dualistic, since this negativity, necessity (ἀναγκή) or matter, is resistant to the intelligence (νοῦς) that works on it, as one can see in the *Timaeus*. Plato's necessity, says Leibniz, must for Christian monotheists be[3]

> internal and is situated in the divine mind. And it is therein that is to be found not only the pristine form of good, but also the origin of evil . . .

But Leibniz, by insisting on the identity of human and divine moral values, does attempt to prevent his God being the direct cause of moral evil, whereas the Augustinians, by separating

[1] V. infra, pp. 195 seq.

[2] Luther, *De Servo Arbitrio*, 1525, sig. N ij vo (referring to Exodus, VII, 3 and Romans IX, 17–18); Bayle, *Dict. Hist. & Crit.*, art. Pauliciens, rem. (I), ed. cit., p. 631: 'Le style des Orthodoxes ne varie point là-dessus: il est fixé de tems immémorial à cet usage, qu'être Manichéen, & faire Dieu auteur du péché, sont deux expressions qui signifient la même chose.'

[3] Leibniz, *Théodicée*, ed. cit., Pt. I, p. 82: 'interne & se trouve dans l'Entendement divin. Et c'est là dedans que se trouve non seulement la forme primitive du bien, mais encore l'origine du mal . . .'

human and divine values, and thus making God's attributes of justice and goodness empty names, leave no barrier against the evil God.

It might be suggested that for Christians the Manichaean evil principle becomes the Devil. Bayle does make this suggestion, but points out that, since the Devil is a created being, whose very existence is entirely dependant on God's will, he cannot be a principle of evil, however important he may be as a second cause of it.[1] He is therefore useless for theodicy, and to attempt to make him the origin of evil is merely to repeat, at a stage further back, the attempt to make Adam's fall the ultimate 'source of all our woes'. The Devil is seldom discussed in theodicies or controversies about hell, perhaps because his status is somewhat doubtful. The Church, chiefly in opposition to Manichaean heresies, has always been careful to insist that he is no more than an angel and can do nothing without God's permission.[2] In this case he is obviously worse than useless for theodicy—it is as if a tyrant employed a cruel Chief of Police and then put the blame on him for his oppressive activities. On the other hand, Satan is usually held to be the highest of all angels, standing at the summit of the created hierarchy, immediately below the Godhead,[3] and he is eternal, not only in that, like other angels and like men, he is immortal, but also in that his kingdom will last for ever. But again, Satan's kingdom, hell, is not only permitted by God, but is an essential part of the plan by which His justice shall be made manifest for all eternity.

[1] Bayle, *Dict. Hist. & Crit.*, art. Pauliciens, rem. (H), ed. cit. p. 631.
[2] See H. I. Marrou, 'The Fallen Angel', in *Satan*, London, 1951 (based on a volume in the series *Collection de Psychologie Religieuse, Etudes Carmélitaines*), pp. 67 seq.
[3] See Walter Farrell, 'The Devil Himself', in *Satan*, p. 10.

Chapter IV

❖-◇-❖-◇-❖-◇-❖-◇-❖-◇-❖-◇-❖-◇-❖-◇-❖-◇-❖-◇-❖-◇-❖-◇-❖-◇-❖-◇-❖-◇-❖-◇-❖-◇-❖

THE MERCIFUL DOCTORS

❖-◇-❖-◇-❖-◇-❖-◇-❖-◇-❖-◇-❖-◇-❖-◇-❖-◇-❖-◇-❖-◇-❖-◇-❖-◇-❖-◇-❖-◇-❖-◇-❖-◇-❖

(i) MITIGATIONS OF HELL

THE doctrine of purgatory, together with the practice, on which it is based, of absolution before penance,[1] does for Catholics provide a safer means of escape from hell than is open to Protestants, and might therefore be considered as a mitigation. But, since all the inhabitants of purgatory are saved, the doctrine is not a mitigation of hell but a modification of heaven, except in that it may somewhat diminish the number of the damned. In fact, it is not presented as a mitigation in Catholic defences of it or in Protestant attacks on it.

Nevertheless the Protestant rejection of purgatory is of great importance in our attempt to discover why the doctrine of hell began to be questioned when it did. First, although there is not much evidence to support this suggestion, it must have been the case that in a personal way the abolition of purgatory produced for many Protestants a painful situation.[2] If a Protestant

---

[1] See Kenneth E. Kirk, *The Vision of God*, London, 1931, pp. 286 seq.

[2] Petersen does mention this situation (*Mysterion*, T. I, Gespräch I, p. 30). Cf. Samuel Richardson, *A Discourse of the Torments of Hell*, n.p., 1660, p. 168: the abolition of eternal torment will be a great comfort 'to many whose children and friends die and leave no testimony of their conversion, the fear that they are to suffer so great and endlesse torment hath greatly sadded and troubled the heart of many a parent and friend'.

was bereaved of a belovèd but by no means saintly friend or relative, he was faced with only two possibilities: either the dead person was fit to go straight to heaven and take his place in the company of the blessèd, or he must go to eternal torment. A Catholic, on the other hand, in the same situation, could reasonably hope that, provided he had been properly absolved, the dead man, however sinful, would go to purgatory, there do penance for his unexpiated sins, and finally be saved. Secondly, purgatory is very similar to a dynamic afterlife, and, if they had not rejected it, the Protestants might easily have transformed it into one. The Catholic purgatory is not morally dynamic; its inhabitants have already been absolved of all their sins and their purgatorial pains are merely the penance they failed to do on earth. Suppose that the Reformation had not been set off by the traffic in Indulgences, but by some other abuse of penitential practices, and that, in consequence, the Protestants, whilst rejecting the whole doctrine of penitential works, had retained the belief in some kind of afterlife intermediate between heaven and hell, then this intermediate state could only have been one of further probation, where those who had not achieved salvation in this life, nor been so wicked as to merit damnation, might still receive the gift of faith or finally damn themselves, i.e. a dynamic afterlife. Such a state is in fact hinted at in the early letter of Luther already cited, where he says that a man may achieve the saving faith in Christ 'in death or after death'.[1] This intermediate state ('mittlerer Zustand') is an essential feature of the Petersens' eschatology, and Petersen, while taking care to emphasize its difference from the Catholic purgatory, frequently expresses his regret that the Protestants rejected purgatory altogether, instead of only its 'superstitious' accretions (i.e. its penitential function)—this was 'throwing the baby out with the bath'.[2] If such an intermediate state is allowed to absorb hell and to extend indefinitely beyond the Last Judgment, one has the most usual scheme for universal salvation; and advocates of this doctrine are always at great pains to point out how their afterlife differs from the Roman Catholic purgatory.

[1] V. supra, pp. 7–8, and infra, p. 237 on Petersen's use of Luther.
[2] Petersen, *Mysterion*, T. I, *Ewiges Evangelium*, p. 6. (the Protestants have 'das Kind mit dem Bade auszgeschüttet'); and cf. infra, pp. 239–40.

Limbo, unlike purgatory, is a real mitigation of hell, since unbaptized infants are in the class of the damned, owing to original sin, but enjoy the exceptional privilege of suffering only the *poena damni* (deprivation of the beatific vision), not the *poena sensus* (sensible torment).[1] This type of mitigation, extended to the whole class of the damned, had several adherents, and is still very popular today, both among Protestants, most of whom are allowed to believe in it, and among Catholics, who are not. It supposes either, as Le Clerc suggested, that sinners will first be punished by sensible tortures, and then, when their sins have been thus expiated, by only the deprivation of the vision of God, in which case, he thinks, their condition will be 'tolerable', though they will still be tormented by regret and envy;[2] or, as in the systems of Calvin or Jaquelot,[3] there are no sensible pains at all, but only the mental torment of deprivation.

The latter, more usual, form of the doctrine runs up against serious scriptural difficulties. 'The worm that dieth not' was nearly always interpreted figuratively, as meaning the stings of envy and regret. But if this is the only kind of torment in hell, then the fire must also mean this, and unfortunately the worm and the fire often occur in the same passage. Swinden, in refuting this mitigation, pointed out that Mark IX, 43-4,

it is better for thee to enter into life maimed, than having two hands to go into hell, into the fire that never shall be quenched: where their worm dieth not, and the fire is not quenched

would mean in non-figurative terms:

It is better to be maimed than to go into hell, into vexation of mind that shall never cease, where their vexation of mind never ceaseth, and the vexation of mind never ceaseth

[1] This doctrine, which seems to have originated with Abelard, is that of Thomas Aquinas; but it was by no means undisputed in the 16th and 17th centuries by those who preferred the Augustinian positive torment of unbaptized infants, such as St Robert Bellarmine and Pétau (see G. G. Coulton, *Infant Perdition in the Middle Ages*, (*Medieval Studies*, No. 16), London, 1922; Leibniz, *Théodicée*, ed. cit., Pt. I, pp. 79 seq., 139 seq.).

The *Limbus Patrum* or *Sinus Abrahae* need not concern us; it has been without inhabitants since Christ released them (see C. Spicq, op. cit., in *L'Enfer*, pp. 113 seq., and Antonius Rusca, *De Inferno et Statu Daemonum ante Mundi Exitium, Libri Quinque*, Mediolani, 1621, pp. 2-3).

[2] V. infra, pp. 192-3.

[3] V. infra, pp. 62 n. (4), 198-9.

61

and he rightly remarked on the 'indecency' of the tautology.[1]

Among the Fathers only a small minority, headed by Origen, are in favour of interpreting hell-fire figuratively as remorse, regret,[2] etc., and it is easy for defenders of the orthodox hell to cite innumerable authorities for the reality of the fire, and even for that of the brimstone mentioned in Isaiah XXX, 33 and elsewhere. Bishop Bilson, for example, in his *Survey of Christ's Sufferings*, writes:[3]

> If God will have *Brimstone* mixed with *Hell Fire* to make it burne not onely the darker and sharper, but also the lothsommer, and so to grieve the sight, smell and taste of the wicked, which have here been surfeited with so many vaine Pleasures, what have you or any Man living to say against it?

and can support his view with an imposing list of authorities. It was such interpretations that Calvin, commenting on the above-mentioned verse in Isaiah, contemptuously dismissed as 'crassae imaginationes'.[4] But why, asked Tobias Swinden,[5]

> must these Truths be exploded as gross Imaginations, since they are delivered in the Scriptures, and received by the Church of *God*?

The answer to this question is by no means obvious. For, as Bayle pointed out to Jaquelot and Le Clerc, an eternal hell of only mental torment is of no use for theodicy;[6] a God who inflicts only this is still cruel (if one considers eternal torment cruel), though perhaps in a less crude manner than the God who also inflicts sensible pain. But can God be said to *inflict* the *poena damni*? In the sense that He is ultimately responsible for it by not giving, or not having given, irresistible grace to the

---

[1] Tobias Swinden, *An Enquiry into the Nature and Place of Hell*, ed. of 1727, p. 37.

[2] See G. Bardy, op. cit., in *L'Enfer*, pp. 154 seq.

[3] Thomas Bilson, *The Survey of Christs Sufferings for Mans redemption*, London, 1604, pp. 46–7, quoted by Swinden, ibid., p. 48. Cf. Rusca, *De Inferno*, 1621, II, xix, pp. 223 seq., chapter entitled: 'An sulphur accensum in gehenna verè foeteat. Id ab aliquibus in dubium reuocari. Communi doctorum sententia, exhalare putidum odorem'; St Ignatius Loyola's 5th Spiritual Exercise, which is a meditation on hell, includes imagining the stench (quoted by P. Dearmer, *The Legend of Hell*, pp. 40–1).

[4] Calvin, *Commentarii in Isaiam*, Genevae, 1551, p. 305.

[5] Swinden, ibid., p. 58.

[6] V. infra, pp. 198–9.

damned, yes; but, in the sense of doing any positive punitive act, no. This is, I think a real distinction, and points to the basic motive behind this mitigation: the wish to believe that God's part in the torments of the damned is purely negative, and that in some way the damned themselves, or their sins, are the only positive cause of their punishment. As we shall see in the debates on free will and predestination, this kind of distinction does not absolve God from cruelty; there is little if any moral difference between allowing the occurrence of a disaster together with the resultant suffering, which you could prevent, and actively causing the disaster and the suffering. But, if we leave out of account God's responsibility for the disaster, that is, for most men having sinned to the point of damnation, and assume that sin must inevitably, 'naturally' cause suffering in the sinner, then the God who merely allows this to happen does seem less savagely cruel than the God who actively increases this 'natural' suffering.

The weak spot in such mitigating systems is the assumption that sin naturally and inevitably brings suffering on the sinner. For, in systems which posit the eternity of hell and no *poena sensus*, it is difficult to imagine the nature of this suffering. Remorse, the stings of conscience, are ruled out, because, if the damned felt these, it would mean they were repentant and therefore on the way to salvation. The separation from God's presence, if it is to produce pain, again leads to the self-contradictory conclusion that the damned are in a state of grace, since they would not suffer from His absence unless they loved Him. Of other natural consequences of sin physical ones, such as disease, do not apply to the afterlife, except for the very literal-minded Whiston, who believes that the wicked will resurrect with the same diseases they had at death.[1] Such physical suffering is anyway ruled out, if there is to be no *poena sensus*. Of the usual regret and envy attributed to the damned only the latter can be retained, since the regret must be aroused by the *poena sensus*—otherwise it would be remorse; and in fact Jaquelot does lay greatest emphasis on envy, as the main torment of the damned.

Perhaps the most satisfactory suggestion is William King's: that the damned are in a state of frustrated madness, always

[1] V. infra, p. 100.

wishing for evil pleasures which they cannot possibly attain, though here the consequences of sin can scarcely be called natural or inevitable.[1] His hell must have been specially designed to drive sinners mad, since in this world there seems to be no general tendency for the wicked to go out of their wits. These difficulties do not arise, as we shall see, in systems which allow for the eventual salvation of the damned, and the theory of an inevitable, natural connection between sin and suffering was a fruitful one.[2]

Leibniz, who mentions Jaquelot's and King's mitigations with vague approval, contributes a typically ingenious and frivolous mitigation of his own. Having cited Augustine's admission, in reply to Origen's using Psalm LXXVII, 9 ('Hath God forgotten to be gracious? hath he in anger shut up his tender mercies?'), that perhaps the sufferings of the damned, though eternal, may eventually be mitigated, Leibniz suggests that the mitigation may be continuous and asymptotically approach complete absence of pain.[3]

There is a mitigation within the orthodox doctrine itself: the damned will not all be punished with the maximum intensity of pain, the torments being graded in accordance with the quantity and quality of their sins.[4] This mitigation is not excessive, since the lowest point on the scale of pain will be beyond anything experienced in this life—as St Augustine writes:[5]

That fire will be more severe than anything a man can suffer in this life

[1] V. infra, pp. 213–4.
[2] One source of this theory is Origen, who uses the analogy of painful diseases produced by intemperate living (*De Principiis*, II, x, 4; *Werke*, ed. Koetschau, Bd. V, Leipzig, 1913, pp. 177–8). Cf. Robert Klein, 'L'Enfer de Ficin', in *Umanesimo e Esoterismo*, Padova, 1960, pp. 47 seq.
[3] Leibniz, *Théodicée*, ed. cit., Pt. III, pp. 153–4; Augustine, *Enchiridion*, c. 112 (Migne, *Patr. Lat.*, T. 40, cols. 284–5). For other mitigations in medieaval and modern times, see C. V. Héris, op. cit., in *L'Enfer*, pp. 253 seq.
[4] The gradation of torments was confirmed by the Councils of Lyons (1274) and Florence (1439) (see *Dict. de Th. Cath.*, art. Enfer, col. 91).
[5] Augustine, In Psalm XXXVII, 2, (Migne, *Patr. Lat.*, T. 36, col. 397); cf. Thomas Aquinas, *Sum. Th.*, III, q. 46, a. 6, ad 3, Suppl., q. 98, a. 3. The same is true of the fire of purgatory; Augustine in this passage is talking about those who shall be saved 'yet so as by fire' (I Cor. III, 15): 'Ita plane quamvis salvi per ignem, gravior tamen erit ille ignis, quam quidquid potest homo pati in hac vita.'

or, in our period, Johann Fecht in his *De Statu Damnatorum*:[1]

> That infernal torment is a kind of most perfect factory for all
> punishments, i.e., that it includes all tortures, however many
> either are or can be conceived, and that it excludes everything
> that might be any kind of relief to the damned or could produce
> any mitigation, is evident . . .

Fecht goes on to give evidence for this statement:[2] first, 'the
accurate description of these punishments everywhere in Holy
Writ', and secondly, the analogy with

> the ineffable joy of life in heaven, which, just as *eye hath not
> known, nor ear heard, neither have entered into the heart of man,
> the things which God hath prepared for them that love him,*
> I Cor. II, 9, so it gives us to understand, by antithesis, that the
> evils of hell cannot be conceived by the soul, or comprehended
> by the mind, or expressed by speech.

Thus if we look at the whole scale of heavenly joys and hellish
pains, we see that it is not continuous but has a gap in the middle
coextensive with the joys and sorrows of this world. This gap
is there partly because there must be a 'great gulf fixt' between
heaven and hell, which would be impossible if there were
borderline cases, but chiefly because of the wish to have the
greatest possible symmetry of contrast between the two states.
If the joys of heaven are beyond our imagining, so must be the
pains of hell, and, as Gregory the Great explains:[3]

> As in the Father's house there are many mansions, in accordance
> with the differences of virtue, so the disparity of crime subjects
> the damned to various torments by the fires of Gehenna.

[1] J. Fechtius, *De Statu Damnatorum*, ed. of 1708, p. 148: 'Infernale supplicium
absolutissimam quandam poenarum omnium officinam esse, id est, cruciatus
omnes, quotquot vel sunt vel cogitari possunt, includere, excludere vero omne id,
quod solatio damnatis qualiscunque esse aut adferre refrigerium possit, palam
est . . .'
[2] Ibid.: 'ex accurata harum poenarum ubique S. Literarum descriptione . . .
ex analogia cum ineffabili coelestis vitae gaudio, quod sicut *neque oculus vidit,
neque auris audivit, neque in cujusquam cor ascendit, quid praeparavit Deus
diligentibus ipsum* (I Cor. II, 9), ita, quam ne cogitanda sint animo, aut com-
prehendenda mente, aut enuncianda sermone inferorum mala, ex contrario nos
intelligere facit . . .''
[3] Gregory the Great, *Moralia*, Lib. IX, c. LXV (Migne, *Patr. Lat.*, T. 75, col.
913): 'Sicut in domo Patris mansiones multae sunt, pro diuersitate virtutis, sic
damnatos diuerso supplicio gehennae ignibus subijcit disparitas criminis.'

Thomas Aquinas extends this symmetry of contrast even to the kind of eternity in each state. True eternity, which entails immutability, belongs only to God, but, through the beatific vision, the blessèd participate in this and can therefore properly be said to enjoy eternal life. In hell, on the other hand, there is a succession of various torments, and it can therefore only loosely be called eternal in that the succession has no end:[1]

> hell-fire is said to be eternal only on account of its endlessness. There is change in their punishments, witness Job 24: they shall go to excessive heat from the waters of the snows.[2] Hence in hell there is not true eternity, but rather time . . .

This variety of torments, of which heat and cold are only one example, leads to another contrast. The blessèd feel neither hope nor fear, since they already possess all that they could hope for and know they will never lose it. The damned, though they too are without hope, do however feel fear, namely, of the future different torments.[3]

The doctrine of the gradation of pains and joys later bore strange fruit in Lessing's discussion of Leibniz and Soner,[4] as we shall see; but on the whole it is not much discussed in our controversies, though it is generally accepted. There are two main reasons for this. First, for strict Lutherans and Calvinists the theory of graded heavenly joys was incompatible with their doctrine of salvation, according to which a man is saved solely by faith through grace, independently of his virtues or merits; but neither Luther nor Calvin did in fact reject the gradation of pains and joys.[5] Secondly, owing perhaps to an incipient change in the attitude to suffering, there is a disinclination to dwell on the details of eternal torment, and this is

[1] Thomas Aquinas, *Sum. Th.*, I, q. 10, a. 3: 'ignis inferni dicitur aeternus propter interminabilitatem tantum. Est tamen in poenis eorum transmutatio, secundum illud Iob. 24. Ad nimium calorem transibunt ab aquis nivium. Unde in inferno non est vera aeternitas, sed magis tempus . . .'

[2] This verse of Job is the main text for freezing as well as burning the damned; it is not nowadays thought to refer to the afterlife (see *Dict. de Th. Cath.*, art. Enfer, cols. 107–8). But it is possible to use other texts (see Walker, 'Ways of dealing with Atheists', *Bibliothèque d'Humanisme et Renaissance*, 1955, T. XVII, p. 275).

[3] *Sum. Th.*, Iª 2ᵃᵉ, q. 67, a. 4.

[4] V. infra, p. 217.

[5] See Walther Koehler, *Dogmengeschichte . . . Das Zeitalter der Reformation*, Zürich, 1951, pp, 488–9, 493–4, 497.

necessary if gradations are to be discussed. Even opponents of eternal torment have no qualms about condemning sinners to several thousand years of torture, but they do not give exact descriptions of it. In consequence, the reader will be glad, or sorry, to hear, this book will be little concerned with the precise nature of infernal punishments.

(ii) SYSTEMS WHICH ABOLISH ETERNAL TORMENT

The greatest possible mitigation of hell is that its torments should come to an end. Since arguments for and against this view constitute the subject of this book, this section will be brief and general.

There is only a limited number of possible ways of eliminating eternal torment. The simplest is to deny personal immortality; but I shall not deal with controversies about the immortality of the soul.[1] The next easiest is to annihilate the wicked at death, that is, to allow only the just to resurrect. This way was adopted by some 16th-century Anabaptists and by some 17th-century Socinians. Or, as Locke, Whiston and some Socinians believed, the wicked will be annihilated only after having suffered a period of torment appropriate in length to their sins.

All the other ways involve universal salvation. Of these the simplest is that everyone should be saved straight away, at death or the Last Judgment. No one has ever proposed this way. All the remaining ways suppose for the wicked a period of torment before salvation. They differ with regard to the effects of the torment and its nature, which may be both physical and mental, as with Burnet and the Petersens, or mental only, as with Sterry and White. Its duration, being usually graded individually according to sins, has to be left vague; but in most cases it is implied that it will be of the order of several thousand years. Another way, deriving from Plato, Origen, or Lurianic Cabalism, includes metempsychosis. Here earthly life performs

---

[1] In the early 18th century a violent controversy was started in England by William Coward and Henry Dodwell, who maintained that the human soul is naturally mortal but will be recreated at the resurrection in order to receive eternal rewards or punishments (see W. R. Alger, *Critical History of the Doctrine of a Future Life*, 4th ed., New York, 1866, pp. 430–1).

some of the punitive and reformatory functions of hell. Logically it could fulfil them all, and hell could be dispensed with. But the wish to keep as much of Christian doctrine as possible led Origen and later believers in metempsychosis, such as F. M. Van Helmont and Lady Conway, to interpolate periods of hell between the successive earthly lives; such periods were in any case already present in Plato's accounts of the afterlife.[1]

It will be noticed that for all these merciful doctors, with the possible exception of some Anabaptists and Socinians, the wicked will receive punishment lasting several thousand years and, in many systems, torments at least as severe as being burnt alive. This suggests that among the many possible motives for wishing to eliminate the eternity of hell a revulsion from the thought of violent and prolonged suffering was not important. But if, as in the systems positing universal salvation, the damned must be reformed, is such suffering perhaps necessary and inevitable ?

The answer to this question points to the great advantage of mental torment over physical. Even in an age which accepted the necessity of cruel punishments for criminals, madmen, and children, it was difficult to believe or argue that severe physical pain could in itself lead to moral amendment, though this proposition was quite often affirmed. Whereas the mental sufferings of remorse or guilt-feelings obviously may do so, and one can argue convincingly that no moral improvement is possible without them. It might, however, be suggested that physical pain will help to produce feelings of remorse and guilt. There is little doubt that prolonged pain does, in most patients, produce a neurotic state of high suggestibility in which religious or other conversion can be easily achieved.[2] This process is, I think, what Petersen means when he talks of the fire of his hell making sinners 'mürbe', soft, ripe to receive grace.[3] Mental suffering has another advantage over physical: its causes can be mainly or entirely internal, whereas physical pain can only be produced by some agent or cause external to

---

[1] Plato, *Republic*, X, 614 A–621 D; *Phaedo*, 107 D–115 A; *Phaedrus*, 246 A–257 B; *Gorgias*, 522 E–537 E. Plato's hell is eternal for the very wicked (*Phaedo*, 113 E).

[2] Cf. William Sargant, *Battle for the Mind*, London, 1957.

[3] V. infra, p. 240.

the soul. If, then, one wished to diminish or eliminate the revengeful, punishing aspect of God, and to regard the torment of the damned as the inevitable, natural consequence of their sins, it was better to have a hell of only mental torment, of remorse and conscience-stricken guilt, which can be regarded as an automatic result of sin and as not directly caused by any punitive action on God's part. This kind of mental torment was not available to theologians who wished to preserve the eternity of hell, since, if the damned feel remorse or contrition, as opposed to regret, they must be on the way to salvation; but for advocates of universal salvation it provided a simple and convincing method of reforming the damned.

The main reason why nearly all schemes for abolishing the eternity of hell retain a long period of severe torment is certainly the wish to preserve as much of the deterrent force of the orthodox hell as possible. By far the greatest barrier to the acceptance of such schemes was their weakening of this deterrent; it was a standard reproach to suggest that debauchees eagerly welcomed them.[1] It was therefore only prudent to lay great emphasis on the torments retained. But in most cases there was also a persistence of vindictive justice, or at least of the emotions and ideas that go with it, namely, revengeful anger and an infantile conception of fairness. This conception is strongly suggested by the parable of Dives and Lazarus:

> Son, remember that thou in thy lifetime receivedst thy good things, and likewise Lazarus evil things: but now he is comforted and thou art tormented.

If the wicked, who have thoroughly enjoyed the pleasures of this life, are in the afterlife to be as happy as the good, who have led lives of suffering and self-sacrifice, it is just not fair; things must be put right by restoring the equal balance of happiness and unhappiness. This idea of fairness in the afterlife presupposes that, at least in this life, sin brings joy and virtue suffering; otherwise the sinners would have to be comforted and the virtuous tormented. This presupposition is the exact opposite of the equally prevalent assumption that sin naturally brings its own punishment. The persistence of revengeful anger, side by side with a belief in the Johannine God of love,

[1] Cf. supra, p. 5.

is extremely evident in some thinkers, such as Petersen,[1] and the conflict between God's anger and love was dramatically acted out by the Camisards and Philadelphians.[2]

In most of the schemes for universal salvation not only are all men ultimately to be saved, but also Satan and his angels. It would indeed be very difficult logically to defend the exclusion of one class of fallen intelligent creatures from salvation granted to an inferior class. This also was a serious obstacle to such systems being widely accepted. It was felt, not without reason, that there was something shocking and absurd about the salvation of devils, especially of the Prince of Darkness himself. The trouble here is due to the ambiguous status of Satan. If he is taken simply to be the chief of the fallen angels, that is, as a rational creature who misused his free will by turning against God and whose will in consequence became perverted, then there seems to be no more reason against his salvation than against Adam's. As Rust argued, if God allowed angels to become devils, why shouldn't He allow devils to become angels?[3] But Satan, as we have noted, comes very near to being a principle of absolute evil, a Manichaean anti-god. If he is so regarded, then to propose his salvation is indeed absurd and nonsensical; only his elimination is possible and desirable.

[1] V. infra, pp. 241–3.
[2] V. infra, pp. 257 seq.
[3] Rust, *A Letter of Resolution*, 1661, pp. 130–1: 'What difference is there between a Devil made Angel and an Angel made Devil. I am sure the Advantage lies on the Ascending Part, rather than on the Descending . . .''; cf. Petersen, *Mysterion*, T. I, Vorrede, pp. (xviii–xix), Gespräch I, pp. 42–3.

Part Two

HISTORICAL

Chapter V

SOCINIANS

THE earliest evidence we have for Socinians believing in the annihilation of the wicked is a *Compendiolum Socinianismi*, dated 1598,[1] and an account of a Colloquy held at Rakow in 1601.[2] This is quite late in the history of the movement. There had been anti-trinitarian churches in Poland in the early 1560's; their city, Rakow, was founded in 1567; Fausto Socini had been in Poland since 1580.[3] It is therefore difficult to guess when and whence they acquired this belief.

One likely source is the Italian Anabaptists. We have the inquisitorial records of an Anabaptist Synod held at Venice in 1550.[4] It was attended by about fifty delegates, mostly from

[1] V. infra, p. 83.

[2] The account is by Valentin Smaltius (Schmalz), who wrote it during the Colloquy of 1601 and the Synod of 1602. Excerpts from this ms. are given in: D. Cantimori and E. Feist, *Per la Storia degli Eretici Italiani del secolo XVI in Europa Testi . . .*, Roma, 1937, pp. 211–75 (on the fate of the unjust: pp. 249–53), and were published in Dutch in 1631 (v. infra, p. 84).

[3] See Earl Morse Wilbur, *A History of Unitarianism Socinianism and its Antecedents*, Harvard, 1945, pp. 326 seq., 357, 393.

[4] See E. M. Wilbur, op. cit., pp. 84 seq.; D. Cantimori, *Eretici Italiani del Cinquecento*, Firenze, 1939, pp. 54 seq.; E. Comba, 'Un Sinodo Anabattista a Venezia anno 1550', in *La Rivista Cristiana*, Firenze, Anno XIII, 1885, pp. 21 seq., 83 seq.; Pio Paschini, *Venezia e l'Inquisizione Romana da Guilio III a Pio IV*, Padova, 1959, pp. 87 seq.

Italy and Switzerland. The sessions lasted forty days, and they agreed on ten points of doctrine, among which were:

> Only the elect resurrect.
>
> There is no hell but the grave; the souls of the wicked perish with their bodies.
>
> The elect sleep until the resurrection.

These points also included a denial of Christ's divinity and of the atonement, i.e. the two main Socinian heresies. Among the delegates was Celio Secondo Curione, author of the already mentioned *De Amplitudine beati Regni Dei*.[1] He was a friend of Matteo Gribaldi, a Professor of Law at Padua, who in 1553 tried to plead with Calvin for Michel Servet's life, and who adopted a version of Servet's christology. Gribaldi was the teacher of Peter Gonesius, one of the first Poles publicly to express anti-trinitarian views, and in Switzerland in the mid 1550's he was associated with Valentino Gentile, Gian Paolo Alciati, and Giorgio Biandrata, all of whom were soon to become active anti-trinitarians in Poland.[2]

Another possible source is suggested by Cloppenburg, one of the many 17th-century theologians who published refutations of Socinianism. In his *Compendiolum Socinianismi Confutatum* (1652)[3] he notes that the doctrine of the resurrection of only the just is a recent Jewish heresy.[4] The freedom of speculation allowed by the Jews did produce by the mid 16th century various doctrines of the afterlife which eliminated eternal torment, such as the cabalistic metempsychosis which later found adherents among Henry More's friends,[5] or the philosophic Judaism of Jean Bodin, who believed in the annihilation of the wicked 'post exacta supplicia'.[6] Judaic

---

[1] V. supra, p. 36.

[2] See E. M. Wilbur, op. cit., pp. 214–38; Stanislas Kot, *Socinianism in Poland*, trans. E. M. Wilbur, Boston, 1957, p. xii; Cantimori, *Erectici*, pp. 202 seq.

[3] Johannes Cloppenburgius, *Theologica Opera Omnia*, Amstelodami, 1684, T. II, p. 404.

[4] He cites evidence given in Menasseh Ben-Israel, *De Resurrectione Mortuorum, Libri III*, Amstelodami, 1636, pp. 176–7.

[5] V. infra, Ch. VIII.

[6] Jean Bodin, *Colloquium Heptaplomeres*, ed. Lud. Noack, Suerini Megaloburgiensium, 1857, pp. 341–4.

influence on Polish anti-trinitarians is at least very probable, since it is known that the Jews there, particularly in Lithuania, proselytized energetically, and it is usually supposed that this is why the Lithuanian anti-trinitarians, headed by Simon Budny, adopted an almost Judaic christology, rejecting any worship of Christ.[1]

Finally it may be relevant that there was a strong Erasmian tradition among the Socinians. Erasmus of course was much too prudent to make any pronouncements about the eternity of hell. Indeed, when he was criticized for the following passage in the *Enchiridion*:[2]

> The flame in which that rich feaster in the Gospel is tortured, and the torments of hell, about which the poets have written much, are nothing else but the perpetual anxiety of mind which accompanies habitual sin

he replied, not very convincingly, that he was writing only of remorse in this life,

> nor was there then any doubt in my mind about the fire of Gehenna.

But the whole tone of his evangelical philosophy of Christ, and his great admiration for Origen,[3] might easily lead disciples to reject eternal torment. The connections between Erasmus and the Socinians are of two kinds. First, as the chief exponent of Christian pacifism, his views were frequently appealed to and discussed in the many debates the Socinians had among themselves and with other churches about a Christian's duty in time of war.[4] Erasmus's biblical criticism also was useful to them in undermining scriptural support for the orthodox Trinity, in

---

[1] See E. M. Wilbur, op. cit., pp. 283–4, 348–9, 367–9.

[2] Erasmus, *Enchiridion Militis Christiani*, c. viii (*Opera Omnia*, ed. J. Clericus, T. V., Lugd. Bat., 1704, col. 56): 'Nec alia est flamma, in qua cruciatur dives ille comessator Euangelicus. Nec alia supplicia inferorum, de quibus multa scripsere Poetae, quam perpetua mentis anxietas, quae peccandi consuetudinem comitatur'; Erasmus, *Supputatio Errorum in Censuris Beddae*, (*Op. Omn.*, T. IX, cols. 699–700): 'nec ulla tum habebat animum meum dubitatio de igne gehennae'; quoted by J. B. Pineau, *Erasme sa Pensée religieuse*, Paris, 1924, p. 130.

[3] See Walker, 'Origène en France', pp. 113–15.

[4] See S. Kot, op. cit., pp. 76, 125, 200.

75

particular his rejection of the *comma Johanneum*.[1] Secondly, there are indirect personal connections. Erasmus's Spanish disciple, Juan de Valdes, was probably responsible for converting Bernardino Ochino to Protestantism; Ochino was a major influence on Socini and was regarded by the 17th-century Socinians as one of their chief ancestors.[2] The friendship and sympathy which existed between Dutch Arminians, such as Konrad Vorst, Grotius, Episcopius, and the Socinians in the first half of the 17th century[3] were, I think, largely due to their both sharing the Erasmian tradition of liberal, tolerant, evangelical, and primarily practical Christianity.

The Socinians were extremely cautious and secretive about their belief in the annihilation of the wicked. In the account of the Rakow Colloquy of 1601 the section expounding the annihilation of the wicked and the resurrection of only the just ends with this caution:[4]

> but this matter must be dealt with cautiously; indeed even Christ Himself and the Apostles adapted themselves to the understanding of the people, as the parable of Dives and Lazarus shows. It was not then the time to upset the Jews, as even now it is not the time, although now and then Christ spoke in such a way that it is quite evident that He is going to raise up only the faithful (John VI, 39–40). And Paul openly stated that he was striving to attain resurrection; in this way something may at times be said to give men a hint of this matter, until at length the age is ripe and men are accustomed to such ways of speaking . . .

[1] See E. M. Wilbur, op. cit., p. 14.
[2] See Marcel Bataillon, *Erasme et l'Espagne*, Paris, 1937, Ch. VII, VIII, and p. 549; E. M. Wilbur, op. cit., pp. 88–93, 256–7.
[3] See J. C. Van Slee, *De Geschiedenis van het Socinianisme in de Nederlanden*, Haarlem, 1914, Ch. IV, V; E. M. Wilbur, op. cit., pp. 541 seq.
[4] Cantimori and Feist, op. cit., pp. 252–3: 'Caute autem de hac re agendum est, quin etiam ipse Christus et Apostoli sese ad captum populi accomodarunt, ut parabola de Lazaro et divite docet. Non erat tunc tempus conturbandi Judaeos, ut etiam nunc non est tempus, quamvis etiam interdum Christus ita loquutus sit, ut satis apertum sit, eum solos fidentes resuscitaturum Joh. 6. Et Paulus apertissime pronuntiavit, se laborare ut aliquo modo pervenire possit ad resurrectionem; sic etiam interdum possunt quaedam dici, quae hanc rem hominibus indicent, donec tandem maturescat aetas et homines hisce loquendi modis assuescant . . .''

As Zeltner, the 18th-century historian of crypto-Socinianism at Altdorf, says,[1]

None of the Socinians has openly and clearly determined or defined anything about this matter, with the sole exception of Soner. . . .

That the Socinians failed to state their doctrine clearly was perhaps partly because, as we shall see, they did not all accept it. But apart from this, they had good reason to be cautious. Limborch, an Arminian and therefore not a bigotted anti-Socinian, writes that some Socinians have adopted[2]

this pernicious opinion which opens the window to sins and indeed to crimes. Whence their Church has hitherto had a bad reputation, as the patron of such a deadly dogma.

Bayle, with more complex intentions, states that[3]

nothing has been more prejudicial to the Socinians than a certain doctrine which they had thought well suited to remove the greatest scandal of our theology for philosophical minds.

This scandal is of course 'the dogma of the infinite torments and tortures of all men, except for a few', inflicted by a God whose

[1] G. G. Zeltner, *Historia Crypto-Socininismi Altorfinae quondam Academiae infesti Arcana ex documentis . . . Martini Ruari Epistolarum Centuriae Duae . . .*, Lipsiae, 1729, Ruar Corresp., p. 170; 'Nemo enim Socinianorum aperte ac diserte aliquid ea de re statuit atque definivit, uno Sonero excepto . . .'

[2] Limborch, *Theologia Christiana*, Amstelodami, 1686, p. 772: 'Huic perniciosae ac peccatis quin et sceleribus quibusve fenestras aperienti sententiae quidam patrocinium suum accommodarunt Doctores, quibus a Fausto Socino Socinianorum nomen inditum. Unde et ipsorum Ecclesia hactenus male audivit, ut dogmatis adeo exitialis patrona . . .'

[3] Bayle, *Dict. Hist. & Crit.*, art. Socin, rem. (L) (ed. cit., p. 234): 'rien n'a été plus préjudiciable aux Sociniens qu'une certaine doctrine qu'ils avoient crue fort propre à lever le plus grand scandale, que les Esprits Philosophiques puissent prendre de notre Théologie . . . le dogme des tourmens & des supplices infinis de tous les hommes, à quelques-uns près. Les Sociniens, déférant trop à la Raison, ont mis des bornes à ces supplices, d'autant plus soigneusement, qu'ils considéroient qu'on feroit souffrir les hommes seulement pour les faire souffrir, & sans avoir en vue ni le profit du souffrant ni celui des spectateurs; ce qui n'a jamais eu d'exemple dans un tribunal bien réglé.' Cf. Bayle, *Oeuvres Div.*, T. III, p. 864: 'il n'y a point de doctrine dans le systême Socinien par laquelle on le rende plus odieux que par celle de l'anéantissement des méchans . . . ces Hérétiques ne prenoient pas garde qu'on les rendroit plus odieux par cet endroit-là, & plus indignes de tolérance, que par tous leurs autres dogmes. Dans le fond il y a très-peu de gens qui se scandalisent du dogme de l'éternité des peines . . .'

chief attribute, according to natural reason, is 'infinite goodness'. Bayle goes on:

> The Socinians, allowing too much to Reason, have put limits to these tortures, and were careful to do so because they considered that men would be made to suffer merely in order to make them suffer, with no intention of profiting either the sufferer or the onlookers; a procedure that is without precedent in any well regulated court of justice.

They hoped thus to gain adherents; but they were sadly mistaken—'These heretics were not aware that by this they would become more hated and more unworthy of tolerance than by all their other dogmas. At bottom there are very few people who are scandalized by eternal torment . . .' Bayle's primary intention here is, as so often, to demonstrate that Christianity is a fundamentally immoral religion; but we may nevertheless accept his evidence about the Socinians, since he was most scrupulously honest about matters of fact.

The situation of the Socinians in the 17th century was such as to make them anxious not to give unnecessary offence, particularly by promulgating a doctrine thought to be socially dangerous. Even while they were still tolerated in Poland, their pacifism, their objection to capital punishment, and their ambiguous attitude to the authority of the State rendered them suspect and unsatisfactory citizens, especially when Poland was at war.[1] In 1638, after the affair of the broken crucifix at Rakow, they were no longer tolerated in Poland, and in 1658 they were finally expelled.[2] Nowhere in Europe, not even in Holland, where large numbers of them settled, were they officially tolerated.

In 1653 the Estates of Holland issued an edict forbidding the communication by any means whatever of Socinian heresies, under pain of banishment.[3] This edict was only one of a series of measures against the Socinians, beginning in 1598 with the banishment of two Socinian missionaries, Ostorrodt and Voidow, and the public burning of their books.[4] This edict of 1653 was

---

[1] See S. Kot, op. cit., passim.

[2] See E. M. Wilbur, op. cit., pp. 451 seq., 474 seq.

[3] See Van Slee, op. cit., pp. 259 seq.; Bayle, *Dict. Hist. & Crit.*, art. Socin, rem. (L) (ed. cit., pp. 232 seq.).

[4] Van Slee, op. cit., pp. 44 seq.; E. M. Wilbur, op. cit., pp. 537 seq. The books could not, at the last moment be found, though the fire for them was already lit.

decreed at the request of the synods of the Reformed Church and of the Faculty of Theology of the University of Leiden, which had reported:[1]

> nothing more deadly and horrible than this heresy can be conceived . . . it differs little or not at all from paganism.

Among the accusations made by these bodies was that of disbelieving in the resurrection of the wicked. When Jonas Slichting, the main Socinian propagandist at this time, answered these accusations in his *Apologia pro Veritate accusata ad illustrissimos & potentissimos Hollandiae & West-Frisiae Ordines, conscripta ab Equite Polono* (1654), he denied this charge, asserting that the Socinians believed in the resurrection of the just[2]

> for the joys of eternal life, of the unjust for the torments of eternal fire (ad vitae aeternae gaudia, injustorum ad ignis aeterni supplicia).

Two years later Cocceius published a reply, *Apologia Equitis Poloni examinata*, in which he refused to accept Slichting's denial and claimed that for the Socinians 'eternal fire' meant abolition, i.e. that, though the fire may be eternal, it will totally consume the wicked.[3] This is exactly the kind of dishonesty of which Felbinger accused them:[4]

> they are extremely crafty and do not account it a vice to dissimulate their opinions, although they are very eager to promulgate their confession of faith. Hence it can happen that one of their number professes, in speech and writing, that he hopes

---

[1] 'Nihil exitiabilius & magis horrendum ista haeresi excogitari potest . . . nihil aut parum differt à Paganismo'; quoted by Bayle, ibid.

[2] Quoted by Limborch, *Theol. Chr.*, 1686, p. 773, and by Bayle, ibid.

[3] Johannes Cocceius, *Equitis Poloni Apologia . . . examinata*, Lugduni Batavorum, 1656, pp. 220–1, quoted by Johann Jacob Rambach, *Historische und Theologische Einleitung in die Religions-Strittigkeiten der Evangelisch-Lutherischen Kirche mit den Socinianern*, Coburg and Leipzig, 1745, 2er Theil, p. 688; cf. Bayle, *Dict.*, art. Socin, rem. (L) (ed. cit., p. 234).

[4] J. Felbinger, *Epistola ad Christianos*, 1672, quoted by Rambach, op. cit., p. 687: 'Sunt versutiae studiosissimi et vitio sibi non vertunt, opiniones dissimulare, etiamsi maximopere ad edendam suae fidei confessionem urgeantur. Unde fieri potest, aliquem ex multis ore et scripto fateri se spem habere ad Deum, futuram esse resurrectionem mortuorum et justorum et injustorum et NB. nihilominus istam resurrectionem secundum suam ipsius praeconceptam opinionem apud se interpretari.'

to God that there will be a resurrection of both the just and the unjust and, N.B., nevertheless, in his heart (apud se), interprets this resurrection in accordance with his own preconceived opinion.

When it is remembered that the 'eternal fire' which consumed Sodom and Gomorrah was a stock example of αἰώνιος not meaning everlasting, and that anyway it did destroy the cities, not torment them for ever, it is difficult not to think that Slichting was deliberately ambiguous.

On the other hand, it may be that Slichting himself, and perhaps by then even a majority of Socinians, did not believe in the annihilation of the wicked. In spite of the Rakow Colloquy of 1601, the Rakow Catechism of 1609, rather tactlessly dedicated to James I of England, mentions the 'eternal punishments' (*poenae aeternae*) of the wicked—an unambiguous phrase.[1] And it may be that Fausto Socini himself accepted eternal torment. None of his adversaries can quote from his published writings any denial of it or of the resurrection of the wicked. But they can and do cite passages which imply this denial, though certainly not conclusively. Calovius, writing in 1638 to the German Socinian, Martin Ruar, to ask just what the Socinians did believe about hell, says:[2]

at times your authors talk ambiguously about the resurrection of the wicked: so that sometimes I am inclined to think that

[1] *Catachesis Ecclesiarum: quae in Regno Poloniae . . . affirmant neminem alium praeter Patrem Domini nostri Jesu Christi esse illum Unum Deum Israëlis . . .,* Racoviae, 1609, pp. 286, 289 (first ed. in Polish: 1605; cf. Wilbur, op. cit., pp. 410–11).

[2] Zeltner, op. cit., Ruar Corresp., p. 170: 'Sed & de resurrectione impiorum ambigue interdum vestri autores loquuntur: ut nonnuquam arbitrer, eosdem annihilationem eorundem credere, vel certe post resuscitationem annihilatum iri reprobos potius quam sempiternis cruciatibus subjiciendos esse. Ita, cum perpetua dissolutio animae & corporis homini naturalis adscribitur a Socino libro contra Puccium, & necessaria eadem statuitur facta per transgressionem Adae, nec vero liberentur ab hac necessitate, praeterquam fideles & pii a Christo secundum ejusdem sententiam, utique concludendum videtur impios ab ea non liberari, adeoque perpetuae dissolutioni obnoxios esse, nec unquam in vitam revocari.' The book of Socini's referred to is: *De Statu primi hominis ante lapsum Disputatio, quam Faustus Socinus Senensis per scripta habuit cum Francisco Puccio Florentino, anno* 1578, in F. Socinus, *Opera*, T. II, pp. 253 seq. (*Bibliotheca Fratrum Polonorum . . .,* Irenopoli, 1656, T. II). Cf. ibid., T.I, p. 455, letter of 1597 from Socini to Johannes Volkelius, in which he admits that in the work against Pucci he was covertly advocating an unpopular doctrine about the death of the wicked and the resurrection of the just.

they believe in their annihilation, or certainly that the reprobate after resurrection will be annihilated rather than be subjected to everlasting torments. Thus, since in Socini's book against Pucci the perpetual dissolution of soul and body is ascribed to man as natural, and this is established as necessary through Adam's transgression, only the faithful and pious being liberated by Christ from this necessity, according to his opinion, it certainly seems to follow that the wicked are not liberated from it, and are thus subject to perpetual dissolution and will never be recalled to life.

This theory of the natural mortality of man, defended at such length by Socini in his polemic against Pucci, is the basis of the doctrine of the annihilation of the wicked propounded at the Rakow Colloquy of 1601. The section of Smaltius's account which deals with this begins:[1]

The dead are reduced to nothing: the body disappears, the spirit returns to Him who gave it, that is God. The soul feels neither pleasure nor pain. And thus, since the form of their life and their life has perished, they are all wholly non-existent.

Eternal life is a privilege of only the faithful, who will be miraculously resurrected. It may seem to some[2]

absurd, if all the unjust are not punished: but it should be considered much more absurd if the wicked were given immortality, which is a most special gift and blessing of God. Moreover, it seems to involve extreme injustice if God gave man, whom He created mortal by nature, immortality merely in order that he should be eternally tormented.

God's justice does not require that He should punish the wicked, but only that He should not punish the innocent. Moreover, the pious suffer no loss by the wicked being let off; no good man should wish for another's perdition.[3] If Cantimori

[1] Cantimori and Feist, op. cit., p. 249: 'Mortui in nihilum redacti sunt: corpus evanuit, spiritus ad eum rediit, qui ipsum dederat, hoc est Deus. Anima nulla nec voluptate nec dolore afficitur. Et sic, quia vitae forma illorum et vita periit, nulli sunt omnes in universum.'

[2] Ibid., p. 251: 'videri potest alicui absurdum, si non omnes iniusti puniantur: sic etiam multo magis absurdum debere haberi, si immortalitas debeat dari impiis, quae est singularissimum Dei donum, et beneficium. Deinde, summa cum iniustitia videtur esse coniunctum si Deus hominem, quem natura mortalem creavit, ideo immortalem faciat ut in aeternum torqueatur.'

[3] Ibid., pp. 251–2.

is right in taking this part of Smaltius's account to have been dictated by Socini,[1] then undoubtedly Socini did not believe in eternal torment. In support of this view is the fact that Camphuysen, who attributed his own disbelief in hell to Socini, translated into Dutch and published this section of the Rakow Colloquy, though without mentioning its provenance or ascribing it to Socini.[2]

On the whole it seems to me likely that there was considerable disagreement on this point among the Socinians, and that they wished to leave the question open, to allow their own adherents to believe what they wanted. This, together with the powerful motive of not giving offence by diminishing the deterrent force of hell, would lead them to use equivocal language whenever possible; and I think that the use of the biblical terms 'eternal fire' or 'unquenchable fire' is deliberately ambiguous. Ruar, in answering Calovius's enquiry, more or less admits that this ambiguity is deliberate, and then himself gives an example of it:[3]

> If there are perhaps utterances of our members about the state of the wicked after the Last Judgment which could be interpreted in a sinister sense, these should not straight away be imputed to each of us, nor am I obliged to defend them except in so far as the authority of Scripture binds me to them. However I notice that, whenever this subject arises, they have kept close to scriptural terms; and thus hardly anything could be objected against them which could not also be objected against Scripture.

[1] See Cantimori and Feist, op. cit., p. 13; this is not clear from the excerpts published by him. Cf. Giovanni Pioli, *Fausto Socini*, Guanda, 1952, pp. 500 seq.
[2] V. infra, pp. 84, 87.
[3] Zeltner, op. cit., Ruar Corresp., p. 178: 'Si quae fortasse extant effata nostrorum de statu impiorum post ultimum judicium, quae sinistrum in sensum trahi possint, ea non statim singulis nostrum imputanda, nec ad ea defendenda magis cogor, quam Sacrarum me Literarum illis astringit auctoritas. Video tamen eos, quoties hac de re sermo incidit, phrasin fere sacrarum literarum retinuisse; eoque vix quicquam illis objici posse, quod non idem & his. Si meam de re tam difficili sententiam nominatim requiris, non nego cum plurimis aliis, quos forte consului, me potius censere, non eos modo, qui cum pietate vitam egerunt, sed & impios atque sceleratos, ad audiendam supremi judicis sententiam, a morte suscitatum iri; & ut illi coeli gaudiis in aeternum fruentur, ita hos igni inextinguibili, quo & mundus ipse conflagrabit cruciandos, servata tamen pro ratione delinquentium justa supplicii proportione.'

Ruar's own opinion is that the wicked as well as the just will resurrect, and as the latter will enjoy eternal bliss,

> so the former will be tormented by that unquenchable fire which will also burn up the world, the torment being justly proportioned to their sins.

Rambach, an 18th-century historian of Socinian polemics, comments on this:[1]

> remember that this word [ignis inextinguibilis] is taken by the Socinians *sensu minus probato*.

The fire may be unquenchable, but are the wicked indestructible?

The consequence of this cautiousness and vagueness is of course that we have very little hard evidence about Socinian opinions on this matter; but there are a few documents which are clear and informative.

In 1652 Cloppenburg published his *Compendiolum Socinianismi Confutatum*.[2] According to his preface this *Compendiolum* was published in Dutch in 1630 as *Kort Begrijp van de Leere der Socinianer*, together with a Dutch translation of Socini's *De Officio hominis Christiani*. Cloppenburg himself owned a manuscript Latin version of it, 'which, written in 1598 by the hands of Ostorrodt and Voidow in Amsterdam, was left to us about 27 years ago'.[3] I have not been able to find the Dutch edition, and unfortunately Cloppenburg does not quote his Latin version *verbatim*, but only summarizes it; one can however get quite a clear picture of the doctrine it contained.

The wicked will not resurrect. After the Last Judgment the wicked then alive, together with Satan and his angels, will be thrown into eternal fire, which will wholly consume them. Scriptural support is sought in passages such as I Thessalonians IV, 14; I Corinthians XV, 23; John VI, 39–47;

[1] Rambach, op. cit., 2er Tl., p. 688.
[2] Cloppenburg, *Theologica Opera Omnia*, Amstelodami, 1684, T. II, pp. 318 seq.
[3] Cloppenburg, ibid., p. 335: 'quod Anno MDXCVIII Amstelodami excussum manibus Ostorrodi & Voidovii, ante annos circiter XXVII nobis relictum fuit.' C. C. Sandius (*Bibliotheca Anti-Trinitariorum*, Freistadii, 1684, p. 99) states that this compendium was thought to have been compiled by Konrad Vorst.

Luke XX, 35, where the resurrection is spoken of as if it were a privilege of the faithful, and of course in Revelations XX, 14 ('And death and hell were cast into the lake of fire. This is the second death'), in spite of Revelations XX, 10. St Paul's words in Acts XXIV, 15, expressing belief in 'a resurrection of the dead, both of the just and unjust', are dealt with by dividing the faithful into just, who lived good lives, such as John the Baptist, and unjust, who lived bad lives but finally repented, such as the thief on the cross. The faithful sleep, or are virtually non-existent, until the Last Day. There will be no resurrection of the flesh, but they will be given celestial bodies like angels, without stomachs, etc.; this is an additional reason why the wicked cannot resurrect. The reasons given against eternal torment are:[1]

> it is absurd that God should be angry forever, and punish the finite sins of creatures with infinite punishments, especially since His glory is not increased thereby.

Ernst Soner was born at Nürnberg in 1572. He studied medicine and philosophy at the University of Altdorf, where later he was 'Professor publicus Medico-Physicus'. He died in 1612 in an odour of Lutheran sanctity; but it was discovered after his death that he had been secretly infecting his pupils with Socinianism. In 1597-8 he had travelled to Holland as a tutor, where he met Ostorrodt and Voidow, the Socinian missionaries who wrote Cloppenburg's copy of the *Compendiolum* and who were perhaps the authors of it. It is likely that it was they who converted him to Socinianism.[2]

Soner's *Demonstratio Theologica* of the injustice of eternal torment was first published anonymously in Dutch in 1631, at the end of Camphuysen's translation of Valentinius Smaltius's *'t Woordt is Vleysch geweest*, together with two other treatises on the afterlife, under the general title of *Van den Stant der Dooden, en Straffe der Verdoemden | nae dit Leven. Verscheyden Tractaten*; these two treatises are in fact translations of the section dealing with the state of the dead in Smaltius's account

---

[1] Cloppenburg, ibid., p. 408: 'quod absurdum sit, Deum irasci in aeternum, & peccata creaturarum finita poenis infinitis mulctare: praesertim cum hinc nulla ipsius gloria illustretur.'

[2] See Zeltner, op. cit., pp. 24–52; E. M. Wilbur, op. cit., pp. 425–6.

of the Rakow Colloquy of 1601.[1] It seems likely that Camphuysen also translated Soner's work. It was published in Latin at Amsterdam in 1654 with several theological treatises by Fausto and Lelio Socini.[2]

The main argument of Soner's treatise has already been mentioned,[3] namely, a *reductio ad absurdum* of the justification of eternal torment by the infinite offence of sinning against an infinite God. This argument, which is, I think, valid, is presented in a severely abstract style; there is no sign of pity or anger, but merely a demonstration that this justification of eternal torment leads, within its own terms and assumptions, to absurd conclusions. Unfortunately Soner badly weakens his case by conceding an absolute right of God as creator to annihilate His creatures ('absolutum Dei imperium').[4] This right or power has nothing to do with justice, which is restricted to the distribution of punishments or rewards proportionate to bad or good deeds. In Soner's system it is clear that the wicked do resurrect, since God will punish them with finite torments proportionate to their sins, and then annihilate them. This annihilation is not a punishment, though it resembles one in that it is inflicted only on sinners. It is imposed by God's absolute power and is neither just nor unjust; in the same way, the eternal life of the blessèd is not really a reward, but a free gift. That is to say: both annihilation and eternal bliss are disproportionate to any human, finite sins or merits; their

---

[1] Smaltius, *'t Woordt is Vleysch geweest* . . . Vertaelt door D. R. C., Rakow, 1631, p. 163: *Van den Stant der Dooden*, comprising: p. 163, *Hoe't gheleghen zy met Lichaem | Ziel | en Geest des Menschen nae de Doodt*; p. 169, *Off alle Menschen van Adam af, tot het eynde des Wereldts toe, van den Dooden sullen opstaen*; p. 186, *Natuerlijck en schriftuerlijck bewijs, dat de eeuwighe straffen der Godtloosen, niet de Rechtveerdicheydt Godts, maer een groote Onrechtveerdicheyt soude mede brenghen* (by Soner). On the first two treatises cf. Rambach, op. cit., 2er Tl., p. 687. There was another edition of this work in the same year, differing only in its title (*Thien Predicatien Over 't begin van't Eerste Capittel des Euangeliums Joannis*). Both these editions also contain the *Extract* from Camphuysen's letter (v. infra p. 86). *Van den Stant der Dooden* and the *Extract* were reedited in Amsterdam in about 1666 (Vrystadt, na het Jaer 1666).
[2] *Demonstratio Theologica, & Philosophica, quod aeterna impiorum supplicia non arguant Dei Justitiam, sed injustitiam*, in *Fausti, & Laelii Socini, item Ernesti Sonneri Tractatus aliquot Theologici, nunquam antehac in lucem editi*, Eleutheropoli, 1654, pp. 36–69.
[3] V. supra, p. 43.
[4] Soner, *Theol. Dem.*, pp. 36–7, 60–2.

occurrence cannot therefore be due to God's justice. Then comes the fatal objection:[1]

> Someone will ask whether God by His absolute power could not decree and inflict on the wicked eternal torments, and even positive eternal tortures?

Soner is bound to allow that the answer to this question is: yes,[2]

> God could perhaps have done this without the reproach of injustice.

The best he can do is to argue that eternal torment would conflict with God's mercy, and that, since all creatures contain some 'ray of divine goodness' (*radius quidam divini boni*), God could not allow a part of Himself to be for ever in evil and misery; whereas, if the wicked are annihilated, this divine ray returns into its source.

Soner was arguing on two logically incompatible assumptions. In order to judge whether actions imputed to God are just or unjust, he is bound to assume that the notions of justice and injustice are anterior to, or independent of God's will. But, by allowing that some of God's actions are outside the scope of justice, he implies the contrary assumption, namely, that God's 'absolute power' makes anything He decides just, or at least not unjust. We have already seen the dangerous consequences of the latter assumption,[3] consequences which are fatal to any attack on the justice of eternal torment; but to attempt to argue on both assumptions at once is hopeless, whatever one's aims.

The Dutch poet Dirk Camphuysen died in 1627. In 1630 appeared a short treatise entitled: *Extract out of D.R.C.'s Letter, Containing: That the opinion of the Annihilation and Finite Punishment of the Unjust, etc. is not so harmful and dangerous; and in consequence that it may well be promulgated,*

---

[1] Ibid., p. 62: 'Quaeret quispiam an non potuerit Deus, pro absoluta sua potestate etiam aeternos cruciatus, & supplicia aeterna etiam positiva impiis decernere, atque irrogare?'

[2] Ibid., p. 63: 'Potuisse quidem hoc Deum fortassis facere sine nota injustitiae . . .'

[3] V. supra, Ch. III, section (vii).

and expounded and propagated for edification. It was not included in De Breen's edition of Camphuysen's theological works of 1638; but there is evidence that Camphuysen intended it to be printed.[1]

As its title indicates, Camphuysen's treatise is primarily concerned, not with the truth of the doctrine of the annihilation of the wicked nor with the timing and manner of the annihilation, but with the moral, religious, and social effects this doctrine produces. He declines to give an opinion on the alternative doctrines of no resurrection for the wicked, or of annihilation after punishment, on the grounds that either gives rise to the same objections with regard to its present effects. But he is most emphatic about his own belief in the general proposition that there is no eternal torment. Although he is not in complete agreement with all Socini's teaching, Camphuysen thinks Socini has done more than anyone else to restore Christianity to its primitive purity; but Socini's greatest achievement, that which has been most productive of true piety, has been to 'see through the thick and universal shadows of the fabled hell and eternal damnation'. Camphuysen goes on:[2]

As for me, I thank for this and praise God the Father of our Lord Jesus Christ from the depth of my heart. For it was this enlightenment on the matter, which by my own understanding I could not attain, which has made me, when I was on the point of rejecting the whole Christian religion, love this religion,

---

[1] *Extract uyt D.R.C. Brief, Inhoudende Dat het gevoelen van de Vernietiging ende Eyndelijcke Straffe der Onrechtvaerdigen, &c. niet soo schadelijck nochte gevaerlijck is; Ende dienvolgens wel mach ontdeckt ende ter stichtinge voorgehouden en verbreydt worden.* See L. A. Rademaker, *Didericus Camphuysen*, Gouda, 1898, p. 149. The 1630 edition of the *Extract*, which begins at p. 35, probably appeared after a 1630 edition of *Van den Stant der Dooden*, which I have not seen. For later editions of the *Extract* see above p. 85, n. 1.

[2] Camphuysen, *Extract*, p. 37: 'maer nergens in dunckt hy my soo uytnemende / ende der Godsaligheyd soo vordelijck / als dat he door die dicke ende alghemeyne duysternissen der gefabuleerder Helle ende oneyndelijcker verdoemnisse ghesien heeft / ende dat uytnemende licht den Menschen herstellt . . . Wat my aengaet / ick dancke ende love deshalven uyt innerlijcker herten God den Vader onses Heeren Jesu Christi. Want die verlichtinge in dit stuck (daer ick door eygen verstandt niet toe konde komen) heeft my / staende op het punct om de gansche Christelijcke Religie te verwerpen / die selve doen lief krijgen / hoogh achten / redelijck vinden / ende tot noch toe uyt alle krachten door Gods genade beleven.'

respect it, find it reasonable, and till now, through God's grace, with all my strength live in accordance with it.

He does cite some scriptural support for his views:[1]

> throughout the New Testament *eternal death* and eternal life are set against each other, and life is allotted to the just and death to the unjust.

The Hebrew meaning of 'eternity' has been misunderstood and some obscure passages in the Apocalypse misinterpreted; this has happened largely through the greed of Papist priests, wishing to frighten money out of people. But he does not deal fully with the question, nor tackle crucial texts such as Matthew XXV.

Camphuysen begins by dealing with the charge that, since this doctrine has been taught, many families have become 'godless'. He takes the unusual line of admitting the truth of the charge, but claiming that it applies to all Christian truths—they make the wicked wickeder, and the holy holier. The true doctrine, for example, of grace as a free gift fills the pious and humble with faith and hope, but is taken by the wicked as a licence to sin. The teaching of Christianity thus makes the difference between sheep and goats more evident. But no one, of course, preaching a Christian truth, intends or wishes it to be perverted by the impious to their own damnation. The result aimed at in promulgating the doctrine of no eternal torment is to increase love towards God through the awareness of His mercy and justice, and to produce great care not to lose eternal life, a reward which God can justly withhold from those who disobey His commandments. This is the result it has had in Camphuysen himself and in many people he knows.[2]

He then examines the cases where this happy result is not obtained. There are two classes of worldly men whom it is impossible to convert: first, the thoroughly debauched and godless; secondly, rational people who lead quite respectable lives but are too lazy and careless to pay attention to religion. What will be the effect of telling these that there is no eternal torment? Members of the first class have no intention of being virtuous and are not attracted by the hope of eternal bliss.

[1] Ibid., p. 42: 'doorgaens in't Nieuwe Testament worden *eeuwige doodt*, en eeuwigh leven tegen malkander ghestelt / en't leven den rechtvaerdigen / de doodt den onrechtvaerdigen toegeëygent.'

[2] Camphuysen, *Extract*, pp. 36–7.

From childhood teaching, however, they retain a 'dull and vague fear of such endless torments';[1] but this is not strong enough to stop them sinning—it merely makes them a little uneasy. The effect of removing this fear is to allow them to sin with more tranquillity and openness, and perhaps to confirm them in their evil ways; that is to say, they become more plainly and fully the goats they always were. The second class usually do not believe in an afterlife at all, and are therefore quite unaffected by any change in it. The worst result, then, of the doctrine of no eternal torment is only to make some anyway irretrievable sinners a little more sinful.

And what about the results of the contrary doctrine? Camphuysen claims that the belief in eternal torment sometimes produces two kinds of bad effect. In the first place, the fear of hell leads people to seek superstitious means of escaping it, to use 'sin-cushions'.[2] By this term he means not only Catholic dogmas and practices, such as purgatory and all that goes with it, but also some Protestant doctrines rejected by the Socinians, such as justification through the merits of Christ. These superstitions are evil from a religious point of view, and are morally pernicious in that they lead people to suppose they can thus escape the consequences of sin and therefore need not try to stop sinning. It is no use for a preacher to threaten such people with hell; for they think to themselves:[3]

'God is merciful; things can't be as strict as all that'—each one thus pushing the eternal torments of hell from his neck, and thinking that they are for others rather than for himself.

The other kind of bad result produced by eternal torment affects those who are pious but weak in understanding. These rightly refuse the sin-cushions; but, owing to false teaching about Christ, they are unable to avoid sin, and therefore believe they are doomed to eternal torment,[4]

[1] Ibid., p. 38: 'een domme ende duystere vreese van soo een oneyndelijcke pijne.'
[2] Ibid., p. 40: 'Sonden-Kussens.'
[3] Ibid., p. 41: 'God is ghenadigh / ten kan niet zijn dat 'et soo nauw soude staen / schuyvende alsoo d'oneyndelijcke Helsche pijne een yeder van sijnen halse / ende meynen datse eer voor anderen / als voor haer selven moet wesen.'
[4] Camphuysen, *Extract*, p. 41: "t welck nootsakelijck soo grooten angst en pijne in de Ziele geeft / dat de Luyden het leven te bange valt / ende alsoo door eygen handen hun selven den doodt aen-doen. Waer van de exempelen niet weynigh / ende eenige my selve bekent zijn.'

which necessarily produces such great fear and agony in the soul, that life is too frightening for them, and they find death by their own hand. Of this there are not a few examples, and some of them known to me personally.

Others do not go as far as suicide, but fall into fits of melancholy and despair, sometimes ending in madness. These are taken to be temptations of the Devil, and in the Reformed Churches one hears prayers for deliverance from these Satanic attacks, which are in fact caused only by the fear of eternal torment.

So far Camphuysen has been considering the moral and religious effects on individuals of belief or disbelief in eternal torment; he then turns to the social effects. It is argued that if the doctrine of no eternal torment is divulged to[1]

> brutal, openly godless men, they will throw off any kind of religious feeling, and turn the whole world upside down, etc.

Camphuysen replies: first, Christianity is not meant to be an instrument of political or social restraint, but to lead men to eternal life; and secondly,[2]

> that the promulgation of this doctrine would lead to disintegration and general chaos in the world and human society, is by no means the case.

He proves the second point by some very interesting observations on society. Even evil-doers who are overtly criminal have some form of religion or superstition; yet this does not restrain them from any crime which they think profitable. Against the eternal torments of hell they have their 'plasters and fabricated remedies', of which we see frequent examples when criminals condemned to death[3]

[1] Ibid., p. 43: 'dat wanneer sulck ghevoelen by de worste en t'eenemal openbare goddelose Menschen / openbaer wierde / die selbe alle Gods-dienstigheyd van haer smijten / ende de gheheele Werelt 't onderste boven keeren &c.'

[2] Ibid., p. 44: 'Maer dat de ontdeckinge van dese Leere strecken soude tot verwerringe ende algemeyne disordre der Werelt en menschlijcke societeyt / en is geensins alsoo.'

[3] Ibid., pp. 44–5: 'Tegen de oneyndelijcke helsche quale hebben sy hare pleysters ende verdichte remedien . . . ende wy klare exempelen hebben in Dieven / Moordenaers / ende andere onbekende quaet-doenders / die onder Beuls handen zijnde / van een sotte Paep hun de Saligheyd laten aenspreken / wanneer nu geenen tijdt noch macht tot bekeeringe meer en is.'

have a silly priest promise them salvation, though there is neither time nor ability left for conversion.

What does restrain evil-doers is the fear of other men, that is, of social or legal punishments. Society is kept together, not by religiously based morals, nor indeed by any kind of morals, but by the wish of everyone who possesses anything, or hopes to do so, to enjoy his possessions in security. Thus even a society of criminals can be stable, or a society of totally irreligious people, such as exists in Brazil.[1] Camphuysen has in mind, as the ultimate basis of society, something like Pascal's *ordre de concupiscence*, or Montaigne's city of criminals; the example of the irreligious Brazilians suggests that perhaps he had read the latter.[2]

Having shown that morally, religiously and socially disbelief in eternal torment produces less bad effects than belief does, Camphuysen is easily able to refute the opinion against which his whole treatise is directed, namely, that, even if the doctrine of no eternal torment is true, it is better not to divulge it, 'or at least to teach it with great circumspection and care';[3] on the contrary, one has a positive duty to preach it, since the opposing doctrine produces superstition, madness and suicide.

Camphuysen showed great shrewdness in attacking the greatest practical barrier to the acceptance of any doctrine of no eternal torment, and his attack was an effective and convincing one. Soner's treatise, too, in spite of the weakness pointed out above, was a successful refutation of the main defence of the justice of eternal torment. But these attacks were not followed up by any later Socinian propaganda. Moreover, these two works had an extremely limited diffusion. Camphuysen's was in a language few people ever bother to learn, and copies of it are very rare; even Bayle, who was so interested in heretics in general and Socinians in particular, only had second-hand knowledge of it.[4] Soner's treatise too was a rare book; though Leibniz had a copy and intended to reedit it,[5] Zeltner had seen

---

[1] Camphuysen, *Extract*, p. 45.

[2] Pascal, *Pensées*, ed. Brunschvicg, Nos. 294, 298, 402, 403, 451, 453. Montaigne, *Essais*, III, ix; II, xii (ed. Villey, Paris, 1923, T. III, p. 231; T. II, p. 218).

[3] Camphuysen, *Extract*, p. 41: 'dat het beter is / dat men dese Leere of t'ene mael verzwijge / of ten mensten met groote omischtigheyd en sorge leere.'

[4] Bayle, *Dict. Hist. & Crit.*, art. Socin, rem. (L) (ed. cit., p. 234).

[5] V. infra, p. 216.

it only in manuscript.[1] The Abbé de Cordemoy, who in 1697 published a refutation of 'une des plus dangereuses erreurs, que le démon puisse suggérer aux hommes', *L'Eternité de Peines de l'Enfer contre les Sociniens*,[2] does not cite a single Socinian author or text. Jurieu and Saurin in their controversy about Socinianism assume that the Socinians deny eternal torment, but they have no first-hand knowledge of the subject, as Bayle pointed out.[3]

[1] Zeltner, op. cit., p. 49.
[2] Paris, 1697.
[3] Bayle, ibid., art. Origène, rem. (C) (ed. cit., p. 541).

Chapter VI

ENGLISH ARIANS

JOHN LOCKE, Isaac Newton, Samuel Clarke, and William Whiston all knew each other. All were Arians, and all disbelieved in eternal torment. Only the youngest of them, Whiston, publicly defended his beliefs, and in consequence it is only of his views on hell that we have any detailed knowledge. These thinkers did not claim any modern predecessors for their heresies, and they may well have arrived at them independently of continental Socinians. But there were earlier English Arians and disbelievers in eternal torment. John Biddle, in his *Twofold Catechism* (1654), affirmed the annihilation of the wicked, and was overtly Arian.[1] Samuel Richardson published in 1658 *A Discourse of the Torments of Hell. The foundation and pillars thereof discovered, searched, shaken and removed*, which his adversary, Nicholas Chewney, described, not unfairly, as 'an old Origenian Heresie new vampt on the Socinian last'.[2] I do not, however, know of any evidence to

[1] John Biddle, *A Twofold Catechism: The One simply called A Scripture Catechism; The Other A brief Scripture Catechism for Children*, London, 1654, pp. 133–8. On Biddle, see Joshua Toulmin, *A Review of the Life, Character and Writings of the Rev. John Biddle, M.A.*, London, 1789; H. J. McLachlan, *Socinianism in 17th-Century England*, Oxford, 1951, pp. 163 seq., 201, 216.

[2] N. Chewney, *Hell, With the Everlasting Torments thereof Asserted . . .*, London, 1660, *To the Reader*. Richardson's book was first published anonymously in London in 1658; an edition of 1660 bore his name. It was reprinted in *The Phenix*, II, 427 seq., London, 1708, and there was a second edition, London, 1720. There were two other refutations of it: Jo. Brandon, τὸ πῦρ τὸ αἰώνιον: *or*

connect these Cromwellian Arians with Whiston and his friends.

Locke wrote a short discourse, headed *Resurrectio et quae sequuntur*, which was first printed in Lord King's biography of him (1829).[1] In this he outlines the following eschatological programme. There will be two resurrections: the first of the just, with spiritual bodies; the second of the unjust, with ordinary bodies. Concerning the latter 'these two things are plainly declared in Scripture':[2]

> 1st. That they shall be cast into hell fire to be tormented there, is so express, and so often mentioned in Scripture, that there can be no doubt about it. Matt. XXV, 41, 46. XIII, 42, 50. XVIII, 8. 2nd. That they shall not live for ever. This is so plain in Scripture, and is so everywhere inculcated—that the wages of sin is death, and the reward of the righteous is everlasting life ... that one would wonder how the readers could be mistaken ...

Locke admits that Matthew XVIII, 8 and XXV, 41, 46 give 'some colour' to the doctrine of eternal torment, and refers to Tillotson on this; but[3] 'everlasting, in a true Scripture sense, may be said of that which endures as long as the subject itself endures', and he gives some of the usual Old Testament references. But he does not attempt to explain away the parallel in Matthew XXV between eternal life and eternal punishment. He is not over-merciful to the wicked:[4]

> how long they shall be continued in that inexpressible torment is not, that I know, anywhere expressed; but that it shall be excessively terrible by its duration as well as its sharpness, the current of Scripture seems to be manifest ...

Locke's *The Reasonableness of Christianity*, published in 1695, is compatible with this eschatology, but does not propound it, and it would be possible to read the book without suspecting

[1] Lord King, *The Life and Letters of John Locke*, London, 1858, pp. 316–23.
[2] Ibid., pp. 319–20.
[3] Ibid., p. 321.
[4] Ibid., p. 322.

Everlasting Fire no Fancy. Being an Answer to a late Pestilent Pamphlet ..., London, 1678; Tho. Lewis, *The Nature of Hell, The Reality of Hell-Fire, and the Eternity of Hell-Torments, Explain'd and Vindicated. In Opposition to a Profane Libel, first published under Cromwell's Usurpation, and lately Reprinted* ..., London, 1720.

that its author disbelieved in eternal torment.[1] Indeed from
his two *Vindications* against Edwards it appears that he was not
accused of this, but only of having Socinian or anti-trinitarian
tendencies.[2] The book begins by stating two poles of erroneous
belief: the first is that Adam's fall doomed all his posterity 'to
eternal infinite punishment'; the second, in reaction to the first,
eliminates the Redemption and regards Christ

> as nothing but the restorer and preacher of pure natural religion;
> thereby doing violence to the whole tenour of the New Testa-
> ment.

The correct view is that Adam and all his descendants were condemned just to death. Christ's Redemption restores prelap-
sarian immortality to the just and faithful;[3]

> but an exclusion from paradise and loss of immortality is the
> portion of sinners.

This last statement is not developed or defended; later he
quotes Matthew XXV without explaining it away, and, in a
eulogy of the moral effects of the Christian afterlife, he writes:[4]

> The view of heaven and hell will cast a slight upon the short
> pleasures and pains of this present state,

a phrase which suggests that heaven and hell are of equal duration. Locke's private opinion on the matter, then, would have
been known only to personal friends, such as Le Clerc, Cudworth's daughter Lady Masham, Shaftesbury, and perhaps
Newton, with whom he corresponded about anti-trinitarian
exegesis.[5]

What Newton and Samuel Clarke thought about the eternity
of hell we know only through Whiston. There is, I think, no
reason to doubt his testimony. In his *Historical Memoirs of the
Life and Writings of Dr Samuel Clarke* (1730), he refers to his

---

[1] The author of *An Account of Mr. Lock's Religion, Out of his Own Writings*,
London, 1720, pp. 187–8, examines the question whether Locke shared the
Socinian belief in the annihilation of the wicked, and is unable to decide it.

[2] Cf. H. J. McLachlan, *Socinianism in 17th-century England*, pp. 327 seq.

[3] Locke, *The Reasonableness of Christianity as delivered in the Scriptures*, in his
Works, 12th ed., London, 1824, Vol. VI, pp. 4–10.

[4] Ibid., pp. 127, 150.

[5] See Isaac Newton, *Theological Manuscripts*, ed. H. J. McLachlan, Liverpool,
1950, pp. 2, 18, 24.

own published arguments *'against* the proper Eternity of the Torments of Hell' of 1709 and 1717, and then goes on:[1]

> And I think I may venture to add, upon the Credit of what I discovered of the opinions of Sir *Isaac Newton* and Dr *Clarke*, that they were both of the same sentiments. Nay, Dr *Clarke* thought that 'few or no thinking Men were really of different sentiments in that Matter'.

Whiston also, in his *The Eternity of Hell Torments Considered* (1740),[2] quotes a comment of Newton's on Revelations XIV, 9–11 ('If any man worships the beast and his image . . ., he shall be tormented with fire and brimstone in the presence of the holy angels, and in the presence of the Lamb: And the smoke of their torment ascendeth up for ever and ever: and they have no rest day nor night . . .'):

> That the degree and duration of the torments of the degenerate and antichristian people, should be no other than would be approved of by those angels, who had ever laboured for their salvation; and that Lamb who had redeemed them with his most precious blood.

This, I think, is intended to imply that these torments will not be eternal.

William Whiston was a mathematician and scientist. He succeeded Newton as Professor of Mathematics at Cambridge, where he himself had been educated. In 1710 he was expelled from the University for his Arian beliefs.[3] In consequence he suffered considerable financial hardship; but he was able to devote his life and energies to propagating his religious views. Whiston's Arianism, like Locke's and Newton's, was an attempt to revive what he believed to be primitive Christianity—in 1715 he started 'A Society for promoting Primitive Christianity', which 'met weekly at the *Primitive Library* at my House in *Cross-Street Hatton-Gardens*'.[4] His religion rested largely on an

[1] Whiston, *Historical Memoirs of the Life and Writings of Dr. Samuel Clarke*, 3rd ed., London, 1748, p. 75.
[2] Whiston, *The Eternity of Hell Torments Considered: Or, a Collection of Texts of Scripture, and Testimonies of the three first Centuries, relating to them*, London, 1740, p. 49.
[3] Whiston, *Hist. Memoirs . . . Clarke*, ed. cit., p. 17.
[4] Ibid., pp. 66 seq.

historical basis: the Scriptures and the Pre-Nicene Fathers. In this respect the theology of the English Arians (or Eusebians, as Whiston preferred to call them) differed from the more radically rational theology of the continental Socinians. An important consequence of this difference was that the English, as we have seen, did not reject the doctrine of the Redemption. Whiston's own conversion to Arianism he ascribed to the historical scholarship of Elie Dupin.[1] He believed that his theology would be generally accepted if he could persuade people to read the Scriptures in the light of primitive Christian literature. In 1712, and again in 1723, he tried to put into effect his 'Grand Proposal',[2] namely, a cheap edition of the Pre-Nicene Fathers with

> some hopes of success, that such an intire set might be gotten into all the parishes of *Great-Britain*.

This predominantly historical approach to religious reform was reinforced by a positive dislike of metaphysics, a term which for him is always pejorative.[3] In consequence, his rejection of eternal torment is based almost solely on scriptural and early patristic authority; he produces no arguments against it, but only historical and textual evidence, accompanied by some emotional outbursts of considerable violence. This dislike of *a priori* reasoning, which of course he shared with Locke and Newton, went with an extremely, even crudely literal turn of mind, which is particularly striking in his *Astronomical Principles of Religion, Natural, and Reveal'd* (1717), an attempt to integrate his Newtonian science into his religious beliefs. In spite of his anti-metaphysical bias, Whiston's great familiarity with the early Fathers led him to adopt some Platonic and Neoplatonic ideas, such as the various vehicles of the soul, or the *prisca theologia*, which he took from Cudworth;[4] and he had great admiration for Henry More and Whichcote, friends and relatives of whom he knew well.[5]

[1] Ibid., p. 8.
[2] Ibid., pp. 98 seq.; Whiston, *Memoirs of the Life and Writings of Mr. William Whiston*, 2nd ed., London, 1753, Vol. I, p. 187.
[3] Whiston, *Hist. Memoirs . . . Clarke*, p. 101.
[4] Whiston, *Astronomical Principles of Religion, Natural and Reveal'd*, London, 1717, pp. 152–3, 194–231.
[5] Whiston, *Memoirs . . . Whiston*, ed. cit., Vol. I, pp. 22–3, 310.

The mainspring of Whiston's courageous and energetic propaganda was his chiliasm, his conviction that by helping to restore pure, primitive Christianity he was preparing the way for, perhaps hastening the Second Coming.[1] He saw not only his own efforts as a prelude to 'the restitution of all things', but also Newton's discovery of the law of gravity, by which the existence of a 'continual *Providence*' was clearly demonstrated— God's 'general, inmechanical, immediate *Power*, which we call the *Power of Gravity*'.[2] Whiston is one example out of several we shall come across of an unexpected connexion between chiliasm and the rejection of eternal torment.

When Whiston was a student at Cambridge (1686–91), he composed ten *Meditations*, of which the ninth is directed against atheists; it ends with eloquent threats of eternal torment, backed up by quotations from Matthew XXV and Mark IX. The tenth is on the death of a certain Mr Hollis, who had died at a party, thus experiencing a sudden change 'from vain jollities to intolerable torments'.[3] But by 1709 he had come to doubt the eternity of hell. In his *Sermons and Essays upon Several Subjects*, published in that year, he suggested, very cautiously, that αἰώνιος, applied to hell, might mean only a very long age, followed by the annihilation of the wicked, and claimed that this was the opinion of most Primitive Fathers and seemed 'most agreeable to the Divine Goodness'.[4] In 1717 he wrote a 'small Paper' in defence of this view, which he does not seem to have published.[5] It was not until 1740 that he published his *The Eternity of Hell Torments Considered: Or, a Collection of Texts of Scripture, and Testimonies of the three first Centuries, relating to them. Together with Notes through the Whole; and Observations at the End.* The only modern predecessor he mentions here is Thomas Burnet, an 'excellent and good natur'd author', who in his *De Statu Mortuorum* endeavoured 'to confute the proper *Eternity*' of hell, but without 'going to the bottom of it'.[6] I think it is in fact likely that Whiston arrived at his

[1] Whiston, *Hist. Mem. . . . Clarke*, ed. cit., pp. 74–5.
[2] Whiston, *Astr. Princ.*, pp. 111–12; *Mem. . . . Whiston*, ed. cit., Vol. I, p. 34.
[3] Whiston, *Mem. . . . Whiston*, ed. cit., Vol. I, pp. 73–4.
[4] Whiston, *Sermons and Essays*, London, 1709, pp. 220–1.
[5] See Whiston, *Memoirs . . . Whiston*, ed. cit., Vol. I, p. 244.
[6] Whiston, *The Eternity of Hell Torments Considered*, p. 2.

very odd afterlife by his own unaided interpretation of Scripture and early Christian literature.

Whiston's use of Scripture is on lines we have already met: a few texts on God's mercy and forgiveness, such as Psalm CIII, 9 and I Timothy II, 4, and on the wages of sin being death are quoted, and all the threats of eternal torment are explained away by claiming that αἰώνιος means only age-long.[1] Whiston deals with the awkward parallel in Matthew XXV by denying that the life of the blessèd is strictly eternal—though it will be considerably longer than the torments of the wicked.[2] This was an entirely novel step, which, not surprisingly, shocked his contemporaries. He is also original in applying his own meaning of αἰώνιος, which he usually translates as 'lasting', to the many early patristic texts he cites. By these means he is able to claim that no Christian writer earlier than Tertullian asserted the doctrine of the true eternity of rewards and punishments. This doctrine, a product of 'Montanist Enthusiasm', was transmitted to 'those ignorant and fatal Hereticks *Marcellus* and *Athanasius*', who were responsible for establishing it in the already decadent Church of the 4th century.[3] Whiston shared with Newton an intense dislike of Athanasius.

The nearest Whiston gets to any rational, as opposed to historical, argument is in a passionate and eloquent invective against eternal torment. The 'astonishing Love of God toward mankind', of which the supreme example is the sacrifice of His only son, 'is so absolutely inconsistent with these common but barbarous and savage opinions' that one would think that no rational being, and certainly no Christian, could ever have held them. These savage opinions are:[4]

that the torments, the exquisite torments of these most numerous and most miserable creatures, are determined without the least pity, or relenting, or bowels of compassion in their Creator, to be in everlasting fire, and in the flames of Hell; without abatement, or remission, for endless ages of ages. And all this for the sins of this short life; fallen into generally by the secret snares of the Devil, and other violent temptations; which they

[1] Ibid., pp. 5–14, 20 seq.
[2] Ibid., pp. 63–4, 106.
[3] Ibid., pp. 86, 89.
[4] Ibid., pp. 18–19.

commonly could not wholly either prevent, or avoid; and this without any other advantage to themselves, or to others, or to God himself, than as instances, (I almost tremble so much as to suppose or repeat it) of the absolute and supreme power and dominion of the cruel and inexorable author of their being, for all the infinite ages of eternity. . . .

In place of this doctrine, which is as absurd and 'reproachful to Christianity' as the Athanasian Trinity, Calvinist reprobation, or Popish transubstantiation,[1] Whiston proposes the following. At death all souls go to Hades, which is inside the earth, where until the resurrection and Last Judgment they have a chance of repentance and amendment. After judgment, the just go to their long, but not eternal, life of bliss, and the still unrepentant wicked to a period of torment, the duration of which is graded in proportion to their sins, and at the end of which they are annihilated. As with Locke, the just resurrect with spiritual bodies, but the wicked with earthly ones. The fire of hell and the worm that dieth not 'are plainly understood to be *literal*'; this is one reason why punishment is deferred until the resurrection, which provides bodies able to be 'eaten up' and burnt.[2] The bodies of the wicked will be raised with the same diseases they had at death, which will give them 'a disposition for becoming a ready prey for those *worms*'. It is, Whiston notes, 'somewhat remarkable' that 'barbarous persecutors of good men' have been 'horribly tormented with such *worms* preying on their wicked bodies', or, like Herod, have suffered from an inward fire, 'till they expired in the utmost agonies'—'a specimen' of their future fate.[3]

In an earlier work, *Astronomical Principles of Religion, Natural, and Reveal'd* (1717), dedicated to 'the Illustrious Sir Isaac Newton, President, and to other members of the Royal Society', he puts forward a conjecture, repeated in the later book,[4] about the way in which the wicked will be burnt and eventually consumed, a conjecture which displays in a striking manner his peculiar synthesis of modern science and scriptural

[1] Ibid., p. 2.
[2] Ibid., p. 109. Whiston suggests that perhaps the wicked may have a second resurrection and a second chance (ibid., pp. 40, 133).
[3] Ibid., p. 110.
[4] Ibid., pp. 110 seq.

literalism. Having given a florilegium of scriptural descriptions of hell, ending with Revelations XIV, 9–11 (quoted above), he writes:[1]

> Now this Description does in every Circumstance so exactly agree with the Nature of a Comet, ascending from the Hot Regions near the Sun, and going into the Cold Regions beyond *Saturn*, with its long smoaking Tail arising up from it, through its several Ages or Periods of revolving, and this in the Sight of all the Inhabitants of our Air, and of the rest of the System; that I cannot but think the Surface or Atmosphere of such a Comet to be that *Place of Torment* so terribly described in Scripture, . . .

This comet will have been formed by the conflagration of our earth, which will occur after the destruction of Gog and Magog (Rev. XX, 7–10). The blessèd will then inhabit the air, purified by the conflagration, of the earth's former orbit, thus having a good view of the comet. It will be

> indeed a terrible but a most useful Spectacle to the rest of God's rational Creatures; and will admonish them above all Things to preserve their Innocence and Obedience; and to *fear him who is* thus *able to destroy both Soul and Body in Hell.*

The presence in Whiston of this bizarre version of the abominable fancy shows that his effort to reach primitive Christianity had made him genuinely archaic, though not more so than some of his adversaries—the abominable fancy appears in the Catholic Francis Blyth's refutation of Whiston's book.[2] It is evident that Whiston has no dislike of physical suffering, even in its most nauseating forms, provided that it be deserved —he was, as one would expect, an ardent advocate of absolute free will.[3] It is a 'barbarous and cruel' opinion to suppose that God torments the damned eternally in punishment for a short life of sin; but it is, presumably, in harmony with His 'astonishing Love toward Mankind' to have them burnt and eaten by worms for several ages. That Whiston had a primitive and infantile conception of God's relation to man is borne out by his

---

[1] Whiston, *Astr. Princ.*, pp. 155–6. Cf. supra, p. 96.
[2] Blyth, *Eternal Misery the necessary Consequence of Infinite Mercy abused*, London, 1740, p. 24.
[3] See, e.g. Whiston, *Hist. Mem. . . . Clarke*, ed. cit., p. 102.

view of providence. In his autobiography he recounts the story
of a certain John Duncalf, who lived not far from the Whistons
and who had[1]

> cursed himself, upon his stealing a bible, and had wished, that
> if he stole it, his hands might rot off, before he died; which
> proved most true, and most affecting to the whole country and
> neighbourhood.

He wishes that accounts of this occurrence might be read 'in this
sceptical age' by all who doubt 'the interposition of a particular divine providence', and that someone would write, as Bacon
suggested, a *Historia Nemesios*, that is, a history of 'the most
remarkable Judgments of God upon the wicked'. Towards the
end of his life, in January 1747, he wrote a letter to the Archbishop of Canterbury on the subject of a murrain which was
destroying cattle; this plague, he suggested, might stop if the
English reformed their manners and stopped cursing the
Eusebians or 'Primitive Christians' in the Athanasian creed.[2]
This is a view of providence that Rabelais was satirizing over
two hundred years earlier.[3] On the other hand, over a hundred
years later Dean Farrar, in his admirably compassionate sermons, *Eternal Hope*, could still regard venereal disease as a
divinely ordained punishment for sexual immorality.[4]

Whiston's treatise produced several refutations. One of them,
Matthew Horbery's *An Enquiry into the Scripture-Doctrine
Concerning the Duration of Future Punishment* (1744), though
primarily directed against Whiston, also examines Marie
Huber, Thomas Burnet, and George Rust, and is one of the
completest defences of the orthodox doctrine to be published
in English. Horbery and Blyth (*Eternal Misery the necessary
Consequence of Infinite Mercy abused*, 1740), both comment on
the lack of rational argument in Whiston, and their refutations
naturally consist mostly of a detailed critique of his use of texts.
Whiston's main defects from a present-day point of view, his
archaic moral outlook and his literal turn of mind, are not
criticized, though Blyth does refer to his 'childish remarks and

[1] Whiston, *Mem. . . . Whiston*, ed. cit., Vol. I, pp. 6–7.
[2] Ibid., pp. 339 seq.
[3] Rabelais, *Gargantua*, Ch. XXVII.
[4] F. W. Farrar, *Eternal Hope*, 1878, p. 141.

pueril conjectures'.[1] His comet is mentioned but not ridiculed, and the only objection to the literal worms is William Dodwell's 'the Conjunction of Fire and Worms, which could hardly subsist together.'[2] His denial of eternal life to the blessèd is of course considered appalling; Horbery calls it a '*horrid* Doctrine' and claims that[3]

> by denying the Perpetuity both of Reward and Punishment, he has done perhaps more than any Man living, to destroy the comfort of good Men, and hinder the Repentance of the Wicked.

All his critics are understandably annoyed at his acceptance of early heretical Fathers, especially Origen, and his branding as heretical later orthodox ones, such as Athanasius.

[1] Blyth, op. cit., p. iii.
[2] W. Dodwell, *The Eternity of Future Punishment*, pp. 31–2.
[3] M. Horbery, *An Enquiry*, pp. 10, 307.

Chapter VII

❖❖

ENGLISH PLATONISTS
(1) Sterry and White

❖❖

URING the Commonwealth, largely owing to Cromwell's personal influence, there was a considerable degree of religious tolerance in England.[1] Among the many and various heresies which this produced was the denial of eternal torment. Two Arians of this period, Biddle and Richardson, have already been mentioned.[2] Gerard Winstanley, the Digger, in his *The Mysterie of God* (1648),[3] advocated universal salvation, and so did Richard Coppin, in several works published in the 1650's.[4] Coppin, a

[1] See Robert S. Paul, *The Lord Protector Religion and Politics in the Life of Oliver Cromwell*, London, 1955.

[2] V. supra, p. 93.

[3] Winstanley, *The Mysterie of God, Concerning the whole Creation, Mankinde* . . ., n.p., 1648.

[4] *Divine Teachings: In three Parts. I. The Glorious Mystery of Divine Teachings between God, Christ, and the Saints. II. Anti-Christ in Man, opposing Emmanuel, or, God in Us. III. The Advancement of all things in Christ and of Christ in all things, with a Discovery of good and evill, inhabiting in Man . . . Being some sparks of the glory that shines and dwels in Richard Coppin*, London, 1649; *Truths Testimony . . . with the Authors Call and Conversion to the truth . . . and his several Tryals for the same . . .*, London, 1655; *A Blow at the Serpent; or a Gentle Answer from Maidstone Prison to appease Wrath . . . Together with the work of four days Disputes, in the cathedral of Rochester . . . between several Ministers, and Richard Coppin, Preacher there . . .*, London, 1656 (also reprinted 1764); *Michael opposing the Dragon: or, A Fiery Dart struck through the Heart of the Kingdom of the Serpent . . . Being a Reply to Edward Garland's Answer of a book, Intitled, A Blow at the Serpent*, London, 1659.

preacher who belonged to no church or sect,[1] maintained his views in public disputations in the cathedral of Rochester in 1655, of which he published an account while in Maidstone jail.[2] He was an interesting thinker, whose views have some similarities to those of Sterry and White.[3] Although Sterry and White may well have known any or all of these contemporaries, there is, to my knowledge, no evidence to confirm this supposition.

In his posthumously published book, *The Restoration of All Things*, Jeremiah White wrote:[4]

> This was the Seal of Love I received from a Dying Saint, who, for weakness, could not speak much, but left this with me, that the Spirit is Love, which I understood not at that time, so well as I bless God I have done since.

There is little doubt that this saint was Peter Sterry, and that White did acquire from him this fundamental belief. But it must have been long before Sterry was on his deathbed, in 1672, that White learnt from him that the supreme attribute of God is love. Though White, born in 1630, was seventeen years the younger, both had been chaplains to Cromwell and fellows of Cambridge colleges—Sterry of Emmanuel, where he was at the same time as John Smith, Whichcote and Cudworth,[5] and White of Trinity.[6] According to the editor of the *Restoration*,

[1] See Coppin, *Truths Testimony*, pp. 11–12.

[2] Coppin, *A Blow at the Serpent*.

[3] Cf. e.g. infra, p. 113, n. 4. To the above mentioned Cromwellian opponents of eternal torment should be added Paul Hobson, a General Baptist, and William Erbery, a Seeker (see H. J. McLachlan, *Socinianism in 17th century England*, pp. 223, 227). All these writers, and particularly Coppin and Winstanley, deserve much more detailed study than I have been able to give them.

[4] J. White, *The Restoration of All Things: or, a Vindication of the Goodness and Grace of God. To be Manifested at last in the RECOVERY of his Whole creation out of their FALL*, London, 1712, pp. 133–4. This first edition was anonymous. There was a second edition, without date, printed for J. Woodward and J. Morphew; a third, 1779, with a preface by John Denis; an American edition of 1844; a fourth English edition, 1851, with a preface by David Thom.

[5] See Vivian de Sola Pinto, *Peter Sterry Platonist and Puritan 1613–1672 A Biographical and Critical Study with passages selected from his Writings*, Cambridge, 1934, pp. 8–10.

[6] From the title-page of: *A Perswasive to Moderation and Forbearance in Love among the Divided Forms of Christians* 'By that late most Eminent Divine, Mr Jeremiah White, Late Fellow of Trinity-Colledge in Cambridge, Preacher to the Council of State, and Chaplain to Oliver Cromwell', London, 1708. This contains a portrait of White, under which is written: 'dyed in the 78th year of his Age, AD, 1707.'

Richard Roach,[1] it was while White was at Cambridge that this conversion occurred. White told him that, having failed to discover any theological system which presented God as love, he was in 'a great Dissatisfaction and Perplexity of Mind', so great that he fell dangerously ill; at the climax of his illness 'a Beam of Divine Grace darted upon his Intellect', which gave him 'a New Set of Thoughts concerning God and his Works, and the way of his dealing with his Offending Creatures', and he recovered his health. This new set of ideas was eventually expounded in the *Restoration*.[2] Though Sterry is not mentioned in this account, it is significant that the *only* works White recommends or cites in his book are Sterry's *A Discourse of the Freedom of the Will* (1675) and his *The Rise, Race, and Royalty of the Kingdom of God in the Soul of Man* (1683).[3] Both these were published posthumously, the latter with a preface headed 'The Publisher to the Reader' and signed J. White, the former with a long preface on God as love, which also is very probably by White. In these two works Sterry does not explicitly assert the doctrine of universal salvation, though he comes very near to doing so, and much that he says implies it unequivocally;[4] it is only from a small manuscript treatise, headed *That the State of Wicked men after this life is mixt of evill, & good things*,[5] that we can learn his views on the afterlife.

Sterry and White had very similar, if not identical, religious beliefs and feelings, and the styles in which they expressed them bear a close family likeness. They write as poets, conveying their meaning as much by rhythm and imagery as by logical argument. By this I do not wish to imply that they are loose or woolly thinkers and writers. They are certainly capable of hard reasoning; Sterry, when examining predestinationist and free will systems, is as relentless as Bayle. Their religious views are

[1] V. infra, pp. 260–1.

[2] Preface to White, *Restoration*, sig. A3 vo.

[3] White, *Restoration*, pp. 148, 201.

[4] E.g. Sterry, *The Rise, Race, and Royalty*, London, 1683, pp. 324–41, 385–6 (cf. passages quoted infra, pp. 108, 111); *A Discourse of the Freedom of the Will*, London, 1675, pp. 168, 211.

[5] Sterry MSS., deposited in Emmanuel College, Cambridge, by Professor De Sola Pinto, Vol. III, pp. 107 seq. On these MSS., see V. De Sola Pinto, 'Peter Sterry and his Unpublished Writings', *Review of English Studies*, Vol. VI, London, 1930, pp. 385 seq. I am most grateful to Professor De Sola Pinto for kindly telling me where these MSS. are.

founded on mystical experience,[1] on insights and emotions which cannot be conveyed in the logical, abstract language of theology or philosophy, but which can be hinted at in the language of poetry. That they were genuine mystics I infer from the high quality of their poetic prose. There may be genuine mystics who express themselves shoddily and tritely; but I do not believe that there are bogus mystics who express themselves powerfully and beautifully. I have insisted on this point because the description of their views which follows must necessarily be inadequate, in the same way that a summary of a good poem would be.

Although their religious views are so similar, the content of their works bearing on the afterlife is not identical. Sterry gives a much more fully developed theory of the preexistence of the soul than White, and some of his basic, recurrent images, such as the bad dream and the shadowy world, appear little or not at all in the *Restoration*. White on the other hand is fuller on topics relating directly to the eternity of hell, such as vindictive justice or the torments of the damned. But these differences do not amount to any divergencies of opinion, and they may largely be due to the fact that White spent the years before his death (1707) condensing and shortening his work so that it should have a greater effect on the public[2]—preexistence of the soul and somewhat mysterious images would be obvious things to cut out. Moreover White, writing forty or fifty years later than Sterry, was aware that taste had changed and that the public no longer appreciated poetic Platonism; in one of several chapters on God as love he writes:[3]

> I could run out at large upon this *Metaphysical* Notion, to prove the Unity of Love must be an infinite Love; but the Age we live in doth not relish *Metaphysical* Learning, and I content myself with the Pleasure of it to my self.

Sterry and White, like most of the Cambridge Platonists,

---

[1] Cf. Sterry, MS. cit., pp. 151–2: 'I appeale now to the experience of all spirituall persons in the burning of their Love-desyres, in the sweete heights, & extacys of their Love-fruitions . . . whither at these times they do not finde, feele & see themselves in a marvellous, & incomprehensible Light, by marvellous, unexpressible groanes carried to the naked person of their God in the Eternity of his Glorys . . .'

[2] Preface to White, *Restoration*, sig. A3 vo.

[3] White, *Restoration*, p. 177.

were brought up as predestinationists. But, unlike the other Platonists, they did not abandon this doctrine in favour of Arminian free will; they managed to combine it with their liberal Neoplatonic theology. This they were able to do by the only possible means: the doctrine of universal salvation. As White says, if this doctrine is accepted, God's

> Universal Grace doth no longer thrust out his Special and Peculiar Favour. Reprobation here will be found combining with Election, yea Damnation it self with Salvation, here all those knots which other systems of Divinity have hitherto tied faster, are in a great Measure loosend.

All the arguments of the Calvinists cannot remove 'an appearing Harshness' from the God who from eternity predestined most of His creatures to eternal torment, and this is why the Arminians have gone 'into another most absurd Extream', ascribing 'a Power unto Man, and a Freedom of Will absolute and independent as to those Acts relating to a future State', and thus making void both grace and the sacrifice of Christ.[1] In Sterry's and White's system the arbitrary, senseless fact of predestination remains, but the believer can look forward to the final consonance, so perfectly sweet that it blots out all the screeching discords that led up to it:[2]

> The rain will be over; the storm pass't away. The sweet, the clear, the Golden, the Glorious smiles of Love will return after the Storm, and Rain . . . Wrath is but for a moment; at longest the moment of this Life, this Shadow, this short Dream of Lifes. The Truth of Life, the Perpetuity of Life, Eternity is for Love.

This retention of predestination was not of course due merely to conservatism. To a Christian mystic the doctrine of predestination offers great advantages: it frees him from having to twist many texts of the New Testament so that they shall mean the opposite of what they appear to say, and it corresponds closely to the psychological character of mystical experience, to its involuntary, 'given' quality. The other Cambridge Platonists were nevertheless obliged to reject it because, unless accompanied by the doctrine of universal salvation, it involves a

---

[1] Ibid., pp. 8, 5.
[2] Sterry, *Rise, Race*, p. 385.

glaringly unjust and cruel God, who can be defended only by making the disastrous separation of human and divine moral values.

The metaphysical framework of Sterry and White's thought is based on a combination of Neoplatonism and Christianity, and belongs to a tradition which goes back to Nicolas of Cusa and Marsilio Ficino, both of whom Sterry cites.[1] In his manuscript treatise Sterry gives a short exposition of this metaphysical system in so far as it concerns the preexistence of souls and their ultimate fate.[2] He begins with a hierarchy of emanations, based on 'Proclus in his Platonicall Divinity', which stretches, without gaps, from the godhead down, through the highest Ideas, the Unities or Henads, to created souls and beyond them to the rest of the creation. Christ is the supreme Unity, which binds the whole system together; his soul is the uncreated mind within the godhead, his body is the totality of the Ideas of all creatures:

> All the Creatures praeexisted in the mediatory state of Christ, where, by the immediate union of the Godhead in Him, they were all spirituall & Eternall, holy, blessed, Divine Eternall Spirits . . . the immediate emanations of the exemplar Ideas in the Godhead . . . This was the Spirtuall and Heavenly Body of Christ.

The visible created world is a shadow of this ideal world, and Christ incarnate 'is the shadowie Head of this shadie Iamge', hidden in it like a seed which will finally spring forth and restore the whole creation, which now 'groaneth and travaileth in pain together',[3] to its original, ideal state. This amalgam of Pauline christology[4] and Neoplatonic emanationism thus leads to a Redemption or *epistrophe* which 'is confirmed to be most Universall' and will include 'the falne Angells as well as the elect Ones'.[5] This restoration of all things, which follows quite naturally, indeed inevitably, within the system, is buttressed

---

[1] Sterry, *Discourse of the Freedom of the Will*, pp. 77, 95.
[2] Sterry, MS. cit., pp. 128–56.
[3] Romans VIII, 22.
[4] Romans VIII, 19–23; Ephesians I, 10, 22–3; Colossians I, 15–18; II, 9–10.
[5] Sterry, MS. cit., p. 162.

by another notion belonging to the same system: man as microcosm. As White explains:[1]

> For if each Soul be a Unity, a Figure, a Shadow, of the Supream
> Unity (not a dead but a living Shadow) and that all Lines of
> Being, and Beauty meet in *this Apex*, and unity of the
> intellectual Spirit; no such Individual Soul can be for ever
> abandoned; *but the whole nature of things* must Suffer therein,
> as it did when Christ was crucified ... If so many Millions of
> these Intellectual Substances be never look'd upon, or visited
> with Redemption, not one Saint is *completely Saved*, for if
> each Spirit be an intire World, all Spirits are in each Spirit ...

For we are members one of another, members of the body of
Christ.[2]

In any theological system which includes the doctrine of
universal salvation one would expect to find a strong emphasis
on the Johannine God of love. It was, as we have seen, usual,
when one was defending the orthodox doctrine, to argue that
there is a conflict between competing divine attributes, justice
on the one hand and mercy or love on the other.[3] The demands
of both must be satisfied, and the resultant compromise is that
the elect are saved by the mercy, and the reprobate are damned
by the justice. Since it was generally agreed that the damned
far outnumber the saved, justice seems to win against love;
some theologians indeed, such as Malebranche, explicitly give
justice absolute priority over all other attributes.[4] There was
naturally a strong tendency among opponents of an eternal hell
to reverse this situation: to allow divine justice the satisfaction
of long and severe torments undergone by the wicked, but to
make love and mercy finally triumphant in the eventual salvation of everyone. There is still a conflict of attributes; but love
wins. What is exceptional in the position held by Sterry and
White is that they remove the possibly of any such conflict by
making love the supreme attribute, out of which all the others
grow and to which they must conform. At that time this was a
most unusual view, and indeed one could hardly expect it to be

---

[1] White, *Restoration*, p. 147.
[2] Ephesians IV, 25; I Corinthians XII, 12 seq.
[3] V. supra, p. 52.
[4] V. infra, p. 206.

common in Protestant theology, dominated as it was by Augustine, who was unable to accept, or even understand, St John's God of love.[1]

White's *Restoration* begins thus:[2]

> The Great Apostle who lay in the Bosom of his *Lord*, and partook of his intimate Favours, as the Disciple of Love, and consequently was most nearly admitted into the Secrets of God . . . tells us, as in singular Expression of the Divine Nature, that it is LOVE.

All the other attributes, such as justice, wisdom, power, 'harmonize in Unity, to make up the Nature of God. And thus Love is All.'[3] This unity has been broken in recent orthodox theology by making the other attributes, in particular justice, coequal with love. This supreme divine attribute is not some unknowably transcendant metaphysical entity, but, on an infinite scale, is of like nature to human affection, charity and compassion. White, referring perhaps to Sterry, writes:[4]

> It was a noble Speech of a great Person, and I should think it must be the sense of every good man's soul, might it be lawful for me to put forth one Act of Omnipotence, that I might redeem poor, sunk, degenerate souls, then would I be content to be buried in the grave of an Eternal Nothing.
>
> And whilst I sometimes entertain myself with such thoughts as these, I feel a secret joy springing in my soul, and whispering to me, if there be so much love in a drop, in a beam, in a creature, there must sure be infinitely more in all respects in the Ocean, in the Sun, in God Himself.

This compassion for the suffering of sinners, and the projection of it into God, are almost unique in the theology of that age; but they are expressed with equal force and beauty by Sterry:[5]

> Poor, and broken Spirits, who lie at the utmost ends of the Earth, mourning as outcasts; hope evermore in Eternal love, wait for it. The love of God will find you out, it will meet with you, and take you on its way.

---

[1] See J. H. S. Burleigh, *The City of God*, London, 1949, p. 180; cf. Augustine, *De Doctrina Christiana*, I, xxxi, and *Comm. in* I John IV, 8 (Migne, *Patr. Lat.*, T. 34, col. 32; T. 35, cols. 2031–2).

[2] White, *Restoration*, p. 1.

[3] White, *Restoration*, p. 2.

[4] Ibid., p. 12, Cf. infra, p. 155.

[5] Sterry, *Rise, Race*, p. 324.

How are the other attributes of God to be harmonized so that 'Love is All'? As far as hell is concerned, the attribute that matters is justice. If God's justice is to arise out of His love and serve the ends of love, it plainly cannot be vindictive; any punishment God inflicts must have the good of the sinner as its sole aim. White attacks vindictive justice and the ascription of it to God with great vehemence. An angry, revengeful God is no God at all, but a projection of men's evil passions,[1]

> but a false Image and Idol which guilty, angry, peevish Man hath set up within it self in the place of God.

All punishment that is not curative or deterrent, that is, which has no positive good as its end, is merely

> to satisfy a peevish Humour which pleases itself in the Misery of those by whom it is offended, and there is a Spirit of Revenge and Cruelty in it, equally, absolutely evil and eternally abhorrent from the Nature of God and all good Men.

He even points to a more sinister emotion than anger behind vindictive justice:[2]

> Sure I am for a Judge here below, to condemn the greatest Malefactor and Murderer with Pleasure and Delight, in the Ruin and Destruction of his Fellow Creature, is to make himself guilty of the same Offence, the same Murder for which he condemns another to Punishment, for Punishment sake; for this is the *Lust* of the Punisher, and cannot be the qualification of any good Being.

Since he has just demonstrated that eternal punishment cannot be either curative or deterrent (after the Last Day), the God whom he is condemning as an angry and sadistic idol seems to be the God of all Christians except the very small minority who secretly disbelieve in the eternity of hell.[3]

God's justice and anger, for White, are an aspect of His love. Nothing is more contrary to love than sin. When the infinite power of God's love meets sin, it burns it and kills it. This

---

[1] White, *Restoration*, p. 186.
[2] White, *Restoration*, p. 189.
[3] White is probably in fact referring to the Calvinist God predestining the reprobate to eternal torment, a God whom he, like Sterry, attacks vehemently; cf. White, ibid., pp. 192–3 (quoting Rust, *A Discourse of Truth*, ed. of 1682, p. 175), and Sterry, *A Discourse of the Freedom of the Will*, p. 190.

loving wrath is directed solely against the sin, not against the sinner:[1]

> thus Love is a Death to everything that should dye. O, how kind is the cruelty of this Death! O, how faithfully cruel is the kindness of this killing Love!

And finally this destructive love will consume all sin, purify all souls, and there will be no more suffering. White believes in the natural, inevitable connexion between sin and suffering. The suffering is the shame and remorse of the sinner when made fully aware of his own state. For the wicked this will happen only after the resurrection, when they will be 'enlightened' by seeing the glory and felicity of the elect.[2] But the most terrible enlightenment will be the direct contact with God's love. The same burning love that will be bliss for the saved will be agony for the wicked, until their sins are burnt up:[3]

> God himself puts forth himself immediately and naked upon them, at once to torment them, and also to sustain them for their Torments ... O! who can express the riches of the Joy and Glory of those Spirits, upon whom God shall appear immediately and nakedly as a Friend, as a Lover in Union with them? And who can express those Pangs, those Horrors, those unspeakable and nameless things which that poor Soul must then sink under, upon whom the same God shall appear with the same nakedness of his Godhead, in a direct contrariety to it, making his Glory it self a Fire upon it.

This theory of the identity of God's love and hell-fire[4] appears also in Sterry:[5]

> If he [sc. God] meet with any pure and sweet Spirit, like himself; he closeth with it, in all manner of gentleness, and softness, as *Two Flames* embrace one another.
> But where he meets with opposition he rageth. He burns

---

[1] White, *Restoration*, pp. 183–4; cf. pp. 210–17.

[2] White, ibid., pp. 130–1. The elect will also see the misery of the damned; White is able to admit the abominable fancy, made harmless by universal salvation.

[3] White, ibid., pp. 226–8.

[4] This theory is also fully expounded by Michel Servet in his *Christianismi Restitutio*, 1553 (Nürnberg repr., 1790, pp. 245–6), and by Richard Coppin (*A Blow at the Serpent*, pp. 35, 37, 70–1).

[5] Sterry, *Rise, Race*, p. 52.

113

upon dark, unclear, untractable Hearts, as *Fire* in the *Iron-works*; till he hath poured them forth into the Temper, and Mold of his Spirit, and Image.

But Sterry gives us a more detailed picture of the sufferings and final salvation of the damned.

The damned are 'empty, deformed Shades', inhabiting a dark shadowy world, remarkably like the underworld of Homer and Virgil, and are tormented with 'restlesse desyres' and 'per-petuall frustrations'. 'As a light & a prospect in a dreame & at a great distance', they see the glories of heaven, become aware of the 'contrarietie of their Life past in Sin unto this Heavenly Image', and are filled with regret and remorse—this is the worm that dieth not:[1]

> This also is the weeping, & wailing, and gnashing of teeth, which our Saviour speakes of inter stridulas umbras.

Then the 'Seed & Life of God' works among them, burning up the sin that opposes it; by its power they suffer the agony of the crucifixion, 'they drinke of the Cup which he did drinke', they share in His resurrection, and are saved. These are sufferings which all, good and bad alike, must go through; the good on this earth and the bad in hell. This is the meaning of the parable of Dives and Lazarus; and Sterry is able to explain the charitable concern of Dives for his seven brothers, so troublesome to orthodox commentators, as the beginning of the redemptive process that will finally save him. As a concession to the value of hell as a deterrent, Sterry affirms that it is better to be Lazarus than Dives; but then at once denies that true holiness, regeneration through Christ, has anything to do with hopes of reward or fears of punishment.[2]

Although universal salvation considerably lightens the moral blackness of predestination, serious problems of theodicy still remain. Everything will end as it began in perfect bliss and beauty; but what is the justification of all the misery and evil in between? Sterry goes into these problems much more thoroughly than White, who seems less seriously troubled by them. The latter suggests a curious version of the abominable

[1] Sterry, MS. cit., pp. 107–9.
[2] Ibid., pp. 115, 111, 114, 116–17; on the terrors of hell, cf. Sterry, *Rise, Race*, pp. 52–3, and White, *Restoration*, pp. 46–7.

fancy: the happiness of the damned, when they are finally saved, will be heightened by the memory of their torments—[1]

> Yea, so shall the Damned rejoyce over that Hell they have been in. They shall reflect on that Fire out of which they are De-livered; and it shall be the food of their Joy. . . .

But, unless this makes them actually happier than the elect, which would lead to antinomian conclusions, it still does not justify God's having allowed or engineered the whole business of sin and hell. White also proposes aesthetic analogies, such as appear in all theodicies from Plotinus to Leibniz:[2] every act of 'this Tragi-Comick Scene' is directed towards 'that last and sweetest Close, that overcoming, that ravishing Love and Good-ness which is the End of them all'.[3] In Sterry too we find the discords of music making the consonances more sweet, the crooked lines and ugly objects in a beautiful picture,[4] the heroes of Homer, Virgil, Tasso, and Spencer, carried to the *utmost extremity* of misery before the happy ending.[5] Such analogies are more convincing in systems which include universal salva-tion than in orthodox ones—at least there is a happy ending, at least the music does not end on an unresolved discord. But I think that no serious thinker could rest content with these analogies; even if we were only spectators of life, which we are not, they demand that we should be very callous ones.

Perhaps the most satisfactory attempt at theodicy made by Sterry is in the form of a Platonic-Cabalistic vision of pre-existent souls, which appears both in his *Discourse of the Free-dom of the Will* and in his manuscript treatise. Its mythical character protects it against the simple deflating questions to which ordinary theodicies are subject. In the published version Sterry's myth begins with an extended cabalistic sexual analogy taken from Henry More and Cudworth.[6] The souls are born of the marriage of the Father with the Word, and are

---

[1] White, *Restoration*, p. 106.

[2] Cf. A. O. Lovejoy, *The Great Chain of Being*, Cambridge, Mass., 1948, pp. 64–6, and infra, p. 211.

[3] White, ibid., p. 105.

[4] Sterry, *Discourse of the Freedom of the Will*, pp. 155–6 (discords in music), 28 (Lazarus, with all his sores, when painted by Titian or Vandyke, is 'a worthy and most agreable entertainment to the eye and fancy of any Princess').

[5] Sterry, ibid., p. 179.

[6] Sterry, ibid., pp. 31–2.

themselves married couples; their bodies, not yet corporeal but some kind of spiritual vestment or 'sensitive Image', are the brides, their minds the bridegrooms. Some of them fall into a deep sleep— 'yet are they still sleeping Beauties and sleeping Loves, beautiful and lovely in their sleep'. And in this sleep they have, like Abraham in Genesis XV, 'disorderly, deformed, distracting Dreams':

> They may see dreadful fires in the midst of this darkness, themselves, their dear Bride the sensitive Image, like Doves, lying dead, and *divided* one from another, like innocent Beasts of Sacrifice slain, and cut into several pieces, with the brands of fire, or turning Lamps passing between them.

In this nightmare-ridden sleep they lie until they are awakened by the sound of a trumpet and an archangel saying: 'Arise and shine, for thy light is come, the glory of the Lord is risen upon thee'.[1]

> Then shall these Bridegroom-Souls, with their beloved Brides, their Bodies, appear after this dark and tempestuous night of their sleep and dreams, in the fresh and pleasant morning of a *new day*, as new Heaven and a new Earth, with their Beauties, all new married anew to eachother.

These souls, before 'their *descent* and *fall*', had shown to them, 'as in a mysticall Glasse', a prospect of their ordeal: 'a vast & howling wilderness of vanity, bondage & corruption, of sin, death & wrath.' But they also received the assurance that God

> would forever preserve that Love which he had to them in eternity, when he beheld them in that *first-born Image* of all loves and lovelinesses . . . and direct their way through this wilderness.

And in the glass they also saw

> a Glory in the Godhead on high unfolding itselfe in this blacke & melancholy Scheme, which, as they come forth from this Scene in the close of it shall open itselfe to them, although now it be altogether incomprehensible.

They know that their ordeal will result in a 'Glory altogether new & before unknowne to them'; and they freely consent to

---

[1] Sterry, ibid., p. 33.

their long sleep and terrible dreams.[1] At the time they make this decision, these souls have already descended from their original state as 'immediate emanations of the exemplar Ideas in the Godhead', and have become 'earthly and shadowy' images inhabiting a 'delightfull' but shadowy Paradise.[2] How and why this occurred we are not told.

The dream, which represents both this life and hell—all that happens to a soul from its Fall till its salvation, is dreamt not only by man but also by God:[3]

> Now God and Man awakened together, as out of a sleep, and the dreams in the sleep, into the same Righteousness, are satisfied with the same likeness in each other, reflected from man as the Son, the Image of God. . . .

Sometimes the dream seems to be only God's. The whole creation is His dream; and the Devil and fallen men and angels are 'only *shadows in a dream*'.[4]

> When the eternal Spirit in whose sleep, like painted forms in a dream, they vainly flutter about, awakeneth himself, he at once dissolveth them into their *own nothingness*.

I think it improbable that what Sterry means here is the annihilation of wicked angels and men; there is nothing else in his work to suggest such a notion, and in his manuscript treatise he explicitly asserts the salvation of fallen angels.[5] It is more likely that the evil of these creatures is dissolved into the nothingness it always truly was, leaving only their original ideal essences.

I called this mythical theodicy satisfactory, not only because its mysteriousness makes it difficult to pick holes in, but also because the image of a dream is psychologically appropriate to theodicy. One of the purposes of most theodicies, including Sterry's, is to make us accept all the misery and ugliness of this world as unimportant compared with some higher, more real order, some magnificent totality, of which we can now have

---

[1] Sterry, ibid., p. 34, and MS. cit., pp. 156–7.
[2] Sterry, MS. cit., pp. 155–6. In the printed version (*Discourse of the Freedom of the Will*, pp. 118, 121), the souls, when they make this decision, are all existing in Adam, before the Fall.
[3] Sterry, *Discourse of the Freedom of the Will*, p. 119.
[4] Sterry, ibid., p. 61.
[5] Sterry, MS. cit., p. 162; cf. supra, p. 109.

only partial glimpses. We resist this demand because we have direct experience of the misery we and other men undergo, and we find it difficult and repellent to imagine another experience that would make this misery seem trivial and unreal. To overcome this resistance an image is required which can express the apparently contradictory notions of the immediate reality of our suffering, and of its unreality compared with some other experience. While one is dreaming, the terrors of a nightmare are as intense and real as those of any other frightening experience (perhaps more so, since we compare waking experiences to nightmares); but when one wakes up one immediately feels—with what joyful relief—that this familiar waking world is the real one, and that the nightmare-world, already fast fading, was sheer illusion. The images of fresh mornings and sunlight that Sterry uses for the apocatastasis[1] reinforce this impression of relief, reality, and familiarity that comes on waking from a bad dream.

But still of course remains the simple awkward question: what was the point of all this misery? why not a pleasant dream? and the psychological objection: is all our suffering as aimless and senseless as the terrors of a dream? The myth also tries to answer these objections, by representing the dream as a voluntarily undertaken ordeal, which will achieve a greater glory for both God and man. As for God, the contrast between His holiness and the deformity of sin displays

> the Beauties in the Face of God with a new heightening, a new lustre, infinitely more sweet and ravishing.

As for man,

> the *shadowy happiness* of the Creature (in Paradise) is *changed* into a *substantial* one;

man is formed into a 'Divine Image, *infinitely newer*, fuller, higher'.[2] Moreover man and God, when both awake from their dreams, are, as we have seen, closer together because the Incarnation has occurred;[3] the coming of Christ was the begin-

---

[1] E.g. passage quoted supra, p. 116.
[2] Sterry, *A Discourse of the Freedom of the Will*, p. 119.
[3] V. supra, p. 117.

ning of the awakening. This is Sterry's chief answer to the above
questions: the ancient paradox, which we shall meet again:[1]

> O certè necessarium Adae peccatum,
> Quod Christi morte deletum est.
> O felix culpa, quae talem ac tantum
> Meruit habere Redemptorem.

Since Sterry is a frank opponent of absolute free will, he is
left, at the end of his theodicy, with a formidable difficulty:[2]

> If God first from the counsel of his own Will alone withdraw
> those beams, which are all our Light and Beauty, and we then
> by the *inevitable necessity* of our Natures wander as deformed
> shades in a wild darkness, through the Regions of Sin, Death
> and Hell: Is not God, now in a moral sense clearly and fully,
> *the sole Author of Sin and Evil*? This is the knot which indeed
> standeth in need of the Rosy Fingers of the Heavenly Morning,
> the beams of the eternal Day to unty it.

Sterry, as we have seen and as he admits here, has no other
reply to this question than to show that free-will systems ultimately reach the same blasphemous answer. God, then, though
He caused it only negatively, by withdrawing His Grace, did
positively intend the whole nightmare, and every sin and agony
in it. Sterry is too honest not to face the obvious antinomian
implications of this admission. If sin is part of God's plan, then
the sinner as much as the saint can claim to be fulfilling God's
will; and this seems 'to confirm the *Ranters* in their *licentious
Principles* and Practices'.[3] The orthodox way out of this
difficulty is not open to Sterry; he cannot argue that sin is due
to man's abuse of free will, and that God ingeniously uses this
evil to good ends. He admits that the weight of this difficulty is
perhaps too heavy for his shoulders. The best he can do is to
assert that sinners have no knowledge of the divine plan, and
that those who do attain this knowledge are infallibly inclined
to virtue. This could only be true if in fact no antinomian sects
existed, and he has just cited the Ranters.

---

[1] This hymn is attributed to St Gregory (see A. O. Lovejoy, 'Milton and the
Paradox of the Fortunate Fall', in his *Essays in the History of Ideas*, New York,
1955, pp. 277 seq.). White also uses this argument (*Restoration*, p. 213).

[2] Sterry, *A Discourse*, p. 146.

[3] Sterry, *A Discourse of the Freedom of the Will*, p. 156, cf. 153. On the
Ranters, see the Appendix to Norman Cohn, *The Pursuit of the Millennium*,
London, 1957.

This admission that God is, in however negative a way, responsible for sin leads Sterry very near to a Boehmenist or Manichaean God—and we know that he owned some of Boehme's works.[1] Sterry is less certain and clear than White in identifying God's anger with His love. He often calls God's punitive acts 'His strange work' (Isa. XXVIII, 21), and explains that this means[2]

> a work in which he is *descended* out of his own Form into some inferiour Form of the Creature, and so become a Stranger to Himself.

These acts of wrath are 'subordinate' appearances of God, as fire rather than light, or as a mixture of light and darkness; the dark fire is Boehme's term for the destructive principle in his dualistic God.[3] Sterry even suggests in unfigurative language that God contains the defective forms of being, i.e. the principles of evil: darkness, absence, death.[4] Then, two pages later, he denies this; sin is only *'privation* of Grace' and cannot be included in God; but then again, this privation, withholding of grace, though it results in man in 'the *highest deformity*', is a perfection and beauty in God. These deformities make up the fulness and variety of the creation, and thus are part of its beauty when seen in the context of eternity.[5] Here Sterry is far from the image of the nightmare and near to the theodicies of 18th-century optimism. He is also dangerously near to a position that would justify an eternal hell; if the variety and contrast provided by sin and misery now make the universe more beautiful, why should they not do so for all eternity?

White provides an answer to this last objection, an answer that we shall come across again as one of Petersen's main metaphysical arguments. Sin and hell began in time and cannot therefore endure eternally. Human souls are not subject to this limitation because, at least as Ideas, they have existed *ab aeterno* in the mind of God.[6] This argument rests on the impossibility of an eternity that has a beginning but no end—the

---

[1] See V. De Sola Pinto, *Peter Sterry*, pp. 57, 62.
[2] Sterry, *Rise, Race*, pp. 153, 171; *A Discourse*, pp. 150–1.
[3] Cf. infra, p. 222.
[4] Sterry, *A Discourse*, p. 151.
[5] Sterry, *A Discourse*, pp. 152–3.
[6] White, *Restoration*, p. 156.

aeternitas a parte post of orthodox theology. This impossibility, which White merely assumes, Sterry tries to prove when he is arguing in favour of preexistence of the soul, by means of showing logical absurdities which the notion involves.[1]

Sterry and White were chiliasts in the sense that they believed or hoped that the Last Day was near;[2] but chiliasm was not a major element in their work, nor motive in their religious activity. We do find in White that link between chiliasm and universal salvation which was the main driving-force of the Petersens and the Philadelphians: the 'most glorious truth' of universal salvation 'will be found so at the last opening of the *Everlasting* Gospel, to recover in that opening a degenerate world';[3] that is to say, there will be a new revelation other than the New Testament, preparatory to the Second Coming, and this revelation will be the doctrine of universal salvation. But this is an isolated idea, not a central theme. The Everlasting Gospel appears on the title-page of White's book; but it seems likely that Richard Roach put it there, since he admits to having altered the title.[4] White, however, did firmly believe in a continuous, growing revelation; we can approach ever nearer to religious truth, though we can never wholly grasp it in this life, and we must not rest in this endless search. From this dynamic conception of theology he drew the moral of extreme tolerance and open-mindedness:[5]

If we cannot yet receive and embrace eachother in our several ages, growths, measures and attainments, it is because we have little, low, dark, narrow and contracted hearts.

[1] Sterry, MS. cit., pp. 118–126.
[2] Sterry, *Rise, Race*, pp. 430 seq.; White, *Restoration*, pp. 97, 112.
[3] White, ibid., p. 7.
[4] Roach, Preface to White, *Restoration*, sig. A3 vo.
[5] White, Preface to Sterry, *Rise, Race*, sig. A3 vo–b2 vo.

Chapter VIII

⸻⸺⸺⸺⸺⸺⸺⸺⸺⸺⸺⸺⸺⸺⸺⸺⸺⸺⸺⸺⸺⸺⸺⸺⸺⸺⸺

ENGLISH PLATONISTS
(2) Henry More and some Friends

⸻⸺⸺⸺⸺⸺⸺⸺⸺⸺⸺⸺⸺⸺⸺⸺⸺⸺⸺⸺⸺⸺⸺⸺⸺⸺⸺

(i) INTRODUCTION

HENRY MORE was a very close friend of Anne Finche, Viscountess Conway. They corresponded regularly and More frequently stayed with the Conways at Ragley. Lady Conway shared her friend's religious and philosophical interests; though they did not always see eye to eye on these matters, their mutual respect and affection were constant. She suffered from violent, almost continuous headache. This terrible affliction, which she bore with great fortitude, certainly influenced her religious views, and it also led her to seek help from anyone who laid claim to unusual medical skill.[1] Among those who made this claim was Baron Francis Mercurius Van Helmont, the son of the great physician J. B. Van Helmont. From 1670 to 1679 he was almost constantly at Ragley, trying unsuccessfully to cure Lady Conway's headache.[2]

Van Helmont was not only a physician, but also an educational theorist, a magician, a Hebrew scholar, a highly speculative

---

[1] On Lady Conway and Henry More, see *Conway Letters*, ed. Marjorie Hope Nicolson, London, 1930, passim.

[2] *Conway Letters*, p. 317.

theologian, and a skilled carpenter, weaver and painter.[1]
His conversation seems to have been fascinating, though confusing, and by all accounts he was a kind and charming person.
Henry More, who met him first at Cambridge in 1670, remarked
that he had a strong 'phancy', but a very good heart.[2] Leibniz
saw him much later, in 1696, when, at the age of seventy-nine,
still 'vif et alerte', he came to Hanover, dressed as a Quaker in
brown cloth and wearing 'un chapeau sans audaces';[3] they had
long talks together, attended by the Electress of Hanover, an
old friend of Van Helmont's, who said of him 'qu'il ne s'enten-
doit pas lui-même'.[4] Leibniz later gave the following judgment
on him:[5]

> His conduct was above reproach, his actions were charitable and
> disinterested; and, but for a few delusions which had remained
> with him, like an hereditary illness, from the impressions of his
> youth, he was an excellent man, whose conversation was very
> instructive to those who knew how to profit by it. His works
> show only what was least praiseworthy in him.

Among Van Helmont's multifarious interests was Cabalism,
especially the 16th-century school led by Isaac Luria, in which
metempsychosis was a dominant theme.[6] Before he came to
England, he was already closely associated with the German
Cabalist, Christian Knorr von Rosenroth; in 1667 they had
published a German version of Boethius's *Consolatio Philosophiae*, of which Van Helmont translated the prose and Rosenroth the verse, and a work of Van Helmont's on the Hebrew
alphabet, with a preface by Rosenroth.[7] Soon after he met

[1] See Leibniz, *Opera Omnia*, ed. L. Dutens, Genevae, 1768, T. VI, Pt. I, p.
331; *Conway Letters*, pp. 309 seq.

[2] *Conway Letters*, p. 329.

[3] 'en sorte qu'on l'auroit plutôt pris pour un artisan que pour un Baron',
Leibniz, ibid.

[4] Leibniz, ibid., p. 333, and cf. pp. 70–2.

[5] Leibniz, *Op. Omn.*, ed. cit., T. V., p. 43: 'Sa conduite étoit sans reproche,
ses actions pleines de charité & de désintéressement; & à quelques chimères près,
qui lui étoient restées des impressions de la jeunesse & comme une maladie
héréditaire, c'étoit un excellent homme dont la conversation étoit très-instructive
pour ceux qui en savoient profiter. Ses ouvrages ne font voir que ce qu'il y avoit
en lui de moins louable.'

[6] See Gershom G. Scholem, *Major Trends in Jewish Mysticism*, Jerusalem,
1941, pp. 276 seq.

[7] See Kurt Salecker, *Christian Knorr von Rosenroth (1636–1689)*, Leipzig,
1931, pp. vii–viii. Rosenroth too was a friend of Leibniz (v. ibid., pp. 11–13).

More, Van Helmont recommended Rosenroth to him.[1] More, who was of course already interested in Cabalism, corresponded with Rosenroth, and they had a friendly debate on the subject of Lurianic Cabalism, of which More was sharply critical. This debate was printed in the *Kabbala Denudata* (1677, 1684).[2] This large compilation, published by Rosenroth and Van Helmont, also contains Latin translations of parts of the *Zohar*, of various 16th-century cabalistic treatises, and of a Lurianic work on metempsychosis, *De Revolutionibus Animarum*.[3] Van Helmont later stated that he was responsible for the inclusion of this last work, and for getting it translated.[4]

While Van Helmont was at Ragley, both he and Lady Conway became Quakers, much to the distress of Henry More, who regarded the Quakers as disciples of the Familists planted by the Catholics in order to disrupt the Church of England.[5] Van Helmont and Lady Conway also became converted to other religious doctrines not held by More: metempsychosis and universal salvation. The main source of these doctrines was Lurianic Cabalism, though it is likely that More's firm belief in the preexistence of the soul and his admiration for Origen were also important influences.[6]

Van Helmont expounded these doctrines in works published between 1684 and 1694.[7] He also arranged the posthumous publication of a treatise by Lady Conway, which appeared in Latin in 1690 and in English in 1692.[8]

In June 1661 appeared *A Letter of Resolution concerning Origen and the chief of his opinions*, which, in spite of a few oddly cautious reservations,[9] is a defence of Origen's major heresies, in particular of preexistence of the soul and universal salvation.

---

[1] *Conway Letters*, pp. 323–4.
[2] *Kabbala Denudata*, T. I, Sulzbaci, 1677, Pt. 2, pp. 14 seq., 62 seq., 173, 225 seq.
[3] *Kabbala Denudata*, T. II, Francofurti, 1684, Pt. 3, pp. 243 seq.
[4] F. M. Van Helmont, *The Paradoxical Discourses*, London, 1685, pp. 98–9, 160.
[5] See *Conway Letters*, pp. 306, 409, 411 seq.
[6] V. infra, p. 131.
[7] V. infra, p. 141.
[8] V. infra, p. 137, note 3.
[9] *Letter of Resolution*, p. 135.

This work has frequently been attributed to George Rust,[1] a former pupil of More's at Cambridge, who in 1661, at Jeremy Taylor's request and on More's recommendation, went to Ireland, in company with the Conways, to be Dean of Connor; he later became Bishop of Dromore.[2] The only evidence I know of in favour of this attribution is Richard Roach's statement, in his preface to White's *Restoration* (1712),[3] that the *Letter of Resolution* is 'known among the Learned to have been written by a Bishop of the Church of England, Famous for his Excellent Tract *de Veritate*.' Roach is certainly referring to Rust's *Discourse of Truth* (1677); he is a well-informed and disinterested witness, but he is writing about fifty years after the publication of the *Letter*. Against the attribution to Rust is the following evidence.

Between September 1661 and January 1662 More corresponded with Lady Conway about the book, the Conways then being in Ireland and in contact with Rust.[4] He recommended it to her, saying 'it is a pretty odd Book, but has some thinges very consyderable in it', and 'I am persuaded it will please you better than any Romance', and he sent her a copy.[5] He wrote in October 1661 that it had been censured in the Consistory by the Vice-Chancellor of the University for unsound opinions, among which was the preexistence of the soul.[6] But in December 1661 he still had not discovered who the author was—[7]

> I have enquired as diligently as I could who should be the Authour of that *Letter of Resolution*, but I could never yett finde it out.

In the General Preface to his *Collected Works* (1662) More again affirmed that he did not know who wrote the *Letter*.[8] These facts may of course mean only that Rust had been very careful to preserve his anonymity. But this is more difficult to

[1] E.g. by M. H. Nicholson, in her preface to the facsimile edition of the *Letter* (Columbia, 1933); she adduces no evidence whatever. The *Letter* was reprinted in *The Phenix: a Revival of Scarce and Valuable Pieces*, London, 1707, pp. 1–85.
[2] See *Conway Letters*, p. 171; M. H. Nicolson, pref. to *Letter*.
[3] White, *Restoration*, sig. A3 vo.
[4] *Conway Letters*, p. 192.
[5] Ibid., pp. 192, 195, 197.
[6] Ibid., p. 194.
[7] Ibid., pp. 196–7.
[8] More, *A Collection of Several Philosophical Writings*, London, 1662, p. xxii.

explain: the *Letter* is addressed to the 'Learned and most Ingenious C.L: Esquire', and the author, having cited Henry More on the nature of the soul, thanks this gentleman 'for giving me the first notice I had of so worthy an Author'.[1] Since More had been Rust's tutor, one would have to suppose, if Rust was the author, that he was here deliberately putting readers off the scent; this might just possibly be the case. Judging from the views expressed in Rust's other works, I think it by no means unlikely that he did write the *Letter*.

Someone else who read the *Letter* with great interest was Joseph Glanvill. In the preface to his *Lux Orientalis* (1662) he explains that some of his learned friends thought well of the theory of preexistence expounded in the *Letter*, but found the subject not fully enough treated there and so asked him to write this fuller account.[2] Glanvill himself in January 1662 had written a letter to an unknown correspondent in which, being 'enamour'd of the Origenist Hypothesis', he asked for certain objections against it to be resolved.[3] He sent a copy of the *Lux Orientalis* to More, together with a Latin dedication. Glanvill and More had in common, besides the doctrine of preexistence, a keen interest and firm belief in supernatural phenomena such as ghosts and poltergeists.[4] This dedication was printed in the 1682 edition of the *Lux Orientalis*, which also contained Rust's *Discourse of Truth* and annotations on both works 'by one not unversed in these kinds of speculation'. The whole volume was dedicated by the publisher to Sir John Finch, Lady Conway's half-brother, because he had been 'so Noble a Benefactor' to Rust.[5] The annotations, of considerable interest, are probably by More.[6] In them he refutes two earlier attacks on preexistence.

---

[1] *A Letter of Resolution*, p. 22.

[2] *Two Choice and Useful Treatises*: the one Lux Orientalis; Or an Enquiry into the Opinion of the Eastern Sages Concerning the Praeexistence of Souls. Being a Key to unlock the Grand Mysteries of Providence. In Relation to Mans Sin and Misery. The Other, A Discourse of Truth, By the late Reverend Dr. Rust Lord Bishop of Dromore in Ireland. With Annotations on them both, London, 1682, sig. B5.

[3] Charles F. Mullett, 'A Letter by Joseph Glanvill on the Future State', in *The Huntington Library Quarterly*, Vol. I, 1937, pp. 447–56.

[4] Cf. More's edition of Glanvill's *Sadducismus Triumphatus*, London, 1681.

[5] *Two Choice . . . Treatises*, dedication by James Collins.

[6] The Annotations end, 'by way of digression', with 'A brief Return to Mr. Baxter's Reply, which he calls a Placid Collation with the Learned Dr. Henry More'.

One of these, by Samuel Parker, had been answered in 1668 in an anonymous publication, *Deus Justificatus*, which comes very near to asserting universal salvation.[1] It was probably by Henry Hallywell, a friend of Rust's and the editor of his posthumous *Discourse of the Use of Reason in Matters of Religion* (1683), which he dedicated to Henry More.[2]

Glanvill's and More's doctrine of preexistence was defended in a work 'originally written in the Latine Tongue by the Learned C.P.' and translated by 'D.F.D.P. upon the recommendation of F.M.H. their friend': *A Dissertation Concerning the Pre-existency of Souls* (1684).[3] I do not know who D.F. was, but I am sure that F.M.H. stands for Francis Mercurius Van Helmont and C.P. for Christian Peganius, a regular pseudonym of Knorr von Rosenroth.

(ii) HENRY MORE

Although More was so closely connected with these advocates of universal salvation, he himself, I think, held to the orthodox doctrine of eternal torment. Richard Roach, however, in his preface to White's *Restoration*, includes More in a list of modern believers in universal salvation, and cites More's *Divine Dialogues* (1668), claiming that[4]

the Vision of Bathynous's Silver and Golden Keys, the Keys of Providence, speaks very favourably of this, yea covertly and at a distance involves it; not only in his direct maintaining the Doctrine of Praeexistence which goes hand in hand with it; but laying down the more general Principles from whence it flows.

The vision of Bathynous,[5] one of the two main speakers in the *Dialogues*, is in the form of a dream he had when young. Having

[1] V. infra, pp. 154–5.
[2] See *Notes and Queries*, 1851, p. 195; *Conway Letters*, p. 293, n. 4.
[3] It bears a strong likeness to the *Adumbratio Kabbalae Christianae*, published at the end of *Kabbala Denudata*, T. II, 1684. Cf. *A Dissertation*, pp. 57–72, with *Adumbratio*, pp. 45–7, containing the same, rather odd, list of authorities: Clement of Alexandria, Origen, Augustine, various Neo-platonists, Ficino, Cardano, Fernel, Pomponazzi.
[4] White, *Restoration*, sig. a–a2 vo.
[5] Franciscus Palaeopolitanus (i.e. Henry More), *Divine Dialogues, Containing sundry Disquisitions & Instructions Concerning the Attributes of God And his Providence In the World*, London, 1668, Vol. I, pp. 477–92.

decided that the three chief attributes of God are power, wisdom and goodness, and that 'the sovereign of these was his *Goodness*, the Summity and Flower, as I may so speak, of the *Divinity*', he was much preoccupied with

> inextricable Puzzles and Difficulties, to make the *Phaenomena* of
> the World and vulgar Opinions of men in any tolerable way to
> consort or sute with these two chiefest Attributes of God, his
> *Wisedome* and his *Goodness*.

While thinking on these matters in a wood one summer morning, he lay down under an oak, fell asleep and dreamed he was still walking in the wood and worrying about the attributes. He met a venerable old man, dressed in purple, who, saying that he was a messenger from God, gave him the two keys. These could be opened by a kind of combination lock involving the use of a key-word; inside each was a scroll of very thin paper. The keyword for the silver key was *Claude fenestras ut luceat domus*, and on the scroll, headed 'the true Systeme of the World', was a diagram, in sky blue and gold, of the Copernican universe. The key-word of the golden key was *Amor Dei Lux Animae* and on the scroll, in letters of gold, were twelve sentences. Bathynous glanced at them all, and had learnt the first six by heart, when he was woken up by two asses braying. These six sentences affirmed the preexistence of souls, absolute free will, that 'the Measure of Providence is the Divine Goodness, which has no bounds but itself, which is infinite', and that 'as much as the Light exceeds the shadows, so much do the Regions of Happiness those of Sin and Misery'.

Roach contends that the braying asses symbolize 'the Rudeness and Clamour of *Narrow* and Ignorant Spirits', and hint at the reason 'why he conceal'd the other part of what might serve to clear up the Providence of God', namely, the doctrine of universal salvation, which would have been asserted in the other six sentences.[1] This seems quite a convincing interpretation, if one has not read the rest of More's dialogues. For Roach does not mention what immediately precedes, and leads up to Bathynous's dream. Hylobares, 'a young, witty, and well-moralized Materialist', is required by Philotheus, the other main speaker, to make a certain admission, which, combined

[1] White, *Restoration*, sig. a2.

with the hypothesis of preexistence, will solve all problems of theodicy. This admission is that vindictive justice is compatible with the goodness of God. Hylobares is asked whether[1]

> you do not think that some free Agents, whether the Spirits of Angels or of Men, may not so misbehave themselves, that if you saw them tumbling in stifling flames of Brimstone, and heard them howling for extremity of Torture, and hideously blaspheming God out of an impenitent vexation of mind and diabolical fixedness in that which is evil, being committed to a State of Devils and of Hell; whether, notwithstanding the dismalness of this Tragicall sight, you cannot easily conceive but that such a state of things, though it were all over the face of the Earth, might consist with the *Justice* and *Goodness* of God?
> Hylobares: With that part of his Goodness which we call *Justice*, you mean, Philotheus.
> Philotheus: Be it so, Hylobares.
> Hylobares: That I was convinced of yesterday, by your Parable of the defloured Virgin . . .

This parable was the story of a 'Vertuous and Beautifull Virgin, royally descended and Princely attired', who was raped by 'some rude Wretch', who then dragged her by the hair through hedges and ditches. At this point a knight errant appears, and Hylobares is asked whether it is enough for the knight to rescue the lady, or

> whether there ought not to be added also some exquisite Torture and shamefull Punishment worthy so hainous a fact, and proportionable to the just indignation any noble spirit would conceive against so villainous a Crime, though neither the wronged person nor punished party were at all bettered by it.

Hylobares of course agrees that there must be some exquisite punishment.[2] The fact that the virgin was manifestly of royal rank points to the main traditional defence of the eternity of hell, namely, that the infinite majesty of God offended by sin justifies an infinite punishment.[3]

In these passages More certainly asserts the compatibility of vindictive justice with a God whose supreme attribute is

---

[1] More, *Divine Dialogues*, I, 472 seq., cf. 502 (admission repeated).
[2] Ibid., pp. 301 seq.
[3] Cf. supra, p. 43.

goodness, and applies this to a hell of traditional fire and brimstone; but he does not in the *Dialogues* categorically affirm its
eternity. In the annotations to Glanvill's *Lux Orientalis* however he does make this affirmation, not in commenting on
Glanvill's timid suggestion of a restoration of all things, but in
dealing with one of the opponents of preexistence, E.W.[1] The
main argument adduced by More and his friends in favour of
preexistence was that it was a necessary hypothesis in order to
exonerate God from responsibility for congenital inequalities.
If God's supreme attribute is goodness, then one must find
some explanation for His allowing some souls to be born as
idiots, or with vicious inclinations, or into pagan societies,
whereas others are born with nice natures into pious Christian
families. If one grants preexistence and absolute free will, then
these inequalities can be explained as punishments and rewards
for the bad or good deeds of a former life. The adversaries of
preexistence begin their attack by denying the supremacy of
goodness among the divine attributes, and producing evidence
to show that some of God's acts are obviously not dictated by
goodness. Among these acts is eternal damnation. E.W. claimed
that, if the penalties for sin were 'rated by pure Goodness',
they would not be eternal, since the pleasures of sin are
transitory.[2]

More begins his reply by remarking that one must be 'chary
and wary' in discussing eternal torment—whether one affirms
or denies it, one is likely to produce disastrous results:[3]

> Some being ready to conclude from their *Eternity*, that Religion
> itself is a mere *Scarecrow* that frights us with such an incredible
> *Mormo*; others to indulge in their Pleasures, because the Com-
> mination is not frightful enough to deter them from extravagant
> Enjoyments, if Hell Torments be not eternal.

It would, on the other hand, be inexcusably frivolous to decide
the question

> as the complesent Parson did about the May-pole: they of his
> Parish that were for a May-pole, let them have a May-pole; but
> they that were not for a May-pole, let them have no May-pole.

[1] E. W., *No Praeexistence*, London, 1667.
[2] E. W., op. cit., pp. 16–17.
[3] More, *Annotations*, pp. 72–4, in *Two Choice . . . Treatises*, 1682.

The authority of Scripture is not decisive, since, according to More, αἰώνιος is ambiguous, even in the parallel between heaven and hell in Matthew XXV. He also mentions the argument, later used by Tillotson, that God is not obliged to carry out His threats.[1] Then comes his own opinion; he challenges anyone to[2]

> demonstrate that a Soul may not behave herself so perversely, obstinately, and despightfully against the Spirit of Grace, that she may deserve to be made an everlasting Hackstock of the Divine *Nemesis*, even for ever and ever. And if she deserve it, it is but just that she have it; and if it be just, it is likewise good.

The principle which makes such punishment just is that of vindictive justice, which, as we already know from the *Dialogues*, is compatible with divine goodness. He also suggests another justification of eternal torment: since preexistent souls lapsed from a heavenly state, those saved after this life might fall again, were it not that 'the certain knowledge of everlasting punishment' puts a 'sure bar to any such negligence as would hazard their settled felicity'.[3]

More's annotations on the *Lux Orientalis* end with a long defence of Origen, especially against his condemnation by the Fifth Oecumenical Council of Constantinople.[4] For further evidence of 'that unspeakable good service he did the Church in his lifetime' More refers the reader to his own preface to his *Collectio Philosophica*. Here one finds a very enthusiastic eulogy of Origen, but with the reservation:

> But I must confess I should be loath to be bound to answer for the *truth* of all those *Opinions* that are *imputed* to him.

Among these opinions is 'his making the Punishment of the Devils and of the Damned not eternal;' and of this, says More, his first editor, Jacques Merlin, quits him 'by the Testimony of at least ten several citations out of his Writings'.[5]

---

[1] Cf. supra, p. 6.
[2] More, *Annotations*, pp. 75–6.
[3] Ibid., pp. 76, 118.
[4] Ibid., pp. 151–63. There was a terrible earthquake in the year of the Council, a sign of divine disapproval (pp. 158–9).
[5] More, *A Collection of Several Philosophical Writings*, 4th ed., London, 1712, p. xxii.

In spite of all these indications that More accepted eternal torment, I think it possible that he at least had some doubts about it, and he would certainly have thought it wrong to express these doubts too clearly, as the following incident shows. In 1668 More promised to send Lady Conway's companion, Mrs Foxcroft, a sister of Benjamin Whichcote, a copy of Hallywell's *Private Letter of Satisfaction* (1667), which he thought would be very much to her taste because it asserts 'a capacity after this life of improving their [sc. the wicked's] time for the attainment of eternall happiness'. This opinion, he says, 'is no good friend to quickness and sedulity for the making our calling and election sure in this [life]'. He had lost the book, and so, being unable to send her 'so sweet a sugar plumb', sent her two of his own *Dialogues* instead.[1]

From his youth More had reflected somewhat anxiously on hell. In the General Preface to his *Collected Works* in Latin (1679) he recounts that when he was at Eton,[2]

> I did thus seriously and deliberately conclude within myself—viz. 'If I am one of those that are predestinated into Hell, where all things are full of nothing but cursing and blasphemy, yet will I behave myself there patiently and submissively towards God; and if there be any one thing more than another that is acceptable to Him, that will I set myself to do with a sincere heart, and to the utmost of my power'. Being certainly persuaded that if I thus demeaned myself, He would hardly keep me long in that place. Which meditation of mine is as firmly fixed in my memory, and the very place where I stood, as if the thing had been transacted but a day or two ago.

In a poem he wrote in his twenties, *Psychathanasia* (1642, 1647), is a series of questions, among which are:

> . . . Why will not God save
> All mankind?

[1] *Conway Letters*, pp. 292–3. More does not give the title of the book, but mentions Hallywell as the 'reputed author' of it. M. H. Nicholson gives the *Deus Justificatus* as the book in question; but this work does not contain the doctrine More describes, whereas the *Private Letter*, also attributed to Hallywell, does (cf. infra, pp. 153–4).

[2] Quoted by John Tulloch, *Rational Theology and Christian Philosophy in England in the 17th Century*, London, 1872, Vol. II, p. 306; the translation is by More's biographer Richard Ward (*Life of the Learned and Pious Dr. Henry More* 1710).

Why be not damned souls devoyd of sense,
If nothing can from wickednesse reclaime,

Rather then fry in pain and vehemence
Of searching agony?

But, although 'I itch until of this knot I be resolv'd', the questions remain unanswered, and 'Such drery drad designes do make my heart to quake'.[1]

In his *Immortality of the Soul* (1659), which purports to be written from a philosophical standpoint, with revelation left out of account, More discusses the punishment and final fate of devils and wicked men.[2] The former may possibly, as Agrippa of Nettesheim suggested, be confined in volcanoes; in any case they will be tortured 'far above what the cruellest Tyranny has inflicted here'. Some of the wicked men will be tormented by pangs of conscience; but the very depraved ones, whose consciences are calloused, will 'be exposed to those grim and remorseless *Officers of Justice* [i.e. devils]', who 'satiate their lascivient cruelty with all manner of abuses and torments they can imagine', 'and thus we see how, in the other life, the proud conceited *Atheist* may at last feel the sad inconvenience of his own Practices and Principles'. For their final state, after the Last Day and the conflagration of the earth,[3] More suggests several possibilities, none of which is eternal torment, and none of which he accepts; most of them involve the eventual annihilation or unconsciousness of the soul. But there is one which he rejects, as a 'Stoic fancy', less certainly than the others: after prolonged torture at the hands of the sadistic devils, and a period of coma, the souls of the wicked are reborn on the new earth that has grown up after the conflagration; here they have another chance of salvation.[4] This scheme, which we shall find again in Glanvill,[5] is of course compatible with eternal torment —some of the wicked may fail this second test, or even a series of tests; but it is at least a very considerable mitigation of the

[1] More, *The Complete Poems*, ed. A. B. Grosart, Edinburgh, 1878, p. 86.
[2] More, *A Collection*, 4th ed., 1712, pp. 205-9.
[3] Cf. More, *An Explanation of The Grand Mystery of Godliness*, London, 1660, pp. 444-6, a horrific description of the conflagration, and of the terror and despair of the wicked.
[4] More, *A Collection*, ed. cit., pp. 249-50.
[5] It also appears in Hobbes' *Leviathan* (see references given above p. 51, note 1).

orthodox doctrine. We must however remember that More is writing here, not as a Christian, but as a Platonic philosopher; all the same, the omission of eternal torment as a possibility is very odd, especially since it appears in Plato.[1]

(iii) 'LETTER OF RESOLUTION CONCERNING ORIGEN', AND GLANVILL

What More calls a Stoic fancy could as accurately be called an Origenist one, and after 1661, when the *Letter of Resolution concerning Origen* appeared, many of his readers would have recognized it as such. This *Letter* is important and exceptional in that it gives a full exposition and defence of Origen's eschatology. Most defenders of Origen emphasize only a few elements in his system, as for example More preexistence and extreme free will, or most later Origenists universal salvation. Rust, if he is the author of the *Letter*, defends not only these doctrines, but also metempsychosis, an infinite series of ages, purely curative justice, and a reformatory hell. All these also appear in Van Helmont and Lady Conway; but, owing to Cabalistic influence, their system of metempsychosis is radically different. In the Origenist system a soul has only one life in each age. At the end of an age the earth is burnt up (II Peter, III, 10–12). This conflagration serves two purposes,[2]

> for that one fire will be the just and salutary punishment of rebellious spirits, and the Restauration of the earth grown old and effete unto an healthful genital strength and verdure.

However wicked these souls may have become, they are not 'beyond the Power of Redress and Recovery'—otherwise they could not be the work of a good creator—and 'the great Punishment they shall undergo at the End of this World may contribute thereto'.[3] Rust's attempt to explain how being burnt alive is a 'salutary punishment' is thus summarized by Richard Roach, who reproduced large sections of the *Letter* in his preface to White's *Restoration*:[4]

[1] Plato, *Phaedo*, 113 E.
[2] *Letter of Resolution*, pp. 81–2.
[3] Ibid., p. 76.
[4] White, *Restoration*, sig. a5.

That tho' the Divine Life is extinguish'd in them, their Reason and Consideration remains; and that their Brutish Desires being slaked by the Tormenting Pains, and the Ideas of their Joys in Sin consum'd or become disgustful to 'em, any Offer of Release would be welcome to'em.

The release that is offered them is to be born again into the new world with another chance of salvation. Since this process is repeated indefinitely, even the most persistent recidivists may eventually be saved and God be all in all.

Rust's chief argument in favour of universal salvation is a powerful one that later gave great trouble to orthodox constructors of theodicies: if God had foreseen that millions of His creatures, through their imperfections, would suffer infinitely more misery than happiness, He would at once have annihilated them, or, more likely, not have created them; for God creates 'out of a Principle of Infinite *Love,* and for the Good and Happiness of the things themselves'.[1] Rust also suggests a shrewd explanation of the untroubled acceptance by some orthodox Christians of the doctrine of eternal torment: they,[2]

> having got easie ways of assuring themselves it shall not be their Portion, do as little pity those Calamitous Souls whose lot it may be, as they darkly fancy God himself does.

Glanvill's *Lux Orientalis* is primarily a defence of the doctrine of preexistence, based overtly on More and the *Letter of Resolution*; but it ends with a long eschatological section, which is presented, with cautious apologies, as a 'Romantick Scheme, or *imaginary Hypothesis*'.[3] Glanvill, like More and Rust, accepts the Neoplatonic theory of the vehicles of the soul.[4] Besides its earthly or fleshly body, the soul has two, more subtle, bodies or envelopes: the aerial vehicle, which is more or less identical with medical spirits, performing the functions of sensation and motor activity; the aetherial vehicle (astral body), which the soul uses for its higher, intellectual activities. At death, the very few souls who have dominated their two lower bodies go

---

[1] *Letter of Resolution,* pp. 72–3.
[2] Ibid., p. 133.
[3] *Two Choice . . . Treatises,* 1682, pp. 92 seq.
[4] Ibid., pp. 114–26. On the vehicles cf. D. P. Walker, 'The Astral Body in Renaissance Medicine', *Journal of the Warburg and Courtauld Institutes,* 1958, pp. 119, 121–3, and the references there given.

back to celestial regions, clad only in their aetherial vehicle. The imperfectly virtuous, in aerial vehicles, remain in the air or atmosphere. The majority, having given themselves up to 'their *degenerate sensual*, and *brutish propensions*', also keep their aerial vehicles, but they are confined within the earth, where there are huge cavities, full of foetid air, the innermost of which is fiery.[1]

> 'tis very probable, that the *wicked* and *degenerate* part of mankind, are after death committed to those squalid *subterraneous* habitations; in which dark prisons, they do severe *penance* for their past *impieties*, and have their *senses*, which upon earth they did so fondly indulge, and took such care to gratify, now persecuted with *darkness, stench,* and *horror.* Thus doth the *divine justice* triumph in punishing those vile *Apostates* suitably to their *deliquencies.*

If the wicked, while in this 'very *wretched* and *calamitous*' condition, should be 'taught by their *miseries* to renounce and forsake their *impieties*', 'meer Philosophy' would lead us to suppose that they might be delivered—'but we know what *Theology* hath determined. And indeed', Glanvill goes on quite cheerfully,[2]

> those *brutish Apostates* are so *fixt* and *rooted* in their *sensual* and *rebellious propensions,* that those who are not yet as far distant from their *Maker* as they can be, are still verging *downwards.*

This appears to settle the wicked for good and all; but there is more to come:

> the *earth* and all the *infernal Regions* being thus monstrously depraved, 'tis time for the *Divine Justice* to show some remarkable and more than ordinary *severity* upon those *remorseless Rebels.*

The central fire bursts out of its cavern and spreads to the whole interior of the earth. The wicked thus

> receive the full reward of their impieties, which doubtless will be the most intolerable and severe torment that can be imagined, these fierce and merciless flames sticking close to, yea, piercing through and through their bodies, which can remove no where to avoid this *fiery* over-spreading *vengeance.*

[1] Glanvill, *Lux Orientalis*, in *Two Choice . . . Treatises*, 1682, pp. 129–32.
[2] Ibid., pp. 135–6.

Their bodies, it should be remembered, are aerial, therefore penetrable by fire and highly sensitive. The fire reaches the earth's surface and burns the wicked then living; just before it gets there, the Second Coming occurs, the bodies of the just then living become purely aetherial and they ascend out of the way of the fire.[1]

This is still not the end, 'if we concult meer *Reason* and the Antient *Eastern Cabbala*'. For the wicked are 'still pretended to be under the eye and tender care of that *Almighty Goodness*', which, we are a little surprised to learn, 'punisheth not out of *malice* and *revenge*', and 'hath so ordered the matter that none of his Creatures shall be lost eternally, or indure such an endless misery, than which *not Being* it self were more *eligible*'. The violence of the long torments at length destroys the union between soul and vehicle, and, since, without some kind of body, souls are totally inactive and unconscious, the damned are at last allowed by that Almighty Goodness to be at rest.[2] Then, under the heading 'The General Restitution', we find an elaborated version of the Stoic fancy, 'represented by the profoundly Learned Dr H. More, with a *copious* and *pompous* eloquence'. Those reborn souls who carry out the '*good Resolutions* that they took while under the lash of the fiery tortures' will eventually 'reascend the *Thrones* they so unhappily fell from, and be circled about with unexpressible felicity'. Those who again follow the path of '*sensuality* and *rebellion*' will meet with 'the same *methods* of *punishment*'.[3] Glanvill, like More, does not state whether recidivist souls have still more chances allowed them, and thus neither asserts nor denies universal salvation.

(iv) LADY CONWAY AND VAN HELMONT

Lady Conway's *Principles of the most Ancient and Modern Philosophy*,[4] which greatly interested Leibniz, is a short, dog-

[1] Ibid., pp. 136–9. Glanvill is pleased that his theory allows him to take the scriptural fire and brimstone literally.
[2] Ibid., pp. 140–1.
[3] Ibid., pp. 142–4.
[4] This was first published anonymously in Latin, *Principia Philosophiae Antiquissimae & Recentissimae . . .*, Amstelodami, 1690, with two other works, under the general title of *Opuscula Philosophica*; one of these was the Latin version of Van Helmont's *Two Hundred Queries* (cf. infra, p. 141). The English

matic treatise, written mostly in a dry, almost scholastic style—
she likes to put objections into syllogistic form and refute them
piecemeal. The earlier chapters are sprinkled with references to
the *Kabbala Denudata*, perhaps added by Van Helmont. The
basis of her thought is a metaphysic, reminiscent of the Tele-
sians of the late 16th century, which attempts to eliminate body-
mind dualism by means of the concept of spirit.[1] Only God is
wholly incorporeal, is purely mind; nothing is purely body.
God is, as it were, a limiting value, which creatures can asymptotically approach by becoming more and more purely intellectual. All creatures are of one more or less animated, sensitive,
subtle substance; at one end of the continuous scale is the
thinking human or angelic spirit, at the other, apparently
inanimate, but still 'spiritual' matter. The Logos or Adam
Kadmon 'is not so immense' as God or Ensoph, but otherwise
performs the orthodox creating and mediating functions of
Christ. Since God is essentially creative and infinite, His
creation is infinite both in time and space; there has always
been an infinite number of worlds and there always will be.[2]

As all creatures are modes of one substance, all kinds of
metempsychosis are possible, limited only by the impossibility
of a creature becoming either God or sheer matter. Lady Conway gives the example of a horse, which through several equine

[1] Cf. D. P. Walker, *Spiritual and Demonic Magic*, London, 1958, pp. 190 seq.
[2] Lady Conway, *The Principles*, pp. 2–44.

version has this title: '*The Principles of the most Ancient and Modern Philosophy*,
concerning *God*, *Christ*, and the *Creatures*, viz. of Spirit and Matter in general;
whereby may be resolved all those Problems or Difficulties, which neither by the
School nor Common Modern Philosophy, nor by the *Cartesian*, *Hobbesian*, or
Spinozian, could be discussed. Being a little Treatise published since the Author's
Death, translated out of the *English* into *Latin*, with Annotations taken from the
Ancient Philosophy of the Hebrews; and now again made *English*. By J. C.
Medicinae Professor,' London, 1692 (J. C. is probably J. Clark, M.D., who
translated *Seder Olam* (v. infra., p. 141)). From the preface of this we learn that
it was written 'not many years ago, by a certain *English* Countess, a Woman
learned beyond her Sex, being very well skill'd in the *Latin* and *Greek* Tongues,
and excellently well vers'd in all kinds of Philosophy . . .', and also that the Latin
edition had been published by order of Van Helmont. It had been found after
her death and transcribed as completely as the small pencilled handwriting would
allow. There is no doubt that this learnèd Countess was Lady Conway. Van
Helmont and More wrote a preface for her book, which was not published with
it, but which is given by Ward in his *Life of* . . . *More*, pp. 203–9.

On Leibniz's admiration for Lady Conway's philosophy, see *Conway Letters*,
pp. 454–6.

lives makes steady moral progress, until its spirit eventually migrates into, or makes itself a human body. Conversely, a man who has led a brutish, sensual life will be 'changed into that *species* of Beasts, to whom he was inwardly most like, in qualities and Conditions of Mind'.[1] The general theory is that sin makes the spirit (i.e. mind and body) grosser, coarser, more corporeal. But Lady Conway gets into difficulties with devils, who, though more sinful than men, have, of course, more subtle, invisible bodies. She suggests that the devils' spirits are more corporeal in that they have become harder, more concentrated and rarefied, like tiny diamonds; whereas the spirits of good, tender-hearted men are literally soft.[2] Anyway, very wicked men become devils and are 'tumbled down to Hell'.[3]

The transmigrations down the scale are punishments, but curative ones:[4]

> All Kinds and Degrees of Sin, have their proper Punishments, and all these Punishments tend to the Creatures Advantage; so that Grace prevails over Judgment . . .

How they are curative is not fully explained. One can see that, having failed to lead a good life as a man, one might do better as, say, a cow—so much less is demanded of one; but it is difficult to understand why a devil has a better chance of achieving moral improvement than a man. We must, however, remember that the devils are in hell-fire, and we have already come across reformatory hells and shall meet more. Moreover Lady Conway held an extreme theory of the moral value of suffering;[5]

> every Pain and Torment excites or stirs up an operating Spirit and Life in every thing which suffers; as we observe by continued Experience, and Reason teacheth us, that of necessity it must be so.

It must be so because pain attenuates or subtilizes any 'crassitude or grossness' in the spirit or body, which thus becomes more refined and active, moving away from the corporeal

[1] Ibid., pp. 48–70.
[2] Ibid., pp. 88–92.
[3] Ibid., p. 69.
[4] Ibid., p. 73.
[5] Ibid., p. 87.

towards the mental pole. The greater the suffering the quicker the progress towards good.

This terrible theory becomes excusable, and even heroic, if one remembers Lady Conway's headache. There is everything to be said for making the best of one's own afflictions; it is only when applied to other people's suffering that the theory becomes pernicious. The headache may also have been a contributory cause to her belief in preexistence and metempsychosis, though the influence of More and Van Helmont was probably the major cause. It would be much easier to bear a painful congenital affliction, if one could regard it, not as meaningless, brute fact, but as a necessary expiation of some personal guilt.

Lady Conway's theory of the necessarily good moral results of pain provides her with a powerful argument against the eternity of hell, and it is in this context that she introduces the theory. Another argument against eternal damnation derives from her metaphysical principles, and, if one accepts those principles, it is convincing. A creature can make limitless advances towards good, because God is infinite and the creature can approach indefinitely nearer to Him without ever becoming Him. But the same infinite progress towards evil is not possible, because 'there is no Being, which is infinitely and unchangeably Evil, as God is infinitely and unchangeably Good'. Thus 'there are limits and bounds to Evil; but none unto Good'.[1] She means, I think, that the moral scale is like the scale of temperature, closed at one end only; there is an absolute degree of cold, but none of heat. Since it is impossible for any creature to be totally inactive, and it cannot move indefinitely towards evil, it must sooner or later start moving towards good. This argument, combined with her theory of pain, leads inevitably to universal salvation of a dynamic kind. The infinite, eternal universe is moving asymptotically towards its Creator.

I have somewhat simplified Lady Conway's system of metempsychosis by omitting one specifically Cabalistic idea: each individual spirit is made up of a multitude of spirits, and each body, which is only degraded, inspissated spirit, of a multitude of bodies.[2] Since, in the process of metempsychosis, and in some

---

[1] Lady Conway, *The Principles*, p. 84.
[2] Lady Conway, *The Principles*, pp. 80 seq., with a reference to *De Revolutionibus Animarum* (*Kabbala Denudata*, T. II, Pt. 3, pp. 256, 268 seq.).

other circumstances, these component parts are detachable from the individual, there results a fragmented chaos of entities, which I find very confusing. This idea plays an important part in Van Helmont's metempsychosis.

With the exception of her theory of pain, one finds the whole of Lady Conway's religious philosophy in Van Helmont, from whom she probably derived it, but with some interesting additions and elaborations. He is more concerned than she with finding scriptural support for metempsychosis, and he goes deeper into the arguments for and against eternal punishment. His views were published in two treatises, the first anonymously, *Two Hundred Queries Moderately propounded Concerning the Doctrine of the Revolution of Humane Souls, and Its Conformity to the Truths of Christianity* (1684), the second under his own name, *The Paradoxical Discourses* (1685).[1] He also ordered the publication of *Seder Olam: or, the Order of Ages* (1693, 1694), which was probably not his own work, but of which he presumably approved.[2]

Van Helmont makes ingenious use of metempsychosis to render less shocking the large-scale slaughter so frequently performed or commanded by God in the Old Testament. Lady Conway had already suggested that the Flood was an act of mercy, since men had become so brutishly depraved that they

---

[1] A Latin version of the *Two Hundred Queries*, also published in London, appeared the same year (*De Revolutione Animarum Humanarum . . . Problematum Centuriae duae . . .*). The preface announces the publication, if the *Queries* are favourably received, of another work on the same subject and a translation of the *De Revolutionibus Animarum*, which had come out the same year in the *Kabbala Denudata*. The former of these is *The Paradoxical Discourses of F. M. Van Helmont, Concerning the Macrocosm and Microcosm, or the Greater and Lesser World, and their Union*, London, 1685. This work was dictated in German by Van Helmont to 'J.B.', and, 'for want of another', translated into English by a 'Hollander'. On pp. 138, 159, Van Helmont refers to the *Queries* as his own work.

[2] *Seder Olam sive Ordo Seculorum, Historica Enarratio Doctrinae*, n.p., 1693; *Seder Olam: or, the Order of Ages. Wherein the Doctrine is Historically Handled. Translated out of Latin, by J. Clark, M.D. upon the Leave and Recommendation of F. M. Baron of Helmont*, London, 1694. The translator evidently did not think that Van Helmont was the author of this work and did not know who was. It begins with what is virtually a summary of the basic principles of Lady Conway's work, but most of it consists of a detailed chiliastic programme, combined with a complicated scheme of metempsychosis. I would guess that it is a work either by Lady Conway or Rosenroth, revised by Van Helmont. The English edition contains an appendix not in the Latin.

would soon all have turned into animals. Van Helmont cites many more examples, which give indirect scriptural support to metempsychosis, since without it God's actions seem to be savagely immoral. The story of Elisha and the bears (II Kings, II, 23–4), he points out, does not show God to be very long-suffering, unless one supposes that He was cutting off the forty-two little children from a life of crime, in order to give them a fresh start in some other life.[1] Likewise God hardened Pharaoh's heart (the crucial *locus classicus* in disputes about predestination)[2] so that the slaughtered first-born of the Egyptians might be born again as Israelites, with a better chance of obeying the true God.[3] The Cabalistic multiplicity of spirits within each individual enables Van Helmont to justify original sin and God's visiting the sins of the fathers on the children. One kind of metempsychosis proceeds from father to child. The child's spirit before its conception was part of the father's spirit. Thus the spirits of the whole human race were contained within Adam, and had an active part in his guilt. This idea is very like the 18th-century embryological theory of preformationism, which Leibniz used to explain the transmission of Adam's sin.[4] As direct scriptural support, Van Helmont can cite some passages from the New Testament which do indeed indicate that some Jews in Christ's time, including the disciples, believed in metempsychosis, such as Mark VIII, 28, Luke IX, 19 (people guessing that Christ is Elias or one of the prophets) or John IX (whether the man was born blind for his own or his father's sin).[5]

Van Helmont's system of metempsychosis is rather more severe on sinners than Lady Conway's. Everyone, in this Age, has a thousand years to live. Since the time of Noah, when God mercifully shortened human life so that there should be less time to sin and more fresh starts, these thousand years are divided into twelve lives. Since the time of Christ no one can be sure that he is not on his last life; there is thus no danger of the doctrine of metempsychosis making people lazy about

[1] *Two Hundred Queries*, p. 6.
[2] Cf. D. P. Walker, 'Origène en France', pp. 115 seq.
[3] *Paradoxical Discourses*, pp. 125 seq.
[4] Van Helmont, *Paradoxical Discourses*, pp. 131–5; Leibniz, *Théodicée*, ed. cit., Pt. I, p. 138, Pt. II, pp. 245 seq.
[5] *Two Hundred Queries*, pp. 77–8.

achieving salvation in their present life.[1] Moreover, if anyone rejects the Gospel, he is 'judicially blinded of God, and given up to a reprobate sense'; his later lives are worse than useless to him, since in them he sins without repentance and thus increases his own damnation. This reprobation accounts for some purely punitive metempsychoses: those born as idiots, or congenitally possessed by unclean spirits. These wicked ones, after their twelve lives, will have one more life, being born at the end of the millennium into the army of Gog and Magog. After the defeat of this army they will be burnt in the conflagration, and then tormented in hell 'for ages of ages'.[2] 'Age' here has the sense of the duration of this world, i.e. 7000 years, which is the same as that of previous and subsequent worlds. 'Ages of ages' means therefore some multiple of 7000 years—a very long, though finite, time. That the punishment of some sinners lasts longer than one Age is proved by Christ's words in Matthew XII, 32:[3]

> whosoever speaketh against the Holy Ghost, it shall not be forgiven him, neither in this world, neither in the world to come.

It is likely that the damned do not know when their torment will end, or even that it will end at all—'a most fearful and terrible aggravation of their punishment.' Van Helmont seems to be unaware that he is spoiling this aggravation.[4]

In spite of the lives condemned to idiocy or diabolic possession, in spite of the many millennia of hell-torments, Van Helmont maintains that all divine punishments are curative:[5]

> Is not the Nature, and end of God's vindictive justice, and indeed of all punishment, to aim at the good of those that are punished? Is not the Nature of all punishment Medicinal? and ought not every Judge among Men sincerely to love those whom he condemns to punishment, and to aim at their good thereby? if God then hath placed this instinct of Justice in Men, hath he not the same infinitely more abundant in himself?

[1] Ibid., pp. 58–9, 68–9.
[2] Ibid., pp. 68–9, 71–2, 75, 94–5.
[3] Ibid., pp. 110, 114, 128.
[4] Ibid., p. 127.
[5] *Two Hundred Queries*, pp. 114–5.

The first of these rhetorical questions shows that for Van Helmont God's justice is vindictive as well as curative; this is a quite reasonable combination and certainly very common in real life, but it is seldom explicitly asserted. He makes no attempt to justify vindictive justice, nor to explain how the more unfortunate metamorphoses could be curative. Since God's punishments, including hell, are always primarily aimed at the salvation of the sinner, there can be no strictly eternal torment; finally, even if after ages of ages of torment, God's purpose must be fulfilled and the sinner saved.

Van Helmont denies that the eternity of hell is necessary to its deterrent value; his own scheme provides a sufficiently appalling deterrent:[1]

> is it likely that those that are not reclaimable by the fear of punishment, torment, and misery unutterable, yea to Men inconceivable for the intenseness of it, for ages of ages, or time infinite to the knowledge of Man, will be reclaimed by the other [i.e. strictly eternal torment]?

He admits that the fear of punishment is 'a just and necessary Motive or means, which is to be used to recall people from going on in their Iniquities'; but there is another, more forceful motive, 'without which the former is of no use at all, that is, the Love and Mercy of God in Jesus Christ'. At least with people who have any 'capacity of a sense of Divine things', it is more effectively edifying to represent God as loving even in His punishments.[2] Even if eternal torment were the only effective deterrent, there would be no excuse for preaching it; Van Helmont firmly rejects the conception of esoteric and exoteric doctrines:[3]

> Is it sufficient ground for preaching this Doctrine, to conceit that it will terrify and affright people from sin? Does God need any Lye of Man's making, to deter people from sin? Or shall we lye for God?

Van Helmont also argues that the doctrine of eternal torment has religious effects of a pernicious kind. 'Atheism seems to be the spreading disease of the Age', and 'one of the common

[1] Ibid., p. 123.
[2] Ibid., pp. 123-4.
[3] Ibid., p. 122.

places or ordinary Themes' by which atheists try to convert others is 'by rendering the common Idea of God (from this conceit of infinite Damnation) inconsistent with itself'. This they can easily do by pointing out that the orthodox God, who is said to be immutable and to have loved all His Creatures when He made them, damns 'the greatest part of them' to eternal torment, His love having been turned into an 'absolute and most implacable Hatred', merely because they 'for some small time did disobey his commands'. The atheist's argument falls to the ground, if eternal torment is eliminated;[1]

> For, remove but this, and what hath the Atheist on that score to quarrel that Ever-glorious Being about ?

We shall come across more statements that the orthodox hell leads to atheism, and it is quite possible that this was already the case, or at least that it led some people away from Christianity.

Another consequence of the doctrine of eternal torment which Van Helmont regards as pernicious is that it induces 'many sober-minded People', who are concerned about 'the Nature of God, who is Love and Goodness it self', to hold a theory of punishment, which, we have already noted, had many advocates, namely, that sin inevitably, naturally brings suffering on the sinner, and hence that God plays no positive part in the torments of the damned—

> this Conceit, that the misery and torment that comes upon the wicked, is only their own act, and no appointment or act of God. As a Man that runs himself wilfully into a ditch that stands before him, to which he is in no way necessitated, or cast by anybody else.

Van Helmont regards this as 'a very false, unsound and absurd Notion', because it destroys 'all justice in God . . . divesting Him of all Will to punish Offenders'.[2] This is a valid criticism of the natural punishment theory, if one accepts Van Helmont's assumptions. If the only way to reform obdurate sinners and thus fit them for eternal bliss is to subject them to prolonged agony, then a good God would positively will such punishment.

---

[1] *Two Hundred Queries*, pp. 119–20.
[2] Ibid., pp. 121–2.

In *Seder Olam: or, the Order of Ages* we find again Van Helmont's and Lady Conway's system of metempsychosis and their denial of eternal torment; but we also find a more detailed and precise description of the course of future Ages, and predictions of the imminent occurrence of the millennium, which is to end this Age.

Since each Age lasts 7000 years (6000 plus the millennium), and since in the sight of the Lord a thousand years are but a day, we may call an Age a Week. After seven Weeks there is a Jubilee Day (making 50,000 years in all), when those not yet saved are pardoned. Fifty-two Weeks make up the Lord's Year, i.e. 365,000 ordinary years, 'within which space of time, whatsoever is of human kind on Earth will doubtless be converted unto God'. This final apocatastasis winds up our universe; but, as there is an infinite number of worlds, the whole process will always be going on, as it always has done.[1]

By means of very complicated calculations the beginning of the millennium is predicted for the year 1777. This will be immediately preceded by the Church of Philadelphia, the sixth of the seven churches in Revelations II–III. This church's reign does not begin until 1702, but her seeds are 'not only now in the world, but her first Fruits also'.[2] The public revelation of metempsychosis is directly connected with the imminence of the millennium. Since people are likely to abuse this doctrine by counting on a second chance (or several more chances), it lay hid, known only to a few 'good Men', until the present time, when such abuse is impossible because everyone has reached his twelfth and last life.[3] What were the 'first Fruits' of the Philadelphian Church? We may be able to suggest an answer to this question when we come to Mrs Jane Lead and her disciples.

(v) PREEXISTENCE AND THE ATTRIBUTES

Henry More and his friends believed in preexistence or metempsychosis first and foremost because, like Bathynous, they were

[1] *Seder Olam* (English ed.), pp. 23–5, 31–5.
[2] Ibid., p. 125. In the Appendix, the dates of the Philadelphian Church are corrected to 1666 to 2000, or 1700 to 2034.
[3] Ibid., pp. 93–4.

worried about the attributes of God. As Glanvill says, in his preface to the *Lux Orientalis*, the doctrine of preexistence changes nothing in traditional theology except that it[1]

> clears the *divine* Attributes from any shadows of harshness or breach of equity, since it supposeth us to have sinned and deserved all the misery we suffer in this condition before we came hither.

They saw clearly that if God were not good and just, as well as wise and powerful, He would be an omnipotent Devil. The danger was urgent because they claimed, as so many others before and since, that supralapsarian Calvinists were in fact worshipping a devil. More, for example, compares their God to the idol to which the Mexicans make human sacrifices:[2]

> To which Idol they do not, as the *Mexicans*, sacrifice the *mere Bodies* of men, but their very *Souls* also; not kicking them down a Tarrass, but arbitrariously tumbling them down into the pit of Hell, there to be eternally and unexpressibly tormented, for no other reason but because this their dreadful Idol will have it so.

The first step away from this devil-worship is to lay the greatest possible emphasis on free will, so that at least some of the guilt for human misery, in this world and the next, is shifted from God to man. This all the Cambridge Platonists, except Sterry and White, did. But, even leaving aside all the other weaknesses of free will, could one honestly maintain that a soul born among, say, these Mexicans had a free choice between obeying or disobeying the commandments of God? The next step, then, is to extend free will backwards beyond birth, so that the Mexican infant has only himself to thank for being born into an evil society. That More and his friends took this step mainly, perhaps solely, in order to exculpate God is indicated by the total emptiness of their theory of preexistence in every other respect; as Glanvill admits, it changes nothing, it does nothing, except 'clear the divine attributes'. A highly significant omission in all these writers is that of the Platonic theory of reminiscence, which is what makes Plato's doctrine of preexistence far from empty. Their chief historical source for

---

[1] *Two Choice . . . Treatises*, 1682, sig. C vo.
[2] More, *Divine Dialogues*, I, 411; cf. I, 407.

preexistence was undoubtedly Plato, the Neoplatonists, and the Platonizing Fathers,[1] and it would have been quite easy to integrate Platonic reminiscence into their system by supposing that the innate ideas of morals, God, etc. were more or less strong in accordance with a virtuous or vicious previous life. But, on the contrary, any memory of a previous existence is explicitly denied,[2] so that any continuity between the soul's two or more existences can only consist in an unintelligible identity of substance. The reason for this omission is that they were just not interested in the theory, except in so far as it allowed God to retain the attributes of goodness and justice.

These two attributes are really one, since justice is only the aspect of goodness that appears when God is dealing with sin. Thus goodness is the supreme attribute, in spite of More's and Van Helmont's retention of vindictive justice. It is perhaps significant that these writers use the term goodness rather than love. It is more obviously absurd to say that God loves His creatures while avenging Himself on them, than to say that He is good while so doing, i.e. 'good' in this context has a much wider connotation than 'love'. There is of course no difficulty, as we saw with Sterry and White, in making God's love compatible with purely curative punishment; but a combination of love and vengeance, except in Freudian psychology, comes near to nonsense, as one can see, if 'love' is substituted for 'goodness', in this passage from More's *Dialogues*:[3]

> free Agents . . . may so behave themselves in the sight of God, that they will become such objects of his Goodness, that it cannot be duely and rightfully expected that it should act according to its pure and proper benign form . . . but must step forth in some of those more fierce and grim forms (I speak after the manner of men) such as *Vengeance* and *Justice*.

Since the doctrine of preexistence was primarily a device for exculpating God, one might ask: why did they need it, when there was already the traditional, orthodox device of original sin—in defence of which Pascal said: 'il faut que nous naissions coupables ou Dieu serait injuste'?[4] The chief reason why our

---

[1] Cf. ibid., I, 508–11, list of authorities for preexistence.
[2] Van Helmont, *Paradoxical Discourses*, pp. 154–5.
[3] More, *Divine Dialogues*, p. 300.
[4] Pascal, *Pensées*, ed. Brunschvieg, No. 489.

Platonists did not want to use original sin was undoubtedly because of its cardinal place in the Calvinist or Augustinian systems they were fighting. There were also additional reasons: first, it is very difficult to explain the transmission of Adam's guilt without again involving God in arbitrary injustice; secondly, original sin fails to account for the inequalities of congenital misfortunes—why some are born more miserable and vicious than others.

The adversaries of preexistence realized that the question of attributes was fundamental, and, as I have mentioned, directed their main attack against the supremacy of goodness among them. This they did with singular ineptitude, and More is easily able to show the hopeless inconsistencies of their position. It seems to me that these adversaries, E.W.[1] and Samuel Parker, had mediocre minds and were not entirely in earnest. The former can be judged only from this one short treatise; it is written in a bizarre, pedantic style, rather like an English version of Rabelais' *écolier limousin*. Parker, who ended up as Bishop of Oxford, had the reputation of being an *arriviste* who was ready to change his religious convictions to suit his career.[2]

Parker's critique of preexistence is the second of two letters addressed to a certain Mr Bisbie. The first letter is entitled *A Free and Impartial Censure of the Platonick Philosophie* (1666); both letters were published together in 1667.[3] The censure of Platonism does not mention any contemporary Platonists, but shows him to be quite well read in Renaissance philosophy. The moral teaching of Plato and Socrates he admits to be admirable, and he has special praise for their love of 'ingenious and sweet-natur'd young Gentlemen', which he compares to Christ's love for St John.[4] It is as a hard-headed

---

[1] Abbot gives Edward Warren as the author of *No Praeexistence or a Brief Dissertation Against the Hypothesis of Humane Souls, Living in a State Antecedaneous to This*, London, 1667; (Ezra Abbot, *Literature of the Doctrine of a Future Life*, New York, 1871, No. 470; this excellent bibliography first appeared as an appendix to W. R. Alger, *Critical History of the Doctrine of a Future Life*, Philadelphia, 1864).

[2] See article in the *Dictionary of National Biography*.

[3] Samuel Parker, *A Free and Impartial Censure of the Platonick Philosophie*, Oxford, 1666; *An Account of the Nature and Extent of the Divine Dominion & Goodnesse, Especially as they refer to the Origenian Hypothesis Concerning the Preexistence of Souls*, Oxford, 1666.

[4] Parker, *A Free and Impartial Censure*, pp. 18–24.

modern scientist (he was a Fellow of the Royal Society) that he
makes his main attack. Plato is full of fanciful metaphysical
speculations; the creation of the Soul of the World in the
Timaeus, for example, is 'prodigiously silly and ridiculous'.[1]
The Neoplatonists were superstitious magicians. 'The supposed Agreement between Moses and Plato' is disproved, and
the whole of the *prisca theologia* contemptuously exploded.[2]
E.W. has the same attitude to Platonism. All the *prisci theologi*
were diabolical magicians, and as for Plato:[3]

> Let any sober & judicious Man but seriously reflect upon the
> strange and garish whimsies, the toyish and absurd futilities,
> the silly and delirious fopperies of admirable *Plato.*

Both Parker and E.W. admit that goodness is one of God's
attributes; indeed, they both make the assertion, for them an
extremely imprudent one, that without this attribute God would
'be but a prodigious Feind, and plenipotentiary Devil'.[4] But
this attribute is not supreme, that is to say, God does not always
and necessarily do what is best; His goodness is subordinated
to His will, and His will is free in the same way that human
wills are free. Henry More and the other Platonists, though
advocates of free will in man, did not of course ascribe it to
God; they regarded it as an imperfection, since its essence is a
liability to sin. The only possible way in which without blasphemy or inconsistence one can say that God's will is free is to
adopt the Augustinian position, that is, to identify God's will
with the good, to deny that there is any criterion of goodness
independent of God's will. Our anti-Platonists do not take this
position; they assume criteria of goodness by which God's will
can be judged, and proceed to show, by examples, that His will
is not always directed towards good. They end, in fact, by
demonstrating that God is a 'plenipotentiary Devil' of an un-
intelligibly capricious kind.

Parker makes an attempt to mitigate this unfortunate conclusion by asserting that[5]

The Rights of God's Dominion over sinless Creatures do not

[1] Ibid., pp. 42–3.
[2] Ibid., pp. 92–8.
[3] E. W., *No Praeexistence,* pp. 78–9, 81.
[4] E. W., op. cit., pp. 6–7; cf. Parker, *An Account,* pp. 14–16, 23.
[5] Parker, *An Account,* p. 14.

extend so far as to warrant his dooming them to a condition
more wretched and forlorn than *Non-existence,*

such as eternal torment. The grounds for this assertion, which
is designed to exclude Calvinist reprobation, are that, while
God has the right to withdraw from His creatures any of His
gifts, including that of existence, He has no right, except as a
punishment, to rob them of more than He has given them.
Apart from this limitation, God has a 'right to that, which no
Creature can do without the grossest and most exorbitant
Injustice', such as transmitting Adam's punishment of mortality and corruption to all his descendants—[1]

> all this God might have done, though *Adam* had never sinned,
> and therefore 'tis no Injustice that God has made his Posterity
> the Heirs of his misfortunes.

Since Parker believes in extreme free will, the nonsensical
libertas indifferentiae, God has also the right to perform random,
senseless acts, such as preferring Jacob to Esau, which 'was a
free determination of his own will, without the intervention of
any extrinsique motive to incline it'. By this stage, we are not
surprised to learn that goodness is not really an essential attribute at all; it 'rather approaches to the nature of a habit seated
in the Divine will, then to the condition of an Essential faculty'.
God never acts in a way contrary to his essential attributes,
such as wisdom, justice, and holiness;[2]

> And therefore if God's Beneficence and Bounty were so natural,
> as that all its exertions were necessary, he could never act
> otherwise; but that he frequently does, as is evident in all the
> Instances of his Anger and Severity, which not only Reason but
> Scripture opposes to Benignity.

One of E.W.'s examples to show that Goodness is not the
supreme attribute has already been mentioned: eternal torment.
He begins his discussion of this by outlining 'that dangerous
error' of Origen:[3]

> that the torments of Hell are Cathartical, and when they have
> once wrought a thorow defaecation of the excruciated Patients;
> they shall all be reprieved from their igneous Prisons . . . into an
> anodynous and peaceable condition.

[1] Parker, *An Account*, pp. 9–11.
[2] Ibid., pp. 35–7.
[3] E. W., op. cit., p. 17.

This 'presumptuous Hypothesis', he rightly observes, rests on the assumption that divine punishments are purely curative, and this assumption 'is so weak and lubricious, that it totters of its own accord, and is ready to reel without a push; to set it going therefore, I shall bestow one upon it'. The push turns out to be merely a flat denial. The punishments of hell, far from being reformatory, make the damned ever more wicked, because 'the exquisite *Acuteness* and deadly anguish' of the torments lead them to blaspheme against God;[1]

> the longer they burn, the more obdurate they will grow; and their acerbous miseries running parallel with their everlasting incorrigibleness shall be a standing testimony of this Truth, that the Great GOD does not always do what is best, but sometimes what he will.

In spite of his lamentable performance in dealing with the attributes, Parker does succeed in showing weak spots in the doctrine of preexistence; but this is not at all difficult to do. He points out that it is absurd to regard congenital misfortunes as punishments for the sins of a preexistent soul, since this soul admittedly has no memory of these sins; one cannot justly, or usefully, punish anyone for actions of which he has no knowledge whatever.[2] It is equally absurd to claim that souls so punished are being given a second chance, since this punishment often consists in being placed in circumstances where they are almost bound to sin.[3] He quotes two of Glanvill's arguments in favour of preexistence: first, that God manifests His goodness in giving sinful preexistent souls another chance of salvation on earth; second, that the goodness of God prevents His putting a pure, freshly created soul into conditions, such as a vicious family or society, which will almost certainly lead it to sin and damnation, and therefore we must suppose a sinful preexistent soul. Parker rightly remarks that the second argument refutes the first.[4] His conclusion, which seems to me valid, is that if[5]

> these Phaenomena be inexplicable without the Origenian Hypothesis [i.e. preexistence], they are so too with it; and if so, then

[1] E. W., op. cit., pp. 18–19.
[2] Parker, *An Account*, pp. 49–50.
[3] Ibid., p. 53.
[4] Ibid., pp. 54–5.
[5] Ibid., p. 57.

the result of all is, that they are not so much Arguments of Preexistence, as Aspersions of Providence.

These objections are equally valid against metempsychosis.

Henry Hallywell's *Deus Justificatus*, in which he criticized Parker's doctrine of the attributes, appeared in 1668; the year before he had published *A Private Letter of Satisfaction to a Friend*, Mrs Foxcroft's sugar-plum.[1] The latter work, which on the title-page bears this quotation from Origen: 'Ἀρχὴ Θανάτου ἤ ἐπὶ γῆς γένεσις (Birth on this earth is the beginning of death), is a plea for supposing a state intermediate between heaven and hell, lasting from death till the resurrection, 'some middle State of Being', in which souls may purify themselves from all bodily inclinations until they are fit for heaven. Like all advocates of such a state, Hallywell is anxious to deny that he is suggesting the Romish purgatory; which in fact he does not, since his middle state is morally dynamic, not merely penitential. Without this state, since few men have the time and opportunity to become saints, 'the infinitely far greater part of men are damned', and this Hallywell finds unacceptable.[2] It is inconsistent with 'that eternal Goodness which is the rule and measure of all the actions of the Deity' to allow the majority of men to be born into circumstances where they have little chance of[3]

> recovering the broken and decayed Image of God in their Souls, for the want of which notwithstanding they shall be thrown into everlasting misery.

Hallywell, faced with the same problem as More and his friends, has extended free will, not backwards beyond birth, but forwards beyond death. This too, though at least a considerable mitigation of hell, does not necessarily eliminate eternal torment, which Hallywell neither asserts nor denies; but an

---

[1] Cf. supra, p. 132. Both these works are anonymous and of doubtful attribution. The *Private Letter*, published without a place name, is attributed to Hallywell by Archibald Campbell, *The Doctrine of a Middle State*, London, 1721, p. 163 (cf. *Notes and Queries*, 1873, p. 255; 1881, p. 324). On the attribution of the *Deus Justificatus: Or, The Divine Goodness Vindicated and Cleared, against the Assertion of Absolute and Inconditionate Reprobation. Together with some Reflections on a late Discourse of Mr. Parkers, concerning the Divine Dominion and Goodness*, London, 1668, v. supra, p. 127 n. 2.
[2] *A Private Letter*, pp. 34–6.
[3] Ibid., pp. 44–5.

acceptance of it is implied by the mention of 'irreclaimable spirits', who are 'sunk below all the principles of Righteousness and Justice, and make it their whole design to obliterate those Ideas from their minds'.[1]

The *Deus Justificatus*, like Rust's *Discourse of Truth*, is a defence of the supremacy of goodness among the divine attributes, directed against the absolute predestinationism of the Calvinists.[2] It is also a very full and eloquent affirmation of that priority of moral ideas over God's will, which is the only safeguard against the disastrous separation of divine from human moral values and which was the basic tenet of all the Cambridge Platonists:[3]

> There are certain immutable and unchangeable laws fixed and radicated in the very centre of the Deity, and which he can no more swerve from, then he can cease to be; and Goodness being the first pregnant root of all things, cannot fail of acting according to it's Essential plenitude and Exuberancy . . .

or, more succinctly:[4]

> I cannot think that God will allow that in himself which he condemns in his Creatures.

Though God's goodness is not different in kind from man's, it must be infinitely greater. Having quoted St Paul's words (Romans IX, 3): 'I could wish that myself were accursed from Christ for my brethren, my kinsmen according to the flesh', Hallywell goes on to state that a good man would be

> content (if it might stand with the goodness of God) to lie in Hell to all Eternity, so that he might be without sin, rather than that any of the sons of men should be forever excluded and debarr'd from the love and favour of God.

If human love and compassion reach thus far, how much further must the love of God extend, the compassion of that 'immense

[1] Ibid., pp. 47–8.
[2] The extremely harsh attacks on the Calvinist God which are so prevalent in the 1660's may well have political motives, especially when, as with Parker and E. W., they are inconsistent with the writer's theological position. In the preface to the *Deus Justificatus* it is argued that the killing of Charles I was due to the proud, factious spirit engendered by predestinationism.
[3] *Deus Justificatus*, p. 33.
[4] Ibid., p. 163.

Ocean of Love, which knows no bounds nor limits'.[1] We are reminded of White's reflections on a 'noble Speech of a great Person', and of his outburst: 'how dare we say to this Ocean of Love thus far shalt thou go, and no further.'[2] Still arguing from the analogy of divine to human love, Hallywell comes yet nearer to universal salvation: a good man wishes all creatures to be happy; God, being omnipotent, can execute this wish:[3]

> What is there left but the malignancy and bitterness of peevish Spirits to hinder or discountenance the Universal happiness of the whole World?

[1] *Deus Justificatus*, pp. 31–2.
[2] V. supra, p. 111, and White, *Restoration*, p. 184.
[3] *Deus Justificatus*, p. 32, cf. p. 110 (a good man would rather save a hundred criminals 'condemned to die, equally culpable', than only ten or twenty of them; *a fortiori* God must wish to save all men).

Chapter IX

❖◇❖

ENGLISH PLATONISTS
(3) Thomas Burnet

❖◇❖

THOMAS BURNET went to Clare College, Cambridge, in 1651, where he was a pupil of Tillotson. When in 1654 Cudworth left that college to become Master of Christ's, Burnet went with him.[1] It was probably from this education that he acquired his open-minded theology and his interest in the early Fathers. By Tillotson, but not, I think, by Cudworth,[2] he might have been led into doubts about eternal torment. He differs from the older generation of Cambridge Platonists in his unphilosophical turn of mind. He is like Whiston in his aversion to metaphysical speculation, and in his enthusiasm for applying modern science to the interpretation of the Scriptures. He also resembles Whiston, whom he knew personally, in the crudity and literalness of his thought. These qualities are most obvious in his famous *Telluris Theoria Sacra* (*Sacred Theory of the Earth*), a work which had numerous progeny in the 18th century.[3]

The first two books of the *Sacred Theory*, published first in

[1] M. Earbery in Burnet, *Of the State of the Dead*, transl. Earbery, 2nd ed., London, 1728, Vol. II, p. 119.
[2] Cf. J. V. Hoppe, *Dissertatio Theologica de Statu Mortuorum et Resurgentium Thomae Burnetio opposita*, Jenae, 1728, p. 2.
[3] See Frank E. Manuel, *The Eighteenth Century Confronts the Gods*, Cambridge Mass., 1959, pp. 135 seq.

1681, are an account of the state of the earth before, during and after the Flood, a subject also treated by Whiston in his *New Theory of the Earth* (1696). In the third and fourth books, which appeared in 1689 and deal with the conflagration of the earth and the subsequent millennium, there are already indications, later noticed by Petersen, that Burnet at least had doubts about the eternity of hell. Like Glanvill and More, Burnet delights in vivid and horrific descriptions of the Last Day. Since the conflagration is both a natural phenomenon and a work of divine vengeance, it is possible to predict where it will begin. The natural requirements for a region's inflammability are: 'Sulphureousness of the Soil, and, an hollow mountainous Construction of the ground'; divine justice demands that the seat of Antichrist should be 'the first Sacrifice to this fiery Vengeance'. Both these conditions are fulfilled by Rome. At the Second Coming, then, the volcanoes of southern Italy will begin to erupt, 'as Fireworks, at the triumphal Entry of a Prince'.[1] The fire spreads rapidly, and, though the just and infants are miraculously saved from it, there is no hope for the majority of mankind:[2]

> We think it a great Matter to see a single Person burnt alive; here are Millions shrieking in the Flames at once.

If we were able to look down on this scene, we should find it 'a lively Representation of *Hell* it self'. Indeed it is clear that, in the *Sacred Theory*, Burnet, like Rust, More and Glanvill, is equating the conflagration with hell. The prime victims of the fire are atheists and the followers of Antichrist (i.e. Roman Catholics), but lesser sinners will also be burnt, the torment being somehow graded in accordance with their sins; and he quotes Matthew XXV, 41 as referring to the conflagration.[3] But these sinners will not apparently, as with the earlier Platonists, be given a second chance on the new earth that succeeds the conflagration, because this earth, restored to its original smooth, egg-like, Paradisal form, will be inhabited by the just during the millennium.

---

[1] Burnet, *The Sacred Theory of the Earth*, 6th ed., London, 1726, Vol. II, pp. 118–20.
[2] Ibid., Vol. II, p. 156.
[3] Burnet, *The Sacred Theory*, Vol. II, pp. 157 seq., 171.

Millennial life will consist largely of 'Devotion and Contemplation', the 'publick devotions' being very splendid and sometimes culminating in a visible appearance of Christ in the sky. As a minor diversion, the blessèd will amuse themselves with the wonders of natural science;[1] but their chief contemplations will be directed towards those things which we now see through a glass darkly, towards questions, to which they will know the answers, such as: 'where, or what, is the state of Hell, where the Souls of the Wicked are said to be for ever?' what will be the last 'Fate and final Doom' of Satan, and 'whether he may ever hope for a Revolution or Restauration?' Besides these hints at universal salvation, there are strong implications of an Origenist succession of reincarnations: 'who knows how many Turns he shall take upon this Stage of the Earth, and how many Trials he shall have before his Doom will be finally concluded?'[2] Preexistence and the 'Revolution of Souls' are also defended in the preface to the Fourth Book.[3] Presumably the reincarnated souls occupy the new earth after the end of the millennium.

Burnet, according to his literary executor, Francis Wilkinson, did not intend to publish his treatise *De Statu Mortuorum & Resurgentium* (*Of the State of the Dead and of Those that are to Rise*).[4] He had a very few copies printed, interleaved with blank sheets, so that he could make additions and corrections, and circulated them among his intimate friends. One of these copies got into a bookseller's hands, and was bought by Dr Richard Mead, who in 1720, five years after Burnet's death, had a small edition privately printed, to which he prefaced an admonition that whoever was shown a copy must be made to promise not to have it transcribed or given to the Press.[5] In spite of this, other editions appeared, and in 1727 Wilkinson published one, where, for the first time, Burnet's additions, written on the blank sheets, are properly distinguished from the main text.[6]

---

[1] Ibid., Vol. II, pp. 287 seq.; cf. Roach's millennium, infra, pp. 248–9.
[2] Ibid., Vol. II, p. 302.
[3] Ibid., Vol. II, pp. 180–1.
[4] Preface to Burnet, *De Fide & Officiis Christianorum*, London, 1727, p. vii.
[5] Mead's preface to Burnet, *De Statu Mortuorum*, London, 1720; cf. article on Burnet in the *Dictionary of National Biography*.
[6] This was reedited in 1728 and 1733. There had been two other printings of Mead's edition, in 1723 and 1726.

In 1728, Matthias Earbery, 'Presbyter of the Church of England', published an inaccurate English translation, accompanied by a running commentary, which is unkind and flippant though sometimes shrewd. There were several more editions in Latin, English, and French.[1]

Wilkinson was probably correct in stating that Burnet did not intend to publish the *De Statu Mortuorum*. At the end of his arguments against the eternity of hell, in which he has cited Origen and a few other merciful Fathers, Burnet addresses to the reader[2]

> that warning, which the above-mentioned Fathers usually give when they deal with this subject. Namely, whatever you decide, in your own mind, about these punishments being eternal or not, the received doctrine and words must be used for the people, and when preaching to the populace, which is inclined to vice and can be deterred from evil only by the fear of punishment

and he later added:

> Therefore, if anyone translates these things, which are addressed to the learned, into the vulgar tongue, I shall consider it done with illwill and evil intent.

This is the ordinary secrecy which, as we have already noted, surrounds any denial of eternal torment, and which leads to the theory and practice of a double doctrine, esoteric and exoteric. But in Burnet the double doctrine occupies an exceptionally large and important place. He comes near to Spinoza's view of the Bible as consisting largely of exoteric doctrine, that is, of fables or useful lies adapted to the childish understanding of

---

[1] There were two editions of Earbery's translation, 1727–8 and 1728. Where this is too inaccurate I quote from the 1733 edition by Wilkinson. There were two other English translations (1729, 1733), and a Dutch (1729) and a French (1731).

[2] Burnet, *De Statu*, 1733, p. 309: 'illud monitum, quod à praefatis Patribus, ubi hoc tractant argumentum, saepius adhiberi solet. Nimirum, quicquid apud te statuas, intus & in pectore, de his poenis, aeternis vel non; receptâ doctrinâ verbisque utendum est cum populo, & cùm peroratur ad vulgus; praeceps nempe in vitium & solâ formidine poenae à malis absterrendum.' Earbery's comment (II, 97) is: 'This looks very like Priestcraft'. Addition: 'Propterea haec, quae doctioribus inscripta sunt, siquis in linguam vulgarem transtulerit, id malo animo atque consilio sinistro factum arbitrabor.' Earbery comments: 'Is there a more universal Language than *Latin*?'

ignorant people; but, unlike Spinoza, he believes that it also contains precious esoteric truths:[1]

> ... the secret and rational Account is different from the vulgar One. It is very frequent in the sacred Scriptures to explain a Thing, and accommodate the Sense thereof to common Understandings; though to the more industrious Searcher of those Scriptures, the latent Truth is brought forth; *We speak Wisdom among them that are perfect* (I Cor. II, 6). ... And we accommodate ourselves in another manner to the Unwise. And in this the divine Wisdom shines forth, in giving Milk to Infants, and more solid Food to grown Persons (Heb. V, 13, 14).

Not only with regard to hell is this the case. The above passage was with reference to the resurrection of the body, and for nearly every doctrine there is a 'vulgar and a rational Hypothesis',[2] of which the former is clearly expressed in the Scriptures, while the latter can only be inferred from hints or extracted by allegorical interpretation—[3]

> It is evident to every one, the Holy Scripture, in treating upon abstruse Subjects is apt ἀνθρωπολογεῖν.

This applies also to Christ's words; he spoke the language 'not of philosophers but of the sons of men', and in particular of the Jews. When, for example, He spoke of hell in Mark IX, 44 and quoted Isaiah LXVI, 24 ('their worm dieth not and the fire is not quenched'), He was merely using an expression familiar to His audience, which He did not change, 'since it seemed not unfitted to restraining the audacity of the impious'.[4]

As I have already pointed out, the double doctrine applied to hell is a special case because the esoteric doctrine directly contradicts the exoteric, and hence the veracity of God, the Scriptures and the whole revelation is impugned. Burnet provides a very remarkable instance of how extremely dangerous the double doctrine could be, especially when combined with a

[1] Burnet, *Of the State*, transl. Earbery, 2nd ed., 1728, Vol. I, pp. 234–5.
[2] Burnet, *De Statu*, 1733, p. 301: 'distinguendum inter hypothesin literalem & rationalem, vulgarem & arcanam.'
[3] Burnet, *Of the State*, 1728, Vol. I, p. 235. On patristic allegorical interpretation Earbery (p. 177) remarks: 'I call it Brooding over a Text till it hatches.'
[4] Burnet, *De Statu*, 1733, p. 300–1: 'cùm non incommoda videretur ad refraenandam audaciam impiorum.'

knowledge of the early Fathers and an open-minded reading of the New Testament. He remarks that

> the primitive Christians were a little mistaken in their Calculation of the Time; for they verily believed the Day of the Lord would come in their Age. . . .

He then gives a battery of patristic and New Testament texts to prove that

> they even believed these Things could happen so soon as to overtake them alive: This *Paul* frequently inculcates, I Thess. IV, 15–17, I Cor. XV, 52. he believed his mortal Body would be swallowed up in Life, that is, in an immortal and glorified Body. . . .

All this arose 'from a wrong Understanding of the Words of Christ', such as Matthew XXIV, 29–30, 34–5, XXVI, 27–8. Then comes the dangerous explanation:[1]

> From comparing these Passages, I do not wonder the Disciples imbibed the Notion of his sudden Coming to judge the Living and the Dead; nor do I wonder that Providence permitted the Errour to grow, so conducive to Piety, Patience, and a Readiness to die for the sake of God. . . .

As Earbery remarks, 'This is a very odd Notion of Providence to send Delusions upon the World.' How much else in the revelation is merely edifying delusion? If Burnet had supposed that Christ, too, was deluded, he would have arrived at Schweitzer's interpretation of the New Testament.

One of the main functions of the double doctrine is to account for the absence of a continuous tradition for any new doctrine one wishes to introduce. If one supposes an esoteric tradition for the new truth, then *ex hypothesi* there will not be an unbroken chain of testimonies to it, but only a few hints here and there, perhaps at long intervals. Glanvill uses this technique for defending preexistence of the soul. This doctrine is not mentioned in Genesis because '*Moses* had here to do with a rude and *illiterate* people', and therefore his account of the creation is

---

[1] Burnet, *Of the State*, 1728, Vol. I, pp. 166–9. Whiston (*The Eternity of Hell Torments*, p. 54) and Francis Lee (apud C. Walton, *Notes and Materials for an adequate Biography of . . . William Law*, pp. 207, 217) both note that the Apostles expected an immediate Second Coming.

'adapted to mean and vulgar apprehensions'. Similarly, it was not preached by the early Christians because

> there were doubtless many Doctrines entertain'd by the *Apostles* and the more learned of their followers, which were disproportion'd to the capacities of the *generality*, who hold but little *Theory*. . . . Among us, *wise men* count it not so proper to deal forth *deep* and *mysterious points* in *Divinity* to common and promiscuous *Auditories*.

Preexistence was 'a *Cabbala* which was handed down from the *Apostolick* ages' to the time of Origen.[1] But here the double doctrine does not involve mendacity, merely discretion and concealment. Burnet, on the other hand, wishing to defend the non-eternity of hell, has to suppose that Christ, the Apostles, and the early Fathers were deliberately deceptive.

In spite of this great emphasis on the esoteric nature of his views on hell, Burnet looks forward to a time when his doctrine will be universally received, when eternal torment will be considered 'no less absurd and odious than is transubstantiation today'.[2] But great caution must be observed. The revelation is dynamic, progressively illuminating mankind; but its progress is very slow, and we must not try to forestall it. Men's minds must be 'gradually accustomed to the stronger beams of truth', before we can preach on the housetops what we heard in the ear (Matt. X, 27).[3] Perhaps Burnet conceived of his own book, shown only to a few suitable friends, as contributing to this gradual illumination. Sinsart, who gives a short refutation of Burnet, remarks:[4]

> Burnet, like a clever seducer, advises that one should procede step by step, so that his new doctrine may, like a cancer, make imperceptible progress.

In the *De Statu*, as in the *Theoria Sacra*, the conflagration is hell, but it is also the Last Judgment. Basing himself mainly on Origen's interpretation of I Corinthians III, 13 ('Every

---

[1] Glanvill, *Lux Orientalis*, in *Two Choice . . . Treatises*, 1682, pp. 37, 42.
[2] Burnet, *De Statu*, 1733, p. 302 (one of the MS. additions).
[3] Ibid., pp. 309–10.
[4] Sinsart, *Defense*, p. 292: 'Burnet en homme d'esprit qui veut séduire, conseille d'aller pas à pas, afin que sa doctrine nouvelle fasse comme un cancer un progrès insensible.'

man's work shall be made manifest: for the day shall declare it, because it shall be revealed by fire; and the fire shall try every man's work of what sort it is'),[1] Burnet explains that the fire will burn only those souls which have combustible matter, i.e. the chaff of sin (Matt. III, 11), simultaneously judging, punishing, and purifying them. He is a little worried by the problem: how this fire, which he asserts to be material, can burn a bodiless soul; but, as he says, this difficulty also occurs in the orthodox hell prior to the resurrection. Nor is it clear where the wicked are punished after the conflagration is over and while the millennium is going on, nor what happens to them when they resurrect. What is clear, is that they will be burnt in ordinary fire, but not for ever.[2] They are not externally tormented before the conflagration, but are in the unhappy state of anxiously and guiltily awaiting the Last Judgment.[3]

Burnet begins his discussion of eternal torment thus:

Human Nature is terrified with the very Name of Eternal Punishments that seem to carry insatiable Revenge, without Correction or Amendment. The Scripture indeed is on the other side of the question.

The golden rule in interpreting Scripture is 'not to recede from the Letter without Necessity'. Eternal torment, therefore, must be accepted, if it is 'not opposed to the plainest and most invincible Arguments'.[4] The chief of these arguments is the dilemma we have already met as expressed by Bayle:[5] either the damned must necessarily sin, in which case they have no free will whatever, cannot properly be said to be capable of sin (i.e. the orthodox static hell), and would be annihilated by a good Creator, or they still have free will and may repent. Burnet rejects the first alternative as[6]

injurious to the Dignity of the Creator, and to the Divine Wisdom and Goodness, to make and form human Nature in

[1] Origen, *Contra Celsum*, V, xv (Migne, *Pat. Gr.*, T. XI, cols. 1202–3). Earbery (I, 176) remarks that the passage from St Paul 'equally proves Souls shall be pickled as burnt'.
[2] Burnet, *Of the State*, 1728, Vol. I, pp. 152–62.
[3] Ibid., Vol. II, p. 79.
[4] Ibid., Vol. II, pp. 80–1.
[5] V. supra, p. 25.
[6] Ibid., Vol. II, p. 82.

such a Manner as to degenerate into a State of incurable Pravity, and with that to be fixed in irrecoverable Misery: This State can be agreeable only to a *Manichean* God.

We are left then with the damned being capable of repentance, and Burnet argues that conditions in hell will be peculiarly favourable to repentance: their sinful disposition[1]

> cannot be so deep rooted but Fire will purge it out: a Remedy as searching as it is powerful and strong . . Moreover in another Life, when the Wicked shall see Christ coming in his Glory . . . there will be no room for their Infidelity; the Fomes peccati in this Flesh will be extinguished; Concupiscence will be no more, and the Food for Vices, for unlawful Pleasures . . . be taken away; why therefore, and with what Motives can they adhere for ever to their Sins, unless they are hardened by Heaven?

Once the orthodox static afterlife is abandoned, it is difficult to refute this argument; this is the best that Horbery, Whiston's adversary, can do against Burnet's reformatory hell:[2]

> It is surprising too, that a Place furthest removed from God, and his heavenly influences, inhabited only by his most accursed Enemies . . . should after all prove the most effectual School of Virtue. There is no good reason to believe that these Punishments will have any such effect.

But Burnet was unwise to keep, like Rust and Glanvill, the traditional flames of hell, because it is difficult to imagine that anyone undergoing pain at least as severe as that of being burnt alive would be able to pay attention to anything else. Sinsart refutes reformatory hells on these lines:[3]

> The intensity of their punishments will so completely occupy their souls that they will not be capable of thinking of anything else. To help us imagine this, let us suppose a man undergoing the sharpest pains of gout or the stone; let us go further,

---

[1] Ibid., Vol. II, p. 83.

[2] Horbery, *An Enquiry*, pp. 256–7.

[3] Sinsart, *Defense*, p. 252: 'La vivacité de leurs peines remplira si totalement leur ame, qu'ils ne seront pas capables de penser à autre chose. Pour rendre ceci sensible, supposons un homme attaqué des plus vives douleurs de la goutte, ou de la gravelle; poussons plus loin, que cet homme souffre les tourmens de la question, croit-on qu'en cet état il s'occupera sérieusement de son salut? mais quelle comparaison de ces maux avec ceux des damnés!'

suppose him to be suffering the torture of the question, do you think that in this state he will seriously concern himself with his salvation? but what comparison is there between these torments and those of the damned!

And elsewhere he asks us to imagine, though these are still 'less than the truth',[1] a man being disembowelled, torn apart by four horses, or burnt alive. Burnet, in arguing that the eternity of hell is incompatible with the 'Goodness & Mercy of God', uses similar comparisons:[2]

> We have read of the Torments of the primitive Christians in the first Ages of the Church; and what the *Sicilian* and other Tyrants have invented; but these are soft to the Torments of Hell, and softer likewise as they are less durable and vehement; eternal Grief has all the Steps and Gradations of the extreamest Misery; were the Boilings of a Fever, the Rackings of the Stone, or the Torments of the Guts to endure only SEVEN Years, what Flesh and Blood could be equal thereto?

Burnet does, however, imply that in his hell there will be periods of relaxation, during which the damned have the opportunity to consider the advisability of repentance. The orthodox hell, he argues, is unbecoming to the wisdom of God, because it 'can serve neither God nor Man'—[3]

> what End can it answer to Man, if there is no room for Repentance, and if his Punishment does not meliorate his Mind; if there is no Intermission of Pain, no Breathings to deliberate and consider upon some Change of Fortune? Let the Punishment be sharp, and even long, but let it have an End . . .

Such arguments imply the rejection of purely vindictive justice and the assumption that all punishments must be curative. But Burnet is not interested in such abstract matters. Nor does he discuss, except superficially, the obviously relevant question of the divine attributes. We find only vague assertions, such as the following:[4]

> We conceive the God of the Christians to be a wise and good Deity, not cruel and hostile to human Nature; nor in his Wor-

[1] Ibid., p. 322, 'au-dessous du vrai.'
[2] Burnet, *Of the State*, 1728, Vol. II, p. 85.
[3] Ibid., Vol. II, p. 82.
[4] Burnet, *Of the State*, 1728, Vol. II, p. 81.

ship has he instituted any Thing barbarous, cruel, or inhumane; he neither wounds nor rends the Flesh, nor, like *Moloch*, pulls tender Infants from their Mother's Breasts into his burning Arms. . . .

As Earbery remarks, 'the Doctor has forgot his Burning Chapter', that is, the chapter where he summarizes the account given in his *Theoria Sacra* of the conflagration, during which, it will be remembered, there will be 'Millions shrieking in the Flames at once'.

Chapter X

ENGLISH PLATONISTS
(4) Shaftesbury

NTHONY ASHLEY COOPER, third Earl of Shaftesbury, should perhaps not appear under the rubric of English Platonist—he might as well be called an English Stoic. But on the whole Cassirer is, I think, right in seeing a close affinity between his philosophical outlook and that of the Cambridge Platonists.[1] He had read and he admired the works of Cudworth and Henry More; the former he must have known through Locke's close friendship with Lady Masham, Cudworth's daughter, since Locke had been his tutor and remained his friend. In 1698 he arranged for the publication of two volumes of Whichcote's sermons, for which he wrote the preface.[2] Like the Cambridge Platonists, he was extremely liberal and tolerant in religious matters, he regarded the Calvinist God as diabolic,[3] and he was concerned, as we have seen, to prevent the separation of divine and human values by asserting the priority of moral ideas over the will of God.[4] On the other hand, the differences are also considerable.

[1] E. Cassirer, *The Platonic Renaissance in England*, pp. 160 seq.
[2] See *A Sketch of the Life of . . . Shaftesbury*, by his son, in *The Life, Unpublished Letters, and Philosophical Regimen of Anthony, Earl of Shaftesbury*, ed. Benjamin Rand, London, 1900, p. xxvii.
[3] V. supra, p. 49.
[4] V. supra, p. 54.

167

First and foremost, judging even from his published writings and still more from his unpublished letters and *Philosophical Regimen*,[1] I doubt whether he was a Christian in any sense that his contemporaries would have accepted, though he could probably have found a place in the present-day English Church, and I would not endorse Berkeley's judgment: 'a man prejudiced against the Christian religion'.[2] Like Sterry and White, he believed in a God whose supreme attribute is love; but, unlike them, he was agnostic about personal survival after death, and he certainly did not believe in an afterlife of rewards and punishments. Secondly, he goes much further than Cudworth and More in his uncompromising insistence on disinterested ethics, on the ideal of *virtus gratia virtutis*, if I may coin a phrase which indicates his tendency to identify moral and aesthetic principles, the good and the beautiful, thus arriving, as Berkeley points out, at the καλοκάγαθία of Aristotle.[3]

It is this conception of virtue as essentially disinterested that enables Shaftesbury to make the most radical attack on hell's strongest point, namely, its value as a deterrent in this life, and indeed on the whole Christian afterlife of rewards and punishments. In his *Inquiry concerning Virtue and Merit* (1699, 1711) he argued as follows.[4] There are two possible reasons why men should obey God:

> either in the way of his power, as presupposing some disadvantage or benefit to accrue from him; or in the way of his excellency and worth, as thinking it the perfection of nature to imitate and resemble him.

In the first case, if,

> through hope merely of reward, or fear of punishment, the creature be incited to do the good he hates, or restrained from doing the ill to which he is not otherwise in the least degree averse, there is . . . no virtue or goodness whatsoever. The creature, notwithstanding his good conduct, is intrinsically of

[1] In *The Life* . . ., ed. Rand, 1900.
[2] George Berkeley, *The Works*, ed. A. A. Luce and T. E. Jessop, London, 1950, Vol. III, p. 132.
[3] Berkeley, ibid., p. 133.
[4] Shaftesbury, *Characteristics of Men, Manners, Opinions, Times,* . . ., ed. John M. Robertson, London, 1900, Vol. I, pp. 266–9. In 1699 Toland, without permission, published the *Inquiry*. The first collected edition of the *Characteristics* appeared in 1711.

as little worth as if he acted in his natural way, when under no dread or terror of any sort.

The grounds for this assertion are:

whilst the will is neither gained nor the inclination wrought upon, but awe prevails and forces obedience, the obedience is servile, and all which is done through it merely servile.

The greater the obedience from such motives, the more abject and self-interested is the obedient creature. If we take the second reason for obeying God and add the first to it, that is, add the motive of fear of punishment or hope of reward to the motive of loving God and wishing to be like Him, we find that we have added nothing to the moral value of good conduct, but on the contrary have made it much more difficult to attain a pure, disinterested love of God and submission to His will. For if anyone resigns himself to death and suffering as part of the

rule and order of the Deity; and if that which he calls resignation depends only on the expectation of infinite retribution or reward, he discovers no more worth or virtue here than in any other bargain of interest. The meaning of his resignation being only this, 'That he resigns his present life and pleasures conditionally, for that which he himself confesses to be beyond and equivalent: eternal living in a state of highest pleasure and enjoyment.'

It might be thought that Shaftesbury is here merely demonstrating an analytical truth: that we do not in fact call virtuous such actions as are motivated by fear of punishment or hope of reward, because the moral responsibility for them rests not on the doer but on the punisher or rewarder, or because we would call all such actions purely self-interested or expedient, and therefore morally neutral or bad. But this is not what he is doing; for it is very doubtful whether in his day this was an analytical truth. Locke, who believed in the annihilation of the wicked but in the eternal bliss of the good, could write in his *Reasonableness of Christianity* that, though the ancient philosophers had 'showed the beauty of virtue', very few people practised it;[1]

but now there being put into the scales on her side 'an exceeding

[1] Locke, *Works*, 12th ed., London, 1824, Vol. VI, p. 150.

and immortal weight of glory'[1]; interest is come about to her, and virtue is now visibly the most enriching purchase, and by much the best bargain.

Shaftesbury, then, was not just pointing out how people did in fact apply terms of moral approval or blame; he was asserting a conception of morals which deliberately excludes an essential, though not necessarily dominant, part of Christian ethics. For him two of the theological virtues may make the third impossible; if there is faith in God's justice and hope of a heavenly reward, there can be no true charity. Virtue consists in doing freely and rationally what we know to be good. We know what is good by an innate faculty for moral intuition deriving from God—'those original ideas of Goodness, which the . . . Divine being, or Nature under him, has implanted in us'.[2] But, though these ideas derive from God, they must for us be logically anterior to, and independent of, the idea of God, for otherwise we could not recognize divinely revealed moral laws as such; and these laws must be obeyed freely and disinterestedly, if we wish to account ourselves virtuous.

It is quite likely that Shaftesbury was thinking of Locke when he used the term 'bargain' in the above passage. Much as he respected him, he believed that Locke's philosophy was pernicious with regard to just this point; by his destructive criticism of innate ideas Locke had removed the basis of disinterested morals, independent of any human or divine authority. He had done so more effectively and dangerously than Hobbes,[3]

for Mr. Hobbes's character and base slavish principles of government took off the poison of his philosophy. 'Twas Mr. Locke that struck at all fundamentals, threw all order and virtue out of the world, and made the very ideas of these (which are the same as those of God) *unnatural*, and without foundation in our minds.

In 1704 Shaftesbury was sent an extract from a farewell letter written by Locke, shortly before his death, to Anthony Collins,

[1] II Cor. IV, 17.
[2] Shaftesbury, *A Letter concerning Enthusiasm*, 1708, in *Characteristics*, ed. cit., Vol. I, p. 25.
[3] Letter of Shaftesbury in *The Life*, ed. Rand, p. 403.

in which occurred the apparently inoffensive statement:[1]

> this life is a scene of vanity, that soon passes away, and affords no solid satisfaction but in the consciousness of doing well, and in hopes of another life.

Shaftesbury seized on the connection, possibly not even intended by Locke, between the last two phrases, and commented on it with great acerbity:

> The piece of a letter you sent me savours of the good and Christian. It puts me in mind of one of those dying speeches which come out under the title of a Christian warning piece. I should never have guessed it to have been of a dying philosopher.

Though Shaftesbury was not, I think, anti-Christian, he certainly despised some kinds of Christian. He went on:

> those who can be conscious of doing no good, but what they are frighted or bribed into, can make but a sorry *account* of it, as I imagine.

He then gave his own dying message to the friend who had sent him Locke's letter:

> our life, thank heaven, has been a scene of friendship of long duration, with much and solid satisfaction, founded on the consciousness of doing good for good's sake. without any farther regards, nothing being truly pleasing or satisfactory but what is thus acted disinterestedly.

Although Shaftesbury concedes that[2]

> the principle of fear of future punishment, and hope of future reward, how mercenary or servile soever it may be accounted, is yet in many circumstances a great advantage, and support to virtue,

this is true only for those subject to strong and evil passions, or habitually depraved, or too feeble to bear the trials of a virtuous life without such support. And it is clear that the disadvantages and dangers of heaven and hell far outweigh their possible advantage to the weak and vicious. A concentration of attention on future rewards and punishments leads us, 'thus transported

---

[1] Shaftesbury, *The Life*, ed. Rand, pp. 345 seq.
[2] Shaftesbury, *Inquiry*, in *Characteristics*, ed. cit., Vol. I, pp. 270 seq.

in the pursuit of a high advantage, and self-interest so narrowly confined within ourselves', to neglect or even deny the naturally pleasant consequences of virtuous behaviour, such as mutual trust and love, so that[1]

> it is customary with many devout people zealously to decry all temporal advantage of goodness, all natural benefits of virtue, and magnifying the contrary happiness of a vicious state, to declare 'that except only for the sake of future reward and fear of future punishment, they would divest themselves of all goodness at once, and freely allow themselves to be most immoral and profligate'. From whence it appears that in some respects there can be nothing more fatal to virtue than the weak and uncertain belief of future reward and punishment. For the stress being laid wholly here, if this foundation come to fall, there is no further prop or security to men's morals. And thus virtue is supplanted and betrayed.

In spite of his insistence on the disinterestedness of true virtue, Shaftesbury, as one can see from the passage just quoted, was aware of the importance of preserving some connexion between virtue and happiness. Though theoretically conceivable, a moral system which promised its adherents only misery would be unlikely to survive for long, nor would such a system be compatible with a beneficent or just God. Shaftesbury lays great emphasis on the joys that his disinterested virtue often brings with it—trust, respect, and affection among those who practise it, and the 'solid satisfaction' of reflecting that one has tried to do good and beautiful actions just because they are good and beautiful.

But why, if he allows these natural, temporal rewards to virtue, does he so contemptuously reject the eternal rewards of Christianity? One answer to this question we have already seen: the eternal rewards lead to a pernicious neglect or even denial of the natural ones. Another answer, though Shaftesbury does not explicitly give it, lies in the following distinctions. The earthly rewards of virtue, on the one hand, are either intrinsic to the virtuous action, that is, the satisfaction of a good conscience, or, if external, they are by no means certain and in fact are often lacking—our disinterested generosity and love may

[1] Shaftesbury, *Inquiry*, in *Characteristics*, ed. cit., Vol. I, p. 275; cf. ibid., pp. 66–7 (*Essay on Wit and Humour*).

be met by ingratitude and contempt, and we may even in some cases be virtually sure that they will be. There is thus still a real difference between expediency and virtue. There is no necessary, inevitable connection between our good actions and our happiness, and it is therefore still possible to know that our motives in doing a good action are not, at least primarily, directed towards the happiness that we may gain by it. The heavenly rewards, on the other hand, are all external to the virtuous action, and they are certain, inevitable and infinitely greater than any earthly reward. In consequence every virtuous action is overwhelmingly expedient, and, even if we wished to have purely virtuous motives, it would, psychologically, be very difficult, if not impossible, to achieve complete indifference to the reward. If virtue and expedience always and necessarily coincide, they are indistinguishable and there seems to be no good reason for having two names for the same thing. Faith and hope have driven out charity.

This consequence of the orthodox afterlife has always troubled Christian mystics in their attempt to attain a pure, that is, disinterested love of God.[1] From St Paul onwards (Romans IX, 3), the difficulty has been met by reaching, or trying to reach, a state of resignation to God's will, in which the reward of heaven is renounced and, in consequence, the torments of hell are accepted.[2] While Shaftesbury was writing his *Inquiry*, a battle over this problem was raging in the French Church. The orthodoxy of this acceptance of one's own damnation was one of the main points of dispute in the controversy about Quietism of which the opposing protagonists were Bossuet, against it, and Fénelon, for it. The strength of Bossuet's view, which eventually triumphed, lay in the paradoxical, even self-contradictory nature of this acceptance. Since the damned suffer the *poena damni*, they are totally deprived of God's grace; hence they can only hate Him, and, exasperated by the *poena sensus*, blaspheme against Him. Thus an acceptance for oneself of the orthodox hell, far from helping to attain a disinterested love of God, looks forward to the eventual attainment of an interested hatred of Him. The terms, however, in which this acceptance is usually expressed imply a hell in

[1] Cf. K. E. Kirk, *The Vision of God*, London, 1931, pp. 142 seq. and passim.
[2] Cf. supra, p. 132 (Henry More's resolution at Eton).

173

which only the *poena sensus* is inflicted. But such a hell, for which there is no authority whatever, would involve God in tormenting those creatures who love Him most purely, thus making Him even more diabolic than the Calvinist God, who at least takes the trouble to force His victims into sin before punishing them. The weakness of Bossuet's view lay in the formidable array of Christian mystics, many of them canonized, who had in fact expressed this acceptance. He claimed that, for orthodox mystics, this acceptance was only an impossible supposition, that is, a hyperbolic figure of speech by which they expressed their attainment of, or wish to attain, disinterested love of God. This opinion, which was embodied in the thirty-third of the articles signed at Issy in 1695 by Fénelon and Mme de Guyon, has two weak points. First, its historical truth is doubtful; there have been saints, such as St François de Sales, who at times accepted, and believed in, their own reprobation. Secondly, if this acceptance is only a figure of speech, it does nothing towards removing the psychological difficulty of disregarding infinite rewards and punishments, or the philosophical difficulty of distinguishing between virtue and expedience.[1]

Berkeley, in the course of discussing ancient sources of Shaftesbury's ethics, remarked that the Stoics in their ideal of disinterested virtue were 'not unlike our modern Quietists'.[2] It is not unlikely that Shaftesbury was thinking of the Quietist controversy, of Mme de Guyon's and Fénelon's attempt to love God disinterestedly in spite of heaven and hell, when he wrote his most emphatic and basic rejection of the orthodox afterlife:[3]

> by building a future state on the ruins of virtue, religion in general and the cause of a Deity is betrayed, and by making rewards and punishments the principal motives to duty, the Christian religion in particular is overthrown, and its greatest principle, that of love, rejected and exposed.

That Shaftesbury's disinterested virtue was a serious threat to Christianity was clearly seen by Berkeley. He also believed that it was socially dangerous, even more dangerous, because

[1] See Bossuet, *Oeuvres*, Paris, 1841, T. XIV, pp. 12, 70 seq., 158, 182–90; Fénelon, *Oeuvres*, Versailles, 1820, T. IV, pp. cv–cvii, cxxxii, cxxxix–cxliv, cxlix; Ronald Knox, *Enthusiasm*, Oxford, 1950, pp. 254–5, 270 seq., 285, 342.
[2] Berkeley, *Works*, ed. cit., Vol. III, p. 136.
[3] Shaftesbury, *The Moralists*, in *Characteristics*, ed. cit., Vol. II, p. 59.

more specious, than Mandeville's cynical theory of the useful-
ness of vice. In *A Discourse addressed to Magistrates and Men in
Authority Occasioned by the Enormous Licence and Irreligion of
the Times* (1738) Berkeley couples Shaftesbury and Mandeville
together as 'two authors of infidel systems', and adds bitterly:[1]

> And yet the people among whom such books are published
> wonder how it comes to pass that the civil magistrate daily
> loseth his authority, that the laws are trampled upon, and the
> subject in constant fear of being robbed, or murdered, or having
> his house burnt over his head.

Berkeley had already attacked these two infidels in his
apologetical dialogues *Alciphron* (1732). The attack on Shaftesbury is surprisingly venomous; though his victim had been
dead for nearly twenty years, Berkeley writes of him as if he
were a personal enemy, who must at all costs be made to appear
contemptible and ridiculous.[2] Since Berkeley was neither a fool
nor a villain, one must suppose that the violence of his attack
was due to his conviction that Shaftesbury's philosophy was one
of the greatest dangers to Christianity then extant.

Berkeley, very wisely, does not attempt to refute Shaftesbury's most fundamentally anti-Christian proposition, namely,
that the Christian afterlife necessarily equates virtue with
expedience or self-interest. On the contrary, he explicitly
accepts it:[3]

> can there be a stronger motive to virtue than the shewing that,
> considered in all lights, it is every man's true interest?

He gives a lyrical description of the universe governed by
Providence, which enforces its rules 'by the highest rewards
and discouragements', so that 'every one's true interest is
combined with his duty' and 'a man need be no Stoic or knight-
errant, to account for his virtue';

> in such a system, vice is madness, cunning is folly, wisdom and
> virtue are the same thing.

---

[1] Berkeley, *Works*, ed. cit., Vol. VI, p. 216.
[2] Cf. e.g. Berkeley, *Works*, ed. cit., Vol. III, pp. 132 (sneer at Shaftesbury's ill
health), 199 (Shaftesbury's prose printed as blank verse).
[3] Berkeley, ibid., p. 120.

This system, in which virtue and self-interest are identical, is the most beautiful one imaginable—

> in contemplating the beauty of such a moral system, we may cry out with the Psalmist, 'Very excellent things are spoken of thee, thou City of God.'

It is beautiful because Berkeley has just identified beauty with utility by expounding a functionalist aesthetic of architecture. The proportions of a building are beautiful in so far as the building is well adapted to its end or use. Thus a universe in which virtue and self-interest are identical is beautiful because it is perfectly adapted to its end, namely, 'the complete happiness or well-being of the whole'.[1] Berkeley is able to adopt Shaftesbury's καλοκάγαθία by making the grand equation: the good is the same as the beautiful, and both are the same as the useful or enjoyable. He does not discuss the question: why do people use different words for the same thing? The answer must presumably be that virtue is a compendious term for long-term expediency.

If one posits a beneficent and omnipotent God, as both Shaftesbury and Berkeley did, then Berkeley's moral system is overwhelmingly the stronger, because any other system must make God unjust or malevolent. If He does not always reward virtue and punish vice, He must sometimes punish virtue and reward vice.

Even if Shaftesbury's disinterested virtue and its aesthetic basis are allowed, Berkeley argues that[2]

> the beauty of virtue, or τὸ καλόν, in either Aristotle's or Plato's sense, is not a sufficient principle or ground to engage sensual and worldly-minded men in the practice of it.

Shaftesbury himself had made this concession—that the Christian afterlife might be useful in restraining inferior people from vicious actions. If this is so, then, Berkeley maintains, it is wrong to publish such views:[3]

> one might expect from such philosophers so much good sense

---

[1] Ibid., p. 129.

[2] Berkeley, *Works*, ed. cit., Vol. III, p. 119. Berkeley (ibid., p. 136) also makes the valid criticism that Shaftesbury's disinterested virtue would be more convincing if he had taken over other Stoic moral concepts connected with it, ataraxia, adiaphora, etc.

[3] Ibid., p. 132.

and philanthropy as to keep their tenets to themselves, and consider their weak brethren, who are more strongly affected by certain senses and notions of another kind that that of the beauty of pure disinterested virtue.

In this case, of course, Berkeley considers Shaftesbury's rejection of the Christian afterlife to be untrue as well as pernicious. But he also defends the general principle of concealing dangerous truths.[1] Hell is still surrounding itself with secrecy and dishonesty.

We may perhaps accept the judgment on Shaftesbury's ethics given by Lysicles, the representative of Mandeville in *Alciphron*:[2]

This doctrine hath all the solid inconveniences, without the amusing hopes and prospects, of the Christian.

[1] Ibid., p. 140.
[2] Ibid., p. 122.

Chapter XI

PIERRE BAYLE AND SOME ENEMIES

LTHOUGH in French religious polemics of the late 17th and early 18th centuries the question of hell, and especially of its eternity, is quite often discussed, the main subjects of these controversies have no immediately obvious connexions with this subject. I shall therefore begin this chapter by pointing out how these connexions arise.

In the years on either side of the revocation of the Edict of Nantes (1685) the debates between Catholic and Protestant theologians became, inevitably, violent and urgent. Differences of doctrine tended to be neglected in favour of the two cardinal questions that were of practical importance with regard to the persecution of the Huguenots: the validity of the authority claimed by each Church, and, closely connected with this, the morality of religious tolerance or intolerance. In their attitudes to these questions the chief Protestant protagonists, Jurieu, Le Clerc, Bayle, Saurin, Jaquelot, differed widely one from another, and this gave rise to a further series of controversies of great interest and acrimony. A third, separate series of discussions, concerned with theodicy, was started by the Manichaean articles in Bayle's *Dictionnaire historique et critique* (1697).

The question of the authority of the two Churches was of great practical importance because, if the Catholics could make good their claim to a continuous tradition of infallibility going back to the scriptural revelation accepted by both sides, then disputes about doctrinal or ecclesiastical divergences would become unnecessary and Protestants, or any other kind of heretics, could legitimately be treated as rebels against the infallibly interpreted authority of God. An infallible tradition of religious truth must, it is obvious, be invariable, or, if it varies, its later stages must not be incompatible with earlier ones. Thus one way of proving the validity of the Catholic Church's authority was to show historically that its doctrine had never varied, and one way of disproving the claims of the Protestants was to show, also historically, that in a comparatively short space of time their doctrine had varied and split itself up into numerous different opinions and sects. These arguments are used by Maimbourg and Nicole, and they are of course the whole point of Bossuet's *Histoire des Variations des Eglises Protestantes* (1688).[1]

One way of answering such arguments is to refute historically the Catholic claim to a continuous and unvarying, or at least not self-contradictory, tradition. This refutation was attempted, with considerable erudition and success, by Jurieu in his *Lettres Pastorales* of 1688.[2] He examined the opinions of pre-Nicene Fathers on certain fundamental doctrines, such as the Trinity, original sin, justification by faith, the state of souls immediately after death, and the punishment of the damned. In the course of examining this last point he naturally discussed Origen's scheme for the eventual salvation of all rational creatures.

Juricu's line of defence against Bossuet was remarkably imprudent.[3] He was sawing off the branch he was sitting on; for these doctrines were as fundamental for Protestant theology

[1] Cf. Jean Delvolvé, *Religion, Critique et Philosophie Positive chez Pierre Bayle*, Paris, 1906, pp. 53 seq., 206 seq.
[2] Jurieu, *Lettres Pastorales*, 3e Année, Rotterdam, 1689, Lettres VI and VII; p. 51 on Origen.
[3] Cf. Bossuet, *Avertissemens* on Jurieu's *Lettres* (Bossuet, *Oeuvres*, ed. Lachat, Paris, 1863, T. XV, p. 199): 'M. Jurieu est l'auteur d'une si belle défense: au moins, dit-il, nous ne périrons pas tous seuls: nous nous sauverons par le nom et la dignité de nos complices; et s'il faut que la Réforme soit convaincue d'instabilité et par là de fausseté manifeste, elle entrainera tous les siècles précédens, et même les plus purs, dans sa ruine.'

as for Catholic, and in some cases more so. By demonstrating that the Fathers of the first two or three centuries had either been ignorant of them or had held erroneous versions of them, he did indeed shake the historical basis of Catholic theology, but he also ruined that of his own. Logically, he was obliged to admit the right of every individual to interpret the Scriptures according to his own lights, since there was no valid tradition of interpretation. Jurieu did not, of course, make this admission; but Bayle, in his *Janua Coelorum reserata cunctis religionibus* (1692),[1] made it for him by showing that Jurieu could not logically, on his own principles, shut the gates of heaven against Socinians or neo-Arians, against Origenists, or even against those who in good faith rejected the Scriptures altogether.

Bayle's purposes were wholly destructive, and he was able easily and serenely to point out the inconsistencies and perils of Jurieu's demonstration that the early Fathers were heretical on many fundamental points, coupled with his refusal to allow tolerance to modern heretics of the same kind. But for a sincere Protestant it was an uneasy and difficult task to criticize Jurieu's use of the early Fathers without admitting that he had in fact destroyed the historical basis of Protestant theology. This task was, however, attempted by Elie Saurin, a competent rationalist theologian, admired even by Bayle,[2] in his *Examen de la Théologie de Mr Jurieu* (1694).[3]

Saurin's main reproach was that Jurieu had not followed the advice of Jean Daillé,[4] a French Calvinist of the earlier 17th century, who had published a widely read *Traicté de l'Employ des Saincts Peres, Pour le jugement des differends qui sont aujourd'huy en la Religion*.[5] Daillé was indeed more prudent than Jurieu, but he too could defend the Protestant position only by means of inconsistencies and evasions. He begins by giving a list of the 'evident' Christian truths which both Catholics and Protestants believe; he is concerned not with these, but only with the points of difference between the two Churches which might be decided by patristic authority.[6]

[1] Published anonymously at Amsterdam. Cf. Delvolvé, op. cit., pp. 206 seq.
[2] Bayle, letter of 1696, in Bayle, *Oeuvres Diverses*, T. IV, p. 724.
[3] La Haye, 1694.
[4] Saurin, *Examen*, pp. 711 seq.
[5] Genève and Paris, 1632.
[6] Daillé, *Traicté*, pp. 1–7.

Among these truths he includes the orthodox doctrines of the Trinity and original sin; he is thus able to evade discussing the highly questionable scriptural and early patristic authority for these two doctrines. Since most of his book is devoted to demonstrating that the Fathers have no positive authority whatever, he leaves these fundamental doctrines with no support except that of General Councils. At one point he seems to accept the authority of the first six Councils, but later rejects it.[1] He allows the Fathers of the first two centuries some negative authority: if they contain no mention of some specifically Catholic belief or practice, such as purgatory or the use of images, they may be used to prove the modernity and hence the wrongness of these beliefs and practices.[2] They may also be read as edifying writers, but their opinions must be accepted only in so far as these agree with Scripture and reason.[3] To show how necessary this caution is, Daillé devotes over fifty pages to describing the doctrinal errors of the Fathers up to and including St Augustine.[4] Among these are the 'grosses & extravagantes erreurs' of Origen, 'le plus dangereux de tous', which are, he says, too well known to require a detailed account.[5] After all this, we are somewhat surprised to find near the end of the book a eulogy of the Fathers as being both edifying and all in agreement on the 'fondemens du Christianisme'.[6]

Saurin, in using Daillé to attack Jurieu, is even more obviously inconsistent; for he accepts Daillé's principle that the Fathers have no authority against Scripture and reason, admits that they are full of errors 'sur les points de la derniere importance',[7] and yet sharply criticizes Jurieu for having given a picture of patristic theology which shows it to be[8]

not a mere corruption, but the complete annihilation of the Christian religion.

In reply to Jurieu's request that he should point out any cases

[1] Ibid., pp. 211–12, 438.
[2] Daillé, *Traicté*, pp. 6–7, 524 seq.
[3] Ibid., pp. 299 seq.
[4] Ibid., pp. 345 seq.
[5] Ibid., pp. 363 seq.
[6] Ibid., pp. 516 seq.
[7] Saurin, *Examen*, p. 718.
[8] Ibid., p. 678: 'non pas une simple corruption, mais le total anéantissement de la Religion Chrétienne.'

where Jurieu has misrepresented the Fathers, he can do nothing but exclaim that it is imprudent and uncharitable thus to denigrate early Christians;[1] just as Bossuet, faced with Jurieu's question: did the Fathers in fact vary in their christology? can only take refuge in a rhetorical question:[2]

> Alas, what stage have you reached, if you need to have it proved to you that the most essential articles, even the Trinity and the Incarnation, have always been acknowledged by the Christian Church?

Saurin was also unwise to point out, as Bossuet did too, that Jurieu's exposure of patristic trinitarian errors left orthodoxy without defence against the Socinians;[3] for his own acceptance of Daillé's principle, that no authority can stand against Scripture and reason, was equally favourable to them.

Jurieu's polemical use of the unorthodoxies of the early Fathers was an indiscretion of the kind which the holders of the double doctrine of hell wished to avoid.[4] In both cases the most important point was considered to be not the truth of the view published, but the wisdom or imprudence of making it known to a lay, theologically untrained public. Nobody could, nor in fact did, attempt to deny the general historical truth of what Jurieu said about the early Fathers, namely, that during the first two centuries of the Christian era doctrine had varied widely on fundamental matters, particularly in Christology and eschatology. Christian scholars had been aware of this for two hundred years. Jurieu was blamed not for saying anything new or untrue, but for publishing these facts in pastoral letters that would be widely read among Protestants and in a form which necessarily emphasized the gravity of the unorthodoxies. When Jurieu claimed:[5]

[1] Ibid., pp. 61, 691 seq.

[2] Bossuet, *Avertissemens*, in *Oeuvres*, ed. Lachat, T. XV, p. 209: 'Helas, où en êtes-vous si vous avés besoin qu'on vous prouve que les articles les plus essentiels & même la trinité & l'incarnation ont toûjours été reconnues par l'Eglise Chrétienne?'

[3] Bossuet, *Avertissemens*, in *Oeuvres*, ed. Lachat, T. XV, p. 191; Saurin, *Examen*, p. 61.

[4] V. supra, pp. 5–7.

[5] Saurin, *Examen*, p. 676: "Il est absurde de me faire un crime d'avoir dit 'qu'Origene & Clement d'Alexandrie avoient aboli l'Enfer pour en faire un Purgatoire'; car tous les savans le disent & l'avancent'. Le crime, ou plûtôt

It is absurd to make out that I have committed a crime in saying 'that Origen and Clement of Alexandria had abolished hell by turning it into a purgatory'; since all scholars say and assert this.

Saurin replied:

The crime, or rather the imprudence, consists in M. Jurieu's having informed the people of a thing which could only scandalize and could not in any way edify.

The debates about religious tolerance involved the question of hell in several ways. It is evident that a belief in the everlasting punishment of everyone outside one's own Church provides a strong justification for religious persecution, the resultant cruelty being as nothing compared with the eternity of torment thus prevented. This justification holds, even if the validity of forced conversions is not admitted, since effective suppression of heresy will stop the contamination of the orthodox and their consequent damnation. In practical terms, it would be difficult for a liberal Catholic who believed that some Protestants might not be damned to justify the use of *dragonnades*.

A slightly different kind of link between intolerance and hell is suggested by Bayle.[1] If God condemns heretics to eternal punishment, they must be His enemies. We are advancing His cause, in our own small way, by beginning their punishment here and now, and by exterminating them we shall prevent their drawing down divine vengeance on our country.

When in a state there are two religions each of which believes that the other is God's enemy and the broad way to eternal damnation, the hostility becomes so great that each sect accuses

[1] Bayle, *Oeuvres Diverses*, T. III, 1727, p. 955: 'lorsqu'il y a dans un Etat deux Religions dont chacun croit que l'autre est ennemie de Dieu, & le grand chemin de la damnation éternelle, les animosités deviennent si grandes, que chaque secte impute à l'autre d'attirer sur toute la Société les malédictions de Dieu; la peste, la famine, les inondations . . . Mais un homme qui se persuade qu'en exterminant les hérésies il avance le regne de Dieu, & qu'il gagnera un plus haut degré de gloire dans le Paradis, après avoir été admiré sur la terre, & comblé de louanges & de présens, comme le protecteur de la vérité; un tel homme, dis-je, foulera aux pieds toutes les regles de la Morale . . .'

l'imprudence consiste en ce que M. Jurieu a donné connoissance au peuple d'une chose qui ne pouvoit que le scandalizer, & qui ne servoit de rien à son édification.'

the other of bringing down the curses of God—plague, famine, flood—on the whole community. . . .

Natural reason or honour may often restrain an atheist from injuring his neighbour:

> But a man who is persuaded that by exterminating heresies he is advancing the kingdom of God, and that he will gain the highest degree of glory in paradise, after having been admired on earth and overwhelmed with praises and gifts, as the protector of truth; such a man, I say, will trample under foot all the rules of morality. . . .

Since all these theologians accepted, at least overtly, eternal punishment for someone or other, the debates on tolerance tend to centre on arguments about the exact areas of certain damnation and possible salvation. This kind of debate has a long history, going back to patristic discussions about the salvation of virtuous pagans, which were taken up again during the Renaissance and continued into this period. The French Protestants, since they were the victims of persecution, were naturally in favour of some measure of tolerance, and were therefore led to allow the possibility of salvation to some Christians outside their own Church. The precise limits of this area of tolerance were usually decided by establishing a few 'fundamental points[1]' in which belief was necessary for anyone to be a Christian at all. Except for some Arminians, Protestants drew these limits so as to exclude the Socinians by making two of the fundamental points a belief in the Nicene Trinity and in eternal punishments and rewards after death.

Jurieu, in his *Tableau du Socinianisme* (1690),[2] denied possible salvation to the Socinians on these grounds. But in earlier works he had granted it to Catholics,[3] mainly because he was anxious to avoid the standard reproach against the Calvinist God, namely, that He was deceitful in arranging for the Gospel to be preached to whole communities whom He had already damned *en bloc*. Jurieu had also refrained from damning the heterodox Fathers, including Origen. Jaquelot, Saurin, and

---

[1] For the earlier history of fundamental points, see J. Lecler, *Histoire de la Tolérance au siècle de la Réforme*, n.p., 1955.

[2] La Haye, 1690.

[3] Jurieu, *Le Vray Systeme de l'Eglise*, Dordrecht, 1686, pp. 169 seq., and Livre I passim. Cf. Delvolvé, op. cit., p. 207.

Bayle all attacked this inconsistency. They maintained that Origen's universal salvation was morally more dangerous than the Socinians' annihilation of the wicked.[1] Bayle argued that, if the Catholics, whom Jurieu admitted to be idolatrous, might be saved, then so might the Socinians, who, though they might fail to hold the orthodox doctrines of the Trinity and eternal torment, at least did not constantly disobey the plain command of God in the decalogue.[2] Bayle's main motive was to show that Jurieu's views on tolerance were at bottom exactly as illiberal as those of his Catholic opponents; he represented a rival orthodoxy, which was equally ready to damn and persecute heretics, and he did in fact defend the execution of Michel Servet.[3] He should have believed in the damnation of all non-Calvinists, including all Catholics, and there is little doubt that, if Jurieu's projected and prophesied Protestant invasion and conquest of France had taken place, the French Catholics, whether saved or damned in the life to come, would have had a thin time in this one.

In the articles *Manichéens* and *Pauliciens* of his dictionary Bayle put forward objections which a Manichaean, or any other kind of religious dualist, might bring against a monotheistic system postulating a good omnipotent God. These objections, which he claimed were unanswerable, were all concerned with the origin of evil and God's responsibility for it. By them he demonstrated convincingly, if verbosely, that it is impossible to reconcile the evils, physical, and moral, of this world with the existence of a good and omnipotent God. The task of answering these objections is difficult enough when God has to be cleared of responsibility for the suffering and wickedness of this world; it becomes, quite literally, infinitely more difficult when He has also to be exonerated from causing the suffering and wickedness of the next world, if these are to be eternal and if, as was generally admitted, the number of the damned greatly exceeded that of the saved. For it was assumed that the theodicy would be satisfactory if one could show that there was far more good than

---

[1] See Bayle, *Dict. Hist. & crit.*, art. Origène, rem. (B) and (C); *Avis sur le Tableau du Socinianisme*, 1690 (Bayle, *Oeuvres Div.*, T. IV, p. 38, states this is by Jaquelot); Saurin, *Examen*, pp. 62, 683–4.

[2] Bayle, *Janua Coelorum*, pp. 116–18, cf. 96–7 (on hell).

[3] Jurieu, *Tableau du Socinianisme*, p. 422.

evil in the universe, more both in duration and in the number of souls concerned; then God would be justified in having created it. Thus hell, containing the great majority of mankind and many of the angels, all in a permanent state of sin, and all suffering some degree of torment for all eternity, was a serious obstacle to any Christian theodicy. Jean Le Clerc took hell to be the only unsurmountable obstacle, and therefore attempted to answer Bayle's objections by assuming an Origenist afterlife. Bayle pointed out that his Manichaean objections were against *Christian* monotheism and that no Christian church or sect accepted Origen's eschatology; but he also maintained that his objections still held even if a limit to the duration of torment were allowed.

In the course of defending the Manichaean objections Bayle brought theologians of many colours into the debate, ranging from the Arminians Le Clerc and Jaquelot, and the Calvinist Jurieu, to the Anglican William King, the Cartesian Catholic Malebranche, and, after Bayle himself was dead, Leibniz.[1] The last three of these will be discussed in the next chapter. While patiently and diligently blowing up his heterogeneous opponents, Bayle steadily maintained his official position, namely, that by destroying any possible rational basis for any kind of Christianity he was helping the cause of strict Calvinism; he had shown that the objections brought against the Calvinist God, who had condemned most men to eternal torment before their creation and even *ante praevisa merita*, applied also to all other Christian Gods. He wrote of himself:[2]

> I may say, by the way, that Mr Bayle can be regarded as having rendered good service to the decisions of the Synod of Dordrecht; for the strongest attack one can make on them is that they attribute behaviour to God which seems quite incompat-

[1] On this controversy, see W. H. Barber, *Leibniz in France from Arnauld to Voltaire*, Oxford, 1955, pp. 71 seq.; Annie Barnes, *Jean Le Clerc*, Paris, 1938, pp. 228 seq.; Delvolvé, op. cit., pp. 313 seq.

[2] Bayle, *Oeuvres Div.*, T. III, p. 679: 'Je dirai en passant que Mr. Bayle peut passer pour avoir rendu un bon service aux canons du Synode de Dordrecht; car la plus forte baterie qu'on puisse leur oposer est, qu'ils attribuent à Dieu une conduite qui ne paroît nullement conforme aux idées que nous avons de la bonté, & de la sainteté & de la justice. Mais on renverse cette baterie dès que l'on montre que les autres hypotheses sur la Prédestination n'ôtent pas la difficulté, & ainsi rien ne doit plus empêcher que l'on ne suive le sens littéral des expressions de l'Ecriture, sur quoi se fondent les rigides Prédestinataires.'

ible with the ideas we have of goodness, sanctity and justice. But this attack collapses as soon as it is shown that the other hypotheses about predestination do not remove the difficulty, and that there is thus nothing to prevent one accepting the literal meaning of the scriptural expressions on which the rigid predestinationists found their position.

This rather casually worn disguise as a pious defender of the Synod of Dordrecht, which in 1619 had established absolute predestination in the Dutch Reformed Church, deceived no one in his own time or during the next two centuries. Although some recent scholars wish to take Bayle as a sincere Calvinist,[1] it seems to me quite evident that his Calvinism is a mask behind which one can clearly see the face.

Bayle's disguise brings us back to the secrecy and dishonesty which we have so often observed surrounding the subject of hell. But dishonesty about hell is of course only a special and acute case of a general tendency to reticence and evasion on the part of theologians when dealing with any controversial subject. Since the writers we are considering were exiled Huguenots living in Holland, they were naturally concerned about their personal safety and livelihood, and anxious to avoid any accusation of unorthodoxy. As far as hell was concerned, they could not afford to be accused of promulgating views which might ruin public morality and even threaten the security of the state. In Holland there was a great measure of *de facto* religious tolerance, but very little *de jure*. As in any community heavily dependent on international trade, the Government was obliged to allow a large number of foreigners to practise their own various religions; but if these were too conspicuous in their devotions, or if they attempted to proselytize, the synods of the Reformed Church pressed for action to be taken against them. Even Catholics could have churches in Amsterdam; but they had to be in warehouses or attics. How precarious was the position of Huguenot refugees in Holland is shown by Jurieu's success at Rotterdam in 1693 in getting Bayle's pension stopped and his right to teach withdrawn.[2]

[1] See Paul Dibon, *Pierre Bayle le Philosophe de Rotterdam*, Paris, 1959, pp. vii seq.

[2] See Delvolvé, op. cit., pp. 216–17. In 1683 Jurieu met Le Clerc in Rotterdam, led him on to express tolerant opinions, and then secretly denounced him to the Vénérable Compagnie at Geneva (see A. Barnes, *Jean Le Clerc*, p. 81).

Arminians, such as Le Clerc and Jaquelot, were particularly vulnerable to accusations of Socinianism. Though the Arminians may genuinely have avoided an Arian christology, rationalism and extreme tolerance were real points of similarity between the two sects, and from the time of Konrad Vorst, Arminius's successor at Leiden, opponents of the Arminians constantly accused them of crypto-socinianism. In some cases there may have been something in such accusations; the Socinians believed that Vorst had written the *Compendiolum Socinianismi*.[1] As early as 1685 Bayle, in a letter to Lenfant, stated that Le Clerc's works were infected with Socinianism, and claimed that the Arminians were generally known as 'the sewer of all the atheists, deists and Socinians of Europe'.[2]

Near the end of his life, Bayle wrote to Shaftesbury:[3]

I pass my time refuting Mr Le Clerc & Mr Jaquelot, whom I find constantly guilty of bad faith.

Bayle not only saw their dishonesty, but also was fully aware of the cause of it, namely, the very real dangers they incurred, as refugee pastors in Holland, from accusations of Socinianism and Origenism. Bayle himself, by keeping to his strict Calvinist and fideist position, which was in itself dishonest, was able to express his opinions on theodicy and hell completely, if backhandedly. I am not of course using the term 'dishonest' to convey my moral judgment on these writers—they could not have published at all had they been entirely honest—but to refer to the evasions and obscurities in their works which are due to this necessary caution.

Le Clerc, in his Origenist reply to Bayle's Manichaean objections, was careful to disavow any belief in Origen's heresies:[4]

[1] V. supra, p. 83, n. 3.
[2] Bayle, *Oeuvres Div.*, T. IV, p. 619: 'l'égout de tous les Athées, Déistes & Sociniens de l'Europe.'
[3] Ibid., p. 884: 'je m'amuse à réfuter Mr Le Clerc & Mr Jaquelot, que je trouve perpétuellement coupables de mauvaise foi.'
[4] Theodore Parrhase (i.e. Le Clerc), *Parrhasiana ou Pensées diverses . . . Avec la Défense de divers Ouvrages de Mr. L. C.*, T. I, Amsterdam, 1699, pp. 303-4: 'Je déclare que je ne veux ni approuver, ni défendre tout ce qu'Origene a dit, ni tout ce que je vai faire dire à un de ses disciples. Je ne m'interesse nullement dans sa réputation, ni dans ses dogmes, & je n'empêche pas qu'on n'en pense ce qu'on voudra. Il ne s'agit pas ici de satisfaire personne là dessus, mais seulement de fermer la bouche aux Manichéens, en faisant parler un Origeniste.'

I declare that I wish neither to approve nor defend all that
Origen has said, nor all that I am going to put into the mouth
of one of his disciples. I have no concern whatever with his
reputation or his dogmas, and I do not prevent anyone thinking
what he likes about them. Here it is a question, not of satisfying
anyone on this point, but merely of shutting the mouths of the
Manichaeans by making an Origenist speak.

Bayle began his refutation of Le Clerc by accepting this
disavowal. If Bayle could put forward Manichaean arguments,
while remaining a good Calvinist, why should not Le Clerc
answer them with Origenist arguments, while remaining a firm
believer in eternal torment?[1] But the two cases are not really
parallel. Bayle was trying not to defend, but to destroy a system
of beliefs, and his objections could as well have been put into
the mouth of an atheist; whereas Le Clerc was supposed to be
defending the Christian God, and the fact that he defended
instead an Origenist God, in whom he claimed not to believe,
must mean that he considered the Christian, eternally punishing
God indefensible. Bayle saw this quite clearly, and, while still
apparently accepting Le Clerc's disavowal of Origenism, managed to imply that it was due only to caution:[2]

No one will disapprove of the care he has taken to distinguish
himself from the Origenist; the interests of his fortune demanded this precaution.

Then, with unpleasant relish, he gave a vivid description of

[1] Bayle, *Oeuvres Div.*, T. III, p. 864.
[2] Bayle, ibid., p. 999: 'On ne condamnera pas le soin qu'il a pris de se dis-
tinguer de l'Origéniste; les intérêts de sa fortune demandoient cette précaution;
car il n'y a point de dogme qui le pût commettre plus dangereusement avec les
Ministres des Eglises Flamandes & Wallonnes, dont il sait bien qu'il est regardé
de mauvais oeil depuis longtems, que de n'exclure personne du bonheur du
Paradis. Le dogme de l'éternité des peines leur paroît trop précieux, & trop
important pour soufrir qu'on y donne atteinte. Ils intéresseroient à cela les
Souverains & les peuples, & leur représenteroient en chaire avec tout le feu de
l'éloquence, que la Religion est le plus ferme fondement des Societez, principale-
ment à cause qu'elle refrène le vice par la crainte de la Damnation éternelle. Ils
représenteroient la même chose aux Etats de chaque Province par des députations
Synodales. La conclusion de leurs sermons, & de leurs harangues, & de leurs
mémoriaux seroit celle-ci: "Tout Origéniste est coupable de leze-Majesté
divine, & de leze-Majesté humaine; il ouvre la porte à tous les crimes; il encourage tous les scélérats"; car il leur aprend à croire que de toute éternité ils
sont destinez de Dieu au bonheur du Paradis'

Le Clerc's fate if he were known to hold the doctrine of universal salvation:

> There is no dogma that could compromise him more dangerously with the Ministers of the Flemish and Walloon Churches, to which, as he well knows, he has been suspect for a long time, than to exclude no one from the bliss of paradise. The dogma of eternal torment seems to them too precious and too important to allow it to be attacked.

These ministers would preach from the pulpit, 'with all the fire of eloquence',

> that religion is the firmest foundation of societies, principally because it restrains vice by the fear of eternal damnation.

They would send synodal deputations to the States of each Province, bearing the message:

> Every Origenist is guilty of lese-majesty against God, and of lese-majesty against humanity; he opens the door to all crimes; he encourages all criminals; for he teaches them to believe that from all eternity they are destined by God to the bliss of paradise.

Bayle may well have believed that this is what would happen to an Origenist in Holland, and he may well have been right. What he certainly did not believe was that disbelief in eternal torment would have a bad effect on morals, or indeed have any predictable effect at all. As I have already mentioned, he tried to demonstrate historically in the *Pensées sur la Comète*, and in several articles of the *Dictionnaire*, that there is no necessary correlation between piety and good moral conduct or, conversely, between atheism and bad moral conduct.[1] When later defending these works, he quoted Jurieu on the Socinian doctrine of the annihilation of the wicked:[2]

---

[1] Cf. supra, pp. 40–1, and Bayle, *Oeuvres Div.*, T. III, pp. 1057 seq. But, when wishing to frighten Le Clerc, Bayle was capable of saying that Le Clerc's only supporters would be 'cette espece de débauchez & de scélérats à qui la crainte des Enfers fait souffrir des inquiétudes' (Bayle, *Oeuvres Div.*, T. IV, p. 31).

[2] Bayle, *Oeuvres Div.*, T. III, p. 773; Jurieu, *Tableau du Socinianisme*, pp. 78, 82: 'On peut dire avec certitude que si la mortalité des ames étoit passé en dogme il n'y auroit plus aucune espece de sûreté dans le monde. Il n'y a point de crime qui ne s'y commît par ceux qui croiroient pouvoir dérober la connoissance de leurs actions à la justice humaine. Ainsi clairement c'est ouvrir la porte à tous les

It can be said with certainty that if the mortality and annihilation of souls became a dogma, there would no longer be any kind of security in the world. There would be no crime that would not be committed by those who believed that they could conceal their actions from human justice. Thus to say that souls are mortal and will be annihilated is clearly to open the door to every kind of disorder.

Jurieu had then, with typical imprudence, raised the objection: why, if this is so, are the Socinians not all criminals? why are there atheists who are 'honnêtes gens'? why were there virtuous pagans? The only answer he could find was:

The devil has various ways of leading men astray, and when he has hold of them in one place, it matters little to him if they escape him in another.

That is to say, as Bayle explains,

It matters little to the devil that those whom he holds by the dogma of the mortality of the soul escape him by good conduct.

Bayle went on to point out that this answer still leaves the objection standing, and added, with malicious complacency:[1]

Moreover, you should know that Mr Bayle attributes to the wisdom of divine Providence what Mr Jurieu attributes to the idleness of the devil.

This refers to the *Eclaircissement sur les Athées* at the end of Bayle's dictionary. Here he put forward the ingenious theory that Divine Providence, in order to preserve human society, has so arranged things that atheists, lacking the deterrent of hell, are naturally virtuous, while the naturally vicious are believers and are thus kept within bounds by the fear of future punishment.[2] Even the most naïf modern scholar must find it difficult here to take Bayle seriously.

[1] Bayle, *Oeuvres Div.*, T. III, p. 773: 'Outre cela vous devez savoir que Mr Bayle attribue à la sagesse de la Providence divine ce que Mr Jurieu attribue à paresse du Démon.'

[2] Bayle, *Dict. hist. & crit.*, ed. cit., T. IV, p. 619.

desordres que de dire que les ames sont mortelles & seront anéanties.' 'Le demon a diverses voyes pour seduire les hommes, & quand il les tient par un endroit, il lui importe peu qu'ils lui échappent par l'autre.' 'Il importe peu au démon que ceux qu'il tient par le dogme de la mortalité de l'ame lui échapent par les bonnes mœurs.'

Bayle also prophesied that the wretched Le Clerc would get into trouble with his own party through having revealed that Arminians were allowed to disbelieve in eternal torment, since[1]

> there would be nothing more fitted to lay that party open to the odious invectives of its enemies than if it was known that its ministers, acting in good faith, could promise paradise to all impenitent sinners.

But the Arminians only tolerate Le Clerc in the same way that they tolerate Socinians, that is, they think them to be in error, but not damnable error, and hope to convert them. Bayle then quotes from Chapter XX of the *Confessio Remonstrantium* (1621, by Episcopius):[2]

> God will then not only irrevocably deprive the wicked and unbelievers of immortal glory, but will also inflict the tortures of hell and eternal torments on them (cruciatus infernales atque aeterna supplicia infliget).

Le Clerc is still too weak in faith ('trop infirme dans la foi') to digest this strong meat.

If we try to look through this mist of secrecy and dishonesty, the purely destructive intentions of Bayle stand out clearly enough, but the aims and beliefs of Le Clerc remain very shadowy. What could be the point of publishing a defence of universal salvation accompanied by a disavowal of it? Did he really believe in this, or did he believe in the mitigated hell he later substituted for it, in which after a period of sensible torments, the wicked are eternally in the 'condition tolérable' of suffering only the *poena damni*?[3]

One reason why it is difficult to answer these questions is that Le Clerc was a follower of Erasmus. All the Arminians were in an Erasmian tradition, but Le Clerc had a closer, more direct relation to Erasmus through his monumental edition of his

---

[1] Bayle, *Oeuvres Div.*, T. III, p. 999: 'il n'y auroit rien de plus propre à exposer ce parti-là aux invectives odieuses de ses ennemis, que si l'on savoit que ses Ministres agissant de bonne foi, pourroient promettre le Paradis à tous les impénitens.'

[2] Ibid., p. 1008; Episcopius, *Opera Theologica*, Paris Altera, 1665, p. 90; cf. infra, p. 193.

[3] Le Clerc, *Bibliothèque Choisie*, IX, 143-4, quoted by Bayle, *Oeuvres Div.*, T. III, pp. 1001-2.

works.[1] Now Erasmus is the fountainhead of the systematic, deliberate vagueness of liberal Protestant theology.[2] A policy of vagueness is the only possible one, if one wishes to preserve the unity of an institution which exists only by virtue of its members holding the same beliefs, and which in fact contains members holding various and incompatible beliefs. The policy begins by affirming the 'fundamental points' which all members do in fact accept, and saying nothing or something inconclusive about all other beliefs. As these points themselves become subject to dispute, the silence or vagueness has to be extended to cover them too. One such point, by Le Clerc's time, was the doctrine of eternal torment, which was already being discussed and mitigated at the Remonstrants' College at Amsterdam in the time of Episcopius, its founder.[3] It is not therefore surprising that Le Clerc should be vague and evasive about it, or that in his translation of the New Testament 'avec des Remarques' he should make no comment on Matthew XXV.[4] Since he did introduce universal salvation into the Manichaean debate, one can only suppose that he considered Bayle's objections valid against any theology including eternal torment, that they seemed to him dangerous, that he therefore decided to take the risk of publicly defending Origenism, and that he hoped by his disavowal to avoid committing himself, or the Arminians in general. Of these suppositions only the last is a little difficult to accept. Le Clerc must have been very much less shrewd than his model, Erasmus, if he could imagine for a moment that Bayle would let him get away with such a feeble subterfuge.

Le Clerc's Origenism is not a complete revival of Origenist eschatology, such as Rust's, but merely the doctrine of universal salvation after an unspecified period of gradated torments. He deals with the scriptural problem not by the usual claim that αἰώνιος need not mean everlasting, but by the much more dangerous argument, employed by Tillotson, that God's threats to the wicked may not be fulfilled.[5] As Bayle pointed

[1] 1703–6, 10 Vols,; cf. A. Barnes, *Jean Le Clerc*, p. 149.
[2] Cf. W. W. Bartley. *The Retreat to Commitment*, New York, 1962, pp. 184, seq.
[3] Episcopius, *Opera Theologica*, 1650, T. I, pp. 67 seq.
[4] *Le Noureau Testament . . . traduit . . . Avev des Remarques . . . par Jean Le Clerc*, Amsterdam, 1703, T. II, p. 111.
[5] Le Clerc, *Parrhasiana*, T. I, p. 312.

out, this argument would deprive the Arminians of one of their favourite weapons against the Calvinist God: that He is deceitful in offering salvation to men He has already decided to damn, since Le Clerc represents God as equally deceitful in[1]

> pronouncing the decree of eternal damnation to people whom He will make eternally happy.

In using universal salvation for theodicy, Le Clerc's main argument is that the physical and moral evils of this world, and of the next, if hell is not eternal, are of so short a duration, compared with the eternity of bliss which all will eventually enjoy, that they do not detract from the mercy and goodness of God. Even if hell lasts for thousands of years, this is still an infinitely short time compared with eternity. Le Clerc uses the analogy of a clockmaker who, if he had made a clock which kept perfect time for a year, except for a few seconds at the start, would rightly consider himself a fine workman.[2] Bayle has little difficulty in demolishing this argument. The analogy with the inevitable imperfection of human workmanship is evidently false—'the accuracy of a supremely perfect Workman excludes absolutely all exceptions'.[3] Nor is the goodness of God vindicated by supposing that He will eventually put an end to all misery; this is only

> the goodness of a father who, because he knew how to mend broken limbs, allowed his children to have falls that broke their arms and legs.

And one cannot explain away the reality of human suffering by contrasting it with an eternity of bliss; Le Clerc must not imagine[4]

> that the torments of hell would be a little thing if they lasted

[1] Bayle, *Oeuvres Div.*, T. III, p. 999: 'prononçant l'arrêt de la damnation éternelle à des gens qu'il rendra éternellement heureux.'

[2] Le Clerc, *Parrhasiana*, T. I., pp. 306–12.

[3] Bayle, *Dict. hist. & crit.*, art. Origène, rem. (E), ed. cit., p. 543: 'la justesse d'un Ouvrier souverainement parfait exclut absolument toutes exceptions.'

[4] Bayle, *Oeuvres Div.*, T. III, pp. 867, 869: 'la bonté d'un père qui parce qu'il sauroit racommoder les membres cassez, permettroit à ses enfans de faire des chûtes qui leur casseroient les bras & les jambes.' 'Que les tourmens de l'enfer soient peu de chose sous prétexte qu'ils ne durent peut-être que 50 ou 60 ans. Ce terme n'est rien en comparaison de l'éternité, mais il est d'une longueur monstrueuse par raport à la sensibilité humaine.'

only 50 or 60 years. This length of time is nothing in comparison with eternity, but it is monstrously long relatively to human sensitivity.

Le Clerc's theodicy rested on two basic assumptions: one was universal salvation, the other was absolute free will, the *libertas indifferentiae*. By means of the latter he hoped to exonerate God from even the few seconds of bad time-keeping—it was the clock's own fault. As I have already tried to show, this kind of free will is in itself a nonsensical concept, and in any case not of great use to theodicy;[1] but I wish to return to it here, since it is one of Bayle's main themes and his attacks on it illuminate his views and intentions. Theologians who held the doctrine of absolute free will believed, as we have seen, that this gave them the right to accuse predestinationists of worshipping a cruel, vindictive, capricious and deceitful tyrant, or, in other words, the Devil. A usual defence against such accusations was to show that the God who allowed free will was, in the last analysis, equally cruel, that He was not truly omnipotent, and that He was plainly not the God of the New Testament.

It is evident that this method of defence is dangerous. Jurieu, who was insensitive to theological dangers, adopted it in his *Jugement sur les méthodes rigides & relâchées d'expliquer la Providence & la Grace*. In this work he made a remarkably frank admission of the absolute impossibility of reconciling God's hatred of sin with His permission of it, and of exculpating Him from the appalling consequences of allowing it. But he also showed that all 'lax systems' finally hit up against the same impossibility, which Calvinism, like St Paul in Romans IX, faced honestly:[2]

> If God has an infinite hatred of sin, why, having forseen it, has He not prevented it? . . . Why has He made men be born who, He well knew, were to damn themselves? . . . Why does He not stop the majority of men in those courses which lead to hell? He could have saved a million people, and let only one be lost.

---

[1] V. supra, pp. 45 seq.

[2] Jurieu, *Jugement sur les methodes*, Rotterdam, 1688, p. 64: 'Si Dieu hait le péché infiniment, pourquoi le prévoiant ne l'a-t-il pas empêché? . . . Pourquoi a-t-il fait naître des hommes qu'il savoit bien se devoir damner? . . . Pourquoi n'arrête-t-il pas la plus part des hommes dans ces courses qui les mènent à l'enfer? Il auroit pu sauver un million de personnes, & n'en laisser perdre qu'une. Au contraire il n'en sauve qu'un cent, & en laisse perdre un million.'

On the contrary, He saves only a hundred, and lets a million be lost.

Bayle is able to quote such passages from his imprudent enemy with full approval—'you can be quite sure that on this point he and Mr Bayle are in perfect agreement'[1]—and with this support continue to demonstrate at great length that all actual and possible Christian Gods are morally repulsive. This he did with the public intention of inducing everyone to 'sacrifice the feeble light of their reason to the authority of religion',[2] and mostly by means of disquieting little stories, such as the notorious comparison of the Socinian God to a mother who takes her pure and free but weak-willed daughter to a ball, leaves her alone in a little room with a 'jeune galant', watches her, through a window, being seduced, and forbears to interfere. This very modern mother must, says Bayle, be held responsible for the loss of her daughter's virginity, as responsible as a mother who deliberately planned the seduction with the young man.[3]

We have already seen Sterry making the same point in another little story,[4] namely, that someone who allows a disaster to occur which he has foreseen and could have prevented is as morally bad as someone who directly causes the disaster. But Sterry believed in universal salvation, so that the disaster (the sin and misery of this world, followed by the purgatorial torment of the reprobate) would end in infinite bliss for everyone. He was able therefore to allow his God to be directly responsible for the disaster and still claim that, at least, His final aim was a perfect and infinite good, though of course the intervening evil remains difficult to explain. In terms of Bayle's analogy, the daughter is going eventually to be happily married, so that it does not matter much whether her mother was excessively negligent or whether she was a procuress. But if the daughter is going, in consequence of her seduction, to lead a miserable life as an unsuccessful prostitute, then Bayle's thesis is more doubtful; for the procuress has engineered a situation which might

---

[1] Bayle, *Oeuvres Div.*, T. III, pp. 775–6: 'vous pouvez donc être très-assuré que sur cet article-là lui & Mr Bayle sont parfaitement d'accord.'

[2] Ibid.: 'sacrifier leurs foibles lumières à l'autorité de la religion.'

[3] Bayle, *Dict. hist. & crit.*, art. Pauliciens, rem, (F), ed. cit., p. 628.

[4] V. supra, pp. 47–8.

not otherwise have occurred, and must bear the prime responsibility for all its consequences, whereas the negligent mother at least shares her responsibility with two other agents, her daughter and the young man, who have acted independently of her influence. In unmetaphorical terms, the Calvinist God, given eternal torment, appears to be morally more disgusting than other Christian Gods; and, when indiscreetly unveiled by worshippers like Jurieu, He certainly did appear so to many people. Saurin, himself a Calvinist, though a moderate and rationalistic one, wrote:[1]

> A God, such as Mr Jurieu represents Him, if there could be such a God, would only be worshipped in the same way that the Japanese worship the Devil.

and Bayle tells how common such judgments were:[2]

> I dare not write to you the things I could find in innumerable works published against the hypothesis of absolute predestination. I do not wish to blacken my paper with these horrors, and I scarcely have the courage to tell you in general that in these books it is asserted that there is nothing more monstrous, or more abominable, than a God such as this system represents Him.

But, as Bayle copiously showed, the Calvinist God does only *appear* more abominable than the others. Bayle's own analogy of the mother and daughter is not exact even for a Socinian God. The negligent mother cannot share her responsibility with the other two agents, because she created them and also the little room at the ball. Even though the Socinian God gave man absolute free will and had no certain foreknowledge of his abuse of it, He must have foreseen the possibility of this abuse; He took a risk that need not have been taken, and plainly must bear the main responsibility for the unfortunate consequences

---

[1] Saurin, *Examen*, p. 347: 'Un Dieu tel que Mr Jurieu le représente, si un tel Dieu pouvoit être, ne seroit adoré que de la même maniere que les Japonnois adorent le Diable.'

[2] Bayle, *Oeuvres Div.*, T. III, p. 807: 'Je n'oserois vous écrire ce qu'une infinité d'ouvrages publiez contre l'hypothese de la Prédestination absolue me pourroient fournir. Je ne veux pas que mon papier porte la charge de ces horreurs, & à peine ai-je le courage de vous dire en général que l'on assure dans ces livres, qu'il n'y a rien de plus monstrueux, ni de plus digne d'abomination qu'un Dieu tel que ce systême le représente.'

which in fact occurred. Here again the question of hell is cardinal. The Socinians might have had a leg to stand on, if the disaster their God risked were to be succeeded by an infinite good, as postulated by believers in universal salvation. But even those Socinians who disbelieved in eternal punishment suggested nothing more cheering than the annihilation of the wicked. The discord stops, but is not resolved; God is still responsible for taking the risk, which turned out badly, of creating millions of creatures who would lead wicked and miserable lives and then be thrown away.

With Arminians, such as Jaquelot, who believed in some kind of eternal hell, and who tried to justify God by means of absolute free will, but without denying His omniscience, Bayle has a still easier task in showing that their God is no better than the Calvinists', that they reach the same conclusions 'in a slightly more roundabout way'.[1] Once again it is hell that is, as Bayle says, 'the chief stumbling-block':[2]

If the infinitely perfect Being had known that, were He to give existence to free creatures, they would have to be punished eternally because of their sins, He would have preferred to leave them in nothingness, or not to allow them to abuse their free will, rather than be obliged to inflict on them punishments which will never end. Common sense tells us that it is better to have no children at all than to have children who laugh at our instructions and orders, and who bring us nothing but distress and dishonour.

And elsewhere he gives a black picture of Jaquelot's God: in Jaquelot's mitigated hell, where the damned are tormented only by regret and envy, there will be[3]

[1] Bayle, *Oeuvres Div.*, T. III, p. 807: 'par un peu plus de détours'.
[2] Ibid., p. 829: 'Si l'Etre infiniment parfait avoit su qu'en cas qu'il donnât l'existence à des Créatures libres, il les faudroit punir éternellement à cause de leurs péchés, il eût mieux aimé les laisser dans le Néant, ou ne leur permettre pas d'abuser de leur franc arbitre, que de se voir obligé de leur infliger des peines qui ne finiront jamais. Le sens commun dicte qu'il vaut mieux n'avoir point d'enfans que d'en avoir qui se moquent de nos instructions & de nos ordres, & qui ne font que nous chagriner & que nous déshonnorer.'
[3] Bayle, *Oeuvres Div.*, T. IV, p. 100: 'un nombre presque infini d'hommes plongez dans une morne mélancolie, & dans une noire haine de leur Créateur . . . Dieu contemplera perpétuellement & éternellement & avec plaisir le triste état de ces malheureux & méchans, & en tirera de la gloire.'

a nearly infinite number of men sunk in gloomy melancholy and black hatred of their Creator . . . God will contemplate perpetually and eternally and with pleasure the sad state of these wretched and wicked people, and will gain glory thereby.

All these debates about the relative moral turpitude of the various Christian Gods turn on the wish to assert or deny a distinction between God's being the author of sin (that is, positively willing and directly causing it) and God's merely permitting it. All sects were bound to admit God's permission of sin, since they all agreed that in fact all men sin and most of them to the point of damnation. All sects, including the Calvinists and Jansenists, refused to admit that their system did make God the author of sin; but, by insisting on absolute predestination, Calvinists and Jansenists made this refusal patently illogical. It was therefore in their interest to deny the distinction between authorship and permission, as we have just seen Jurieu and Bayle doing. They did, I think, succeed in proving that this distinction is not valid when applied to an omnipotent God, and that, even in human situations, the distinction is at the most only one of a slight degree of guilt. Their denials that God is the author of sin are a purely verbal safeguard against accusations of blasphemy; and Bayle, when refuting Arminians, such as Jaquelot, argues in favour of frankly admitting that God positively wills sin, as Luther had done when debating with Erasmus about the heart of Pharaoh ('Stat verbum Dei: Indurabo cor Pharaonis').[1] But there can be no doubt that Bayle, though he can cite Luther, Bèze and even Jurieu in his support,[2] argues for this admission, not to justify strict Calvinism, but to show that all possible Christian Gods are morally disgusting.

In one of the Manichaean articles in his *Dictionnaire*, that on Paulicians, Bayle quotes a passage from Jurieu's *Apologie pour les Réformateurs* (1683) where, in answer to Maimbourg's assertion that the immorality of the Calvinist God leads to atheism, Jurieu claims that, even if it were true that Calvinism 'shows us a cruel, unjust God punishing and chastising innocent

---

[1] Bayle, ibid., T. III, p. 807–8; cf. supra, p. 142, n. 2.
[2] Bayle, ibid., pp. 841–5.

creatures with eternal torments', this doctrine would not lead to atheism because[1]

> it raises the Divine to the highest degree of greatness and superiority that can be conceived. For it abases the creature before the Creator to such a point, that in this system the Creator is bound by no sort of law with regard to the creature, but can do with it as seems good to Him, and make it serve His glory in any way He pleases, without its having the right to gainsay Him.

Bayle is very shocked at this 'monstrous doctrine'. He then runs through some of the complicated and often absurd devices by which theologians have tried to establish a freedom of will that would make man alone responsible for his sins, and asks:

> Why so many suppositions? What has been the measure, what has been the rule of all these goings-on?

This is the answer:[2]

> It is the wish to exculpate God; for it has been clearly understood that all religion is here at stake, and that, as soon as one dared to teach that God is the author of sin, one would necessarily lead men to atheism.

Bayle then, when in refuting 'lax systems', such as Jaquelot's, he argued in favour of admitting God to be the author of sin, knew what he was doing. Even in this same article he had already asserted that, though a Calvinist or a Jansenist might be sincere in his denial that his system made God the author of sin,[3]

---

[1] Jurieu, *Histoire du Calvinisme . . . Ou Apologie pour les Reformateurs,* Rotterdam, 1683, T. I, p. 524: 'elle pose la divinité dans le plus haut degré de grandeur & d'élévation où elle peut estre conceue. Car elle anéantit tellement la créature devant le Créateur, que le Créateur dans ce systeme n'est lié d'aucune espece de loix à l'esgard de la créature, mais il en peut disposer comme bon luy semble, & la peut faire servir à sa gloire par telle voye qu'il luy plaist, sans qu'elle soit en droit de le contredire.'

[2] Bayle, *Dict. Hist. & crit.,* art. Pauliciens, rem. (I), ed. cit., p. 632: 'Pourquoi tant de supositions? Quelle a été la mesure, quelle a été la regle, de tant de démarches?' 'C'est l'envie de disculper Dieu; c'est qu'on a compris clairement qu'il y va de toute la Religion, & que dès qu'on oseroit enseigner qu'il est l'auteur du péché, on conduiroit nécessairement les hommes à l'Athéisme.'

[3] Ibid., rem. (F), p. 628: 's'il prend la peine de définir exactement ce qu'il faudroit que Dieu eût fait, afin d'être l'auteur du péché d'Adam, il trouvera que selon son Dogme Dieu a fait tout ce qu'il faloit faire pour cela.'

if he takes the trouble to define exactly what God would have had to do in order to be the author of Adam's sin, he will find that, according to his dogma, God has done all that needed to be done for that.

He also explains why 'all religion is here at stake': if, by making God the author of sin, you ascribe to Him the qualities[1]

of a lawgiver who forbids man to commit crime, and who nevertheless pushes man into crime, and then punishes Him for it eternally, you make Him into a nature in which one could have no trust, a deceiving, cunning, unjust, cruel nature; He is no longer an object of religion; what would be the point of calling on Him and trying to be good? This is therefore the way to atheism.

[1] Ibid., rem. (I), p. 633: 'd'un Législateur qui défend le crime à l'homme, & qui néanmoins pousse l'homme dans le crime, & puis l'en punit éternellement, vous en faites une nature en qui l'on me sauroit prendre nulle confiance, une nature trompeuse, maligne, injuste, cruelle: ce n'est plus un objet de Religion; de quoi serviroit de l'invoquer, & tâcher d'être sage? C'est donc la voie de l'Athéïsme.'

Chapter XII

THEODICY
Malebranche and Leibniz

ONE way of escape from the blasphemous conclusion to which Bayle tried to force all Christians is to save the goodness of God at the expense of His omnipotence—to suppose that there are some insurmountable obstacles to His goodness. If Manichaean dualism is to be avoided, these limitations must be internal. One such limitation has already been mentioned: that which is caused by a conflict of attributes, namely mercy and justice.

An internal conflict of a different kind is the basis of Malebranche's theodicy, expounded mainly in his *Traité de la Nature et de la Grâce* (1680). Malebranche starts from the same assumption, that God's attributes must be manifest in all His acts, but the conflict arises not between attributes but between means and ends. God wishes to create a universe that manifests as far as possible His own perfection, but the means of creating and governing it must be in accordance with His wisdom. This somewhat tyrannical attribute, which is personified in the second person of the Trinity, demands that these means shall be as simple as possible. Since God cares more about these means than the end, He can only create and maintain the universe by 'volontés générales', i.e. by a few universal, invariable laws, even if this results in a highly defective creation. Why God should care more about the perfection of the means than that of the ends, unlike anyone else making anything, is not explained. But if this is granted, the theory works well enough as an explanation of the physical ills of the universe. Rain, for example, falls both on fields, where it is needed, and on roads and sea, where it is not, and it may even cause floods. This is because rainfall is determined by physical laws instituted by God, which He must not, owing to the dictates of His wisdom, constantly interrupt with miracles. The general will of the laws, in this instance, is to provide rain for crops in fields so that men may have food; where this purpose is frustrated by floods or drought, the resultant evil is not willed by God, but is merely a consequence of His necessarily producing everything according to simple, unchanging laws, dictated by His wisdom.[1]

As an explanation of moral evil, that is, of God's permission of sin and the consequent damnation of most of mankind, the theory is more complicated and less convincing. Malebranche compares the incidence of rainfall to that of grace, which is often given to those who are too hardened to profit by it or who do not persevere to salvation, and is sometimes apparently refused to those whom it might save. 'It droppeth as the gentle rain from heaven Upon the earth beneath', and, since many of the places are not well-cultivated fields and it may happen to miss some fertile places, this rain of grace produces only a small crop of saved, little wheat and many tares. But, in the order of grace, the occasional (second) cause, corresponding to natural laws in the physical world, is far from being absolutely simple and regular in its action. This cause is the soul of Christ, that is, Christ in His human nature, joined to the Word or wisdom. In this capacity Christ's knowledge has two limitations: first, though through the Word He knows ideally all possible objects, He does not know what actually exists at any moment; secondly, as man, His soul is finite and cannot therefore pay attention to everything at once. These two limitations account for his sometimes giving insufficient grace to save a potentially redeemable man, or giving grace to one who will not make

[1] Malebranche, *Oeuvres Complètes*, T. V, *Traité de la Nature et de la Grâce*, ed. G. Dreyfus, Paris, 1958, pp. 27–37. Henry More had already used the rain analogy (*Divine Dialogues*, Vol. I, p. 187).

proper use of it, or failing to give any grace at all to large numbers of men.[1]

Even if one accepts this extraordinary theory that the damnation of the majority of mankind is due to Christ's all too human failings—'we would all be saved, if we had no Saviour', as Bossuet said[2]—the problem of God's permission of sin is still not solved. God created man capable of sin, foresaw that he would sin, and instituted the curious system whereby Christ, though doing His best, is able to save only a small minority of men. Even if one allows that this system is the simplest possible, dictated by divine wisdom, there still remains the question: why did God create at all? For Malebranche is careful to assert that He was free not to do so. The answer to this question is the paradox of the *felix culpa*, that is, the theory that the sin of Adam was a good thing because it eventually produced the Incarnation and Redemption.[3]

God, according to Malebranche, can love only Himself and can therefore act only with the ultimate purpose of increasing His glory. Everything created is necessarily infinitely inferior to Him and thus even the most perfect of created universes would not glorify Him. The only way in which the created universe can glorify God is by God Himself joining Himself to it, in the person of the Word incarnate, and thus raising it, or part of it, above the status of a created, imperfect thing. Thus the sole purpose of the creation was the Incarnation and the formation of the Church, whose members also partake of the divinity of Christ, becoming the body of which He is the head.[4] But why should the Incarnation involve the 'certè necessarium Adae peccatum', all the sin and misery and damnation? That is to say: why could the Word only be made flesh in order to expiate the sins of men?

---

[1] Malebranche, ibid., pp. 49–54, 71 seq. This grace from Christ is one which works on the will by producing pleasure ('Grâce de délectation'). There is also a grace from God, given like sunlight, and unlike rain, to all men; but this consists only of an intellectual illumination, which has no direct effect on the will and cannot therefore, in our fallen state, lead to salvation; we may therefore leave this kind of grace out of account (ibid., pp. 100 seq.).

[2] Quoted in introduction to Malebranche, op. cit., p. xxxiii: 'nous serions tous sauvés, si nous n'avions pas de Sauveur.'

[3] Malebranche, op. cit., pp. 42–3, 70, 182; cf. supra, p. 119.

[4] Ibid., pp. 38 seq.

In the *Traité de la Nature et de la Grâce* Malebranche does not ask or answer this question; or, at the most, he hints at an answer by means of a scriptural metaphor, which is not fully elucidated. Christ is said to be a victim or sacrifice worthy of God, and to be constructing a temple, the living Church, in which He will be both victim and High Priest.[1] The sacrifice is presumably necessary in order to repair the sin-damaged stone with which the temple is built. But why not have prevented the stones being damaged and thus the necessity of the sacrifice? One could still have had the temple and the Chief Priest; for, in the *Entretiens sur la Métaphysique* (1688), Malebranche states that,[2]

> even if man had not sinned, a divine person would not have failed to unite Himself to the universe in order to sanctify it . . .

and in this work he also attempts some answers to the question. The first answer is like one we will meet again in Leibniz:[3]

> God has foreseen and allowed sin . . . this is a certain proof that the universe restored by Jesus Christ is better than the same universe in its original state; otherwise God would never have allowed His work to be corrupted.

As theodicy, this answer simply begs the question. Since the aim of any theodicy is to prove the goodness or justice of God in spite of His having created an apparently defective universe, it is assuming what is to be proved, if one argues that the universe cannot really be defective, or must be the best possible one, *because* we know that a good omnipotent God created it. But later in the *Entretiens* we get a genuine answer, which explains why a repaired universe is better than an undamaged one, and why therefore God permitted sin: it is that the achievement of Christ is greater, and hence God's glory greater, in sanctifying a corrupted universe, in divinizing creatures in a state worse

---

[1] Ibid., pp. 39–40.

[2] Malebranche, *Entretiens sur la Métaphysique*, Rotterdam, 1688, p. 325; also in *Eclaircissements* to the *Traité*, ed. cit., p. 182: 'quoy que l'homme n'eust point péché, une personne divine n'auroit pas laissé de s'unir à l'Univers pour le sanctifier . . .'

[3] Malebranche, *Entretiens*, p. 326: 'Dieu a prévu & permis le péché . . . c'est une preuve certaine que l'univers réparé par Jesus-Christ vaut mieux que le même univers dans sa premiere construction: autrement Dieu n'auroit jamais laissé corrompre son ouvrage.'

than non-existence, i.e. sin, than in sanctifying an uncorrupted universe by joining Himself to it. Christ, by recreating good creatures from a state worse than nothingness, has accomplished something more glorious than the original *creatio ex nihilo*.[1] This argument, though it has a long and respectable history, seems dangerous because, if the glory of Christ's redemption increases in proportion to the evil of the universe redeemed, it follows that God should have created, not the best of all possible worlds, but the worst, or one that was certain to become so. This may be what Malebranche thought. He believed that those animals, such as lice and snakes, which molest or destroy man, were created with a view to punishing man's future sins.[2] This certainly suggests a universe which is designed to reach a maximum of physical and moral evil, of sin and the misery to punish it, at which point Christ, with thus the maximum of glory, redeems a small minority of these worse than non-existent creatures.

Even if we concede the crudely anthropomorphic moral scale by which goodness is measured according to the evil overcome, why so many damned and so few redeemed? and will not the eternal glory of Christ be diminished by the eternal sin and misery of all those who were lost owing to His ignorance or inadvertence as a man? Malebranche gives rather vague answers to these obvious questions. As for the first: God does wish to save all men, but[3]

> His wisdom, or the justice He owes to Himself, makes Him, so to speak, powerless.

His wisdom, as we know, demands the use of simple, regular second causes, in this case, Christ as a man, who was unable to distribute sufficient grace to save everyone; but what about His justice? Here, I think, is the reason why Malebranche thought neither question worth a full answer. Justice is the supreme moral attribute of his God, indeed the only one, in

---

[1] Malebranche, *Entretiens*, p. 592; Malebranche also suggested that man's total corruption serves to eliminate his pride; but this is irrelevant to theodicy. If God had prevented man sinning, he would not have been liable to pride.

[2] Ibid., p. 441.

[3] Malebranche, *Réponse à la Dissertation de Mr. Arnauld*, quoted by Sinsart, *Defense*, p. 162: 'sa sagesse, ou la justice qu'il se doit à lui-même, le rend, pour ainsi dire, impuissant.' Cf. *Traité*, ed. cit., p. 47.

that the others are wholly subordinated to it or derive from it. God[1]

> is neither clement, nor merciful, nor good, according to vulgar notions, since He is just both essentially, and by the natural and necessary love He bears to His divine perfections.

These other attributes, 'as they are ordinarily conceived, are unworthy of the infinitely perfect Being'. God's justice consists in evaluating every being according to its natural perfection or imperfection, and in punishing or rewarding any being which, respectively, falls below or rises above its place in the hierarchy;[2]

> A man whose affections are disordered through bad use of his freedom is brought back into the Order of justice which God owes to His divine perfections, if this sinner is miserable in proportion to his disorders.

Thus God can only be good within the limits of His justice; He is infinitely good to the good,[3]

> but He is just and, if one may say so, infinitely wicked to the wicked.

This justice is, then, retributive purely and simply and 'according to vulgar notions'. Malebranche nowhere discusses the validity of such justice, nor does he explain why the punishment or reward restores the creature to its place in the natural order. If retributive justice is God's sole moral attribute, it can be manifested just as well by punishing as by rewarding, since it does not conflict with any opposing attribute, such as mercy, and it must therefore be a matter of indifference to Him, and to Malebranche, whether there are far more damned than saved, or not. Once the many wicked are suffering in proportion to their sins, and the few blessèd happy in proportion to the merits of Christ, everying is in 'l'Ordre immuable' again, and that is all that matters.

Leibniz also believed in vindictive justice, and he does once

[1] Malebranche, *Entretiens*, p. 308: 'n'est ni clement, ni misericordieux, ni bon selon les idées vulgaires, puis qu'il est juste essentiellement, & par l'amour naturel & necessaire qu'il porte à ses divines perfections.' Cf. ibid., p. 304.

[2] Ibid., p. 307: 'Un homme dont le coeur est déréglé par le mauvais usage de sa liberté, rentre dans l'Ordre de la justice que Dieu doit à ses divines perfections, si ce pécheur est malheureux à proportion de ses désordres.'

[3] Malebranche, *Entretien I. sur la mort*, quoted by Sinsart, *Defense*, p. 154: 'mais il est juste, & s'il est permis de le dire, infiniment méchant aux méchans.'

in the *Théodicée* (1710) give a brief defence of it: vindictive justice[1]

is founded only on the appropriateness which requires a certain satisfaction for the expiation of a bad action . . . a relationship of appropriateness, which satisfies not only the injured party, but also the Wise Men who see it, in the same way that a piece of beautiful music or good architecture satisfies a well-made mind.

This somewhat obscure statement contains, I think, two distinct arguments. First there is an argument from an analogy with aesthetic pleasure, as throughout the *Théodicée*: the infliction of just vindictive punishment pleases persons of good taste because it exhibits the same symmetry or right proportions as good music or architecture, namely a proportion between the harm done by the criminal and the harm suffered by him as punishment. This proportion is not necessarily one of exact symmetry, as in the *lex talionis*, since the relative social status of the parties, or other considerations, may make an unequally proportionate punishment more proper, as in the case where God is the injured party. This analogical argument goes back to Aristotle, who uses mathematical proportions in explaining corrective justice.[2] Here one origin of vindictive justice can be seen. Aristotle is plainly treating all crimes on principles strictly applicable only to crimes or transactions involving property or money, as he openly admits. In this latter class of crimes exactly proportional vindictive justice needs no defence, because, if the punishment is a fine of the same value as the property misappropriated or greater, the fine can be given as compensation to the party who has been robbed, and thus the bad consequences of the crime are really annulled. By calling any injury suffered 'loss' and any injury inflicted 'gain' Aristotle can apply the same rules to crimes for which no exact compensation is possible, i.e. all crimes not involving property. If a man has been injured by a blow, his

---

[1] Leibniz, *Théodicée*, ed. cit., Pt. I, p. 123: 'n'est fondée que dans la convenance qui demande une certaine satisfaction pour l'expiation d'une mauvaise action . . . un rapport de convenance, qui contente non seulement l'offensé, mais encore les Sages qui la voient; comme une belle musique ou bien une bonne architecture contente les esprits bien faits.'
[2] Aristotle, *Nicomachean Ethics*, Bk. V, c. ii–iv.

'loss' is thus considered to be made good by the 'gain' of a similar injury inflicted on the striker.[1]

This brings us to the second argument in Leibniz's defence; perhaps there is a 'gain' which 'satisfies the injured party', who thus receives some real compensation for his injury. This gain must consist in the pleasurable satisfaction of his vengeful anger, which may also, by sympathy, be enjoyed by the 'Sages' who look on. This emotional origin of vindictive justice is explicitly admitted by Leibniz in a letter of 1697. Here he is considering the universe as a city governed by God, in which every good deed is rewarded and every bad one punished. The punishments are not to be merely curative or deterrent, but must exhibit 'that harmony which is fulfilled by just revenge'. God is the punisher and it is His anger that is being satisfied;[2]

> for if one abstracts from anger the imperfection which consists in the clouding of reason and the sense of pain, and only the will to avenge is left, it can be attributed to God, following the example of Holy Writ.

The limitations of God's omnipotence suggested in the *Théodicée* are of a similar kind to Malebranche's, although Leibniz had, he asserts, worked them out independently:[3] they are however both more complex and more vague. The vagueness is perhaps justified by the limited aims which Leibniz states at the beginning of his book.[4] He was too sophisticated a thinker to attempt a positive theodicy, as Malebranche, King, and others had done. His aim is merely to prove that a theodicy is not impossible, that the objections brought by Bayle against a good and omnipotent God are not absolutely irrefutable, as he claimed; if they were, they would prove that the basis of Christianity, and of natural religion as then conceived, was false. Leibniz, therefore, is not obliged to provide a demonstrative

---

[1] Ibid., V, iv. The extension to all punishments of principles properly applicable only to fines, damages etc. is made easier for Aristotle by the wide meaning of the word ζημία (financial loss, fine, punishment in general).

[2] Leibniz, *Opera Omnia*, ed. Dutens, Genevae, 1768, T. VI, p. 84: '... judico ultra emendationem peccantis, & exemplum alios praeservans, spectari posse & debere in poena harmoniam ipsam, quae vindicta demum justa impletur ... Quodsi igitur irae detrahatur imperfectio, quae in rationis obnubilatione dolorisque sensu consistit, tantumque vindicandi voluntas relinquatur, Deo tribui potest, scripturae sacrae exemplo.'

[3] Leibniz, *Théodicée*, ed. cit., II, 100, 104.

[4] Ibid., Preface, I, vi, xxii seq., xxxvi.

refutation of these objections, but only to show that they could conceivably be answered. If he can do this, he has shown that Christianity cannot conclusively be proved to be false, and the way is open to faith. He wishes also to suggest that this faith in a good and omnipotent Creator is in fact true; but the main purpose of the book is the negative one of showing that it cannot be proved to be false. This negative, limited aim accounts in some measure for the appearance of frivolity, even puerility, in some of his arguments against Bayle's objections, an appearance which was heightened by his wish to make his book entertaining as well as edifying—'I thought it necessary to brighten up a subject which, by its seriousness, might be depressing'[1]— and which even led some contemporaries, such as Le Clerc and Pfaff, to suppose that he really agreed with Bayle and was writing a deliberately feeble refutation. In view of what is known of Leibniz's thought and life in general, this supposition must be mistaken, although it is not easy to explain away the letters which Pfaff claimed had passed between himself and Leibniz.[2]

Though Leibniz approved of Malebranche's theodicy and admitted its likeness to his own, there are important differences between the two. For Malebranche God's omnipotence is limited by His wisdom insisting on simplicity and regularity of means, which necessarily produce evils in the created universe. For Leibniz the limitation consists in God's being obliged by His goodness to choose the best of all possible worlds. The vagueness of the term 'best' gives him more elbow-room than Malebranche's limitation, and enables him to avoid the very questionable assumption that a universe governed by simple, invariable laws must necessarily include sin and misery. Indeed Leibniz explicitly asserts that among the possible worlds there may be some 'without sin and without misery'; but 'but these same worlds would in other respects be very inferior in good to ours'.[3] He does at one point try to reconcile

---

[1] Leibniz, *Théodicée*, ed. cit., Pref., p. xxxxii: 'j'ai cru qu'il falloit égayer une matière, dont le sérieux peut rebuter.'

[2] See Dutens' Preface to Leibniz, *Op. Omn.*, 1768, pp. vii–ix; cf. the very odd suggestion that Bayle and Le Clerc were in antichristian collusion (Bayle, *Oeuvres Div.*, T. III, p. 1003).

[3] Leibniz, *Théodicée*, Pt. I, p. 78: 'sans péché & sans malheur . . . ces mêmes Mondes seroient d'ailleurs fort inférieurs en bien au nôtre'; cf. Pt. II, p. 263.

Malebranche's theodicy with his own by suggesting that the distinction between God's ends and means should not be made.[1] The simplicity of God's means, dictated by His wisdom, may also be regarded as an end, as an essential part of the beauty of the universe. Since the universe is a process, not an unchanging thing, everything occurring in it is both means and end. Thus Malebranche's universe becomes the best of all possible ones, and not a highly defective creation botched by God's preference for simple ways.

Quite reasonably, Leibniz says that he cannot show in detail the grounds for the assertion that a universe without sin and misery would be very inferior to ours, since this would require comparing together an infinite number of infinite series; but he must, even with his limited aims, suggest some possible grounds for it, and he does so. One of these is *'ab effectu*, since God has chosen this world as it is'.[2] Leibniz uses this argument, a flagrant *petitio principii*, much more often and more obviously than Malebranche. Although, as I have said, it is impossible to suppose that the *Théodicée* is deliberately feeble and therefore destructive in intention, it is very odd that he should make such use of this patently fallacious argument, particularly since it is one employed by Bayle when wearing his Calvinist mask[3] and refuted by him when attacking William King in the *Réponse aux Questions d'un Provincial*,[4] a work constantly quoted by Leibniz.

But Leibniz does suggest other answers, which consist mainly of rather casually presented aesthetic analogies: musical harmony must include discords, beautiful pictures have dark patches, a satisfying whole may contain separate parts that are ugly;[5] we never see the whole (infinite in extent and time), and therefore we judge unfairly the irregularity of the parts.[6] The argument implied by these analogies is based on a value-judgment fundamentally different from Malebranche's. The evils are justified not because they are inevitable if God must create and rule by invariable laws, but because they make the total

[1] Ibid., Pt. II, p. 104.
[2] Leibniz, *Théodicée*, ed. cit., Pt. I, p. 78: *'ab effectu*, puis que Dieu a choisi ce Monde tel qu'il est.' Cf. p. 30.
[3] Bayle, *Dict. hist. & crit.*, ed. cit., art. Pauliciens, rem, (E), pp. 625, 627.
[4] Bayle, *Oeuvres Div.*, T. III, p. 669.
[5] Leibniz, ibid., Pt. II, pp. 108 seq.
[6] Ibid., Pt. II, p. 92.

universe more beautiful; they perform a good function and are not there merely as a necessary by-product of God's laws or as a condition *sine quâ non* of greater goods. God might have produced a universe without irregularities;[1]

> I reply that it would be an irregularity to be too smooth—that would offend against the rules of harmony.

Leibniz may mean this judgment to apply only to meta-physical evil, that is, the defects inevitable in any creature because it is not God. In this case, he is just expressing the then very widespread belief in the goodness of maximum variety or plenitude in the creation: that it is good that every possible creature from the most to the least defective should be actualized in the great chain of being.[2] For, when dealing with specifically moral evil, Leibniz sometimes asserts that it is only permissible, to God or man, if it is the condition of preventing a greater moral evil or of producing a greater moral good.[3] The only precise example we are given of God's justifiable permission of sin is the *felix culpa*;[4] but this is not made the central, unique justification of the creation, as in Malebranche, and we are given to suppose that there are many other similar, though perhaps less spectacular, cases. Sometimes, however, in direct contradiction to this limitation of the justifiable permission of sin, Leibniz puts moral evil on the same level as physical and metaphysical evil, and argues that moral evil may have been permitted in order to gain a metaphysical good, i.e. the perfection of everything created, inanimate as well as living and intelligent.[5] An example would presumably be the creation of delicious fruits, necessary to the maximum perfection of the vegetable world, but producing the sin of gluttony in man.

Thus Leibniz, by means of the vagueness of 'best' in the best of all possible worlds, oscillates between the conception of evil as a necessary condition of greater goods and evil as a necessary part of the beauty of the whole universe. The former conception is compatible with Malebranche's system, the latter,

[1] Ibid., Pt. II, p. 108: 'Je réponds que ce seroit une irrégularité d'être trop uni, cela choqueroit les règles de l'harmonie.'
[2] Cf. A. O. Lovejoy, *The Great Chain of Being*, passim.
[3] Leibniz, *Théodicée*, ed. cit., Pt. I, pp. 90–1.
[4] Ibid., Pt. II, p. 263.
[5] Ibid., Pt. II, pp. 104–5.

which is much more prevalent, is not. It is, I think, because of this vagueness that Leibniz does come near to achieving his limited, negative aims. He does not justify God, but he does perhaps show that one cannot conclusively condemn Him.

But even to this limited, negative achievement there is an important qualification to be made. Not everyone would accept his second conception of evil, i.e. his assertion that a universe containing sin and misery is better than one without them; and, since this is ultimately a matter of taste, he might as well have stated 'Whatever is, is good',[1] and left it at that. If one's taste is for a universe without sin and misery, if the admission 'Il le faut avouer, le mal est sur la terre'[2] is made with real anguish, Leibniz's theodicy is largely irrelevant, and Bayle's objections still stand; where it is not irrelevant, it is basically the same as Malebranche's and has the same weaknesses.

Leibniz's main positive aim in the *Théodicée*, namely, his attempt to preserve the identity of human and divine moral values, has already been discussed in Part I of this book, as have also some of his justifications or mitigations of eternal torment.[3] He was fully aware that this doctrine was a major barrier to any theodicy, and he cites without comment various thinkers who reject it: Origen, Le Clerc, Petersen, F. M. Van Helmont, Hobbes.[4] But in the *Théodicée* there is no sign that he himself disbelieved in the eternity of hell. Among his justifications of it the most prevalent is that based on the infinite plurality of worlds, inhabited by happy sinless creatures, in comparison with which the great majority of damned in our world is infinitesimal.[5] Why our world should be so much wickeder and nastier than all the others is not explained. A slightly more convincing defence of hell is derived from the principle of vindictive justice coupled with the unorthodox assumption that the damned go on freely sinning.[6] The difficulty here, as we have already seen, is to ensure that they do continue to sin.

It is to solve this difficulty that Leibniz expounds the curious

[1] Pope, *Essay on Man.*
[2] Voltaire, *Poème sur le Désastre de Lisbonne.*
[3] Supra, pp. 53–4, 57; 24, 36, 64.
[4] Leibniz, *Théodicée*, ed. cit., Pt. I, pp. 83, 123, 133–4; Pt. II, pp. 154, 278–9.
[5] Ibid., Pt. I, p. 86.
[6] Ibid., Pt. II, p. 149.

defence of eternal torment in the famous *De Origine Mali* (1702) of William King, Archbishop of Dublin. King suggests that the habitual depravity of the damned, together with the upsetting effect of their punishment, has led them into 'a kind of phrensy and madness'. This madness is not so extreme as to rob them of the power to make choices, but is strong enough to ensure that these choices are always sinful and frustrated. The damned are thus[1]

> sensible of their misery, and strive against it with all their power; but while they do not observe, or believe that it is founded in perverse election, they may hug themselves in the cause the effects whereof they abhor; being still wise in their own opinion, and as it were pleasing themselves in their misery . . . The divine goodness therefore is not to be charged with cruelty for letting them continue in that existence, though it be very miserable, when they themselves will not have it removed: or for not altering their condition, which they utterly refuse to have altered.

This picture of the peculiar behaviour of the damned is easier to accept, if one can also accept King's conception of free will. This is an extreme form of the *libertas indifferentiae*: there is no causal relation between an election of the will and its object; the election itself makes the object pleasing, though, if it be a bad choice, the object may be unattainable or destructive.[2] The damned, then, owing to their madness, constantly choose to do wicked and impossible things, are constantly tormented by frustration, and fail to notice the connection between their perverse, sinful choice and their torments. This conception of free will is one which Leibniz, of course, could not accept, and which he explicitly rejects in the *Théodicée*.[3] Nevertheless he writes of King's justification of eternal torment:[4]

> These thoughts are not to be despised and I have sometimes had similar ones, but I do not care to make a decisive judgment on them.

[1] Leibniz, ibid., Pt. II, pp. 152–3, 342–3; William King, *An Essay on the Origin of Evil*, 5th ed., London, 1781, p. 416.

[2] King, op. cit., pp. 216 seq., 236 seq. (God's free will), 418 (damned's free will).

[3] Leibniz, *Théodicée*, ed. cit., Pt. I, pp. 54–5, 98 seq., Pt. II, pp. 295, 308 seq., 321–2.

[4] Leibniz, ibid., Pt. III, p. 343: 'Ces pensées ne sont pas à mépriser, & j'en ai eu quelquefois d'approchantes, mais je n'ai garde d'en juger décisivement.'

Among Leibniz's many friends and acquaintances was J. W. Petersen. Leibniz read Petersen's vast defence of universal salvation, Μυστηριον ἀποκαταστασεως παντων (1700–10), with pleasure and profit ('cum voluptate et fructu'),[1] and very much enjoyed talking with him when he met him in Berlin in 1706.[2] He also greatly admired Petersen's Latin poetry, and in September 1711, through a mutual friend Johannes Fabricius, he suggested that Petersen should write a Christian epic in Latin hexameters, to be called the *Uranias*, which would, in twelve books, recount the creation, the fall, the redemption, the history of the Church, the millennium, hell, and heaven, and the[3]

> twelfth Book would conclude all by the ἀποκατάστασιν πάντων, even the wicked being reformed and brought back to happiness and God, and God ordering everything in everything without exception . . . such a work would make the author immortal, and could be of marvellous use in moving men's souls by hope of better things and in arousing the sparks of a truer piety.

By the end of the same year Leibniz was astonished to learn that Petersen had already finished the epic, and feared that he might have hurried too much; he also suggested that he should see it before publication. His fears were justified; the poem had great beauties, but also innumerable weak spots, *chevilles*, and solecisms, which he set himself to correct.[4] In March 1712 he wrote:[5]

> I should like the most learnèd author to emend and perfect the 12th Book himself, because in it he deals with an opinion which I certainly do not condemn, but which I would not like to make

---

[1] Leibniz, *Op. Omn.*, 1768, T. V, p. 278, letter of October 1706 to Johannes Fabricius. Leibniz goes on: 'Itaque ego ipse Recensionis Autor fui ac concinnator, quam doctissimus Eccardus noster suis relationibus Menstruis Germanicis aliquando inseruit.' I have not been able to find this review.

[2] Leibniz, ibid., p. 279.

[3] Ibid., pp. 293–4: 'Duoddecimus concluderet omnia per ἀποκατάστασιν πάντων, malis ipsis emendatis & ad felicitatem Deumque reductis, Deo jam omnia in omnibus sine exceptione agente . . . Tale opus immortalem praestaret auctorem & mirifici usûs esse posset ad animos hominum movendos spe meliorum, & verioris pietatis igniculos suscitandos. Haec a te ingeri Viro optem, cum efficacibus hortamentis.'

[4] Ibid., pp. 295–6.

[5] Ibid., p. 297: 'Optarem ut ultimum librum suum Uraniados ipsemet emendaret perficeretque Auctor doctissimus, quia in eo sententiam tractat, quam ego quidem minimè damno, meam tamen facere nolim.'

my own (sententiam quam ego minimè damno, meam tamen facere nolim).

The poem was published some years later, in 1720,[1] Leibniz having lost it in an old trunk and found it again.[2]

What are we to make of this? If Leibniz did believe in eternal torment, as is indicated by his defence of it in the *Théodicée* and by the last phrase in the letter just quoted, why did he encourage Petersen to write a work which would advocate universal salvation? I think the most probable solution to this problem is suggested by Leibniz's remarks on the edifying effects of the projected epic. He may, perhaps through reading Petersen's *Mysterion* or Bayle's Manichaean objections, have been persuaded that the doctrine of universal salvation would be more conducive to true piety than that of eternal torment, while remaining convinced that the latter doctrine was in fact true. If this conjecture is correct, Leibniz's attitude would be an extension of that expressed by Luther,[3] an upside-down case of the usual secretiveness about hell: the exoteric, useful but untrue doctrine is universal salvation, while eternal torment is the esoteric, dangerous but true doctrine. Leibniz is ready to encourage someone else to tell a useful lie, someone for whom it is not a lie; but he is not ready to tell it himself.

Leibniz had also intended to publish Soner's treatise against the justice of eternal torment. But here his intentions seem to have been different. It was to have been accompanied by a preface, which Lessing later published. In this preface Leibniz gives as his reason for publishing the treatise, that it has the reputation of being irrefutable merely because it is so rare, men being wont to esteem highly what they have never seen. By being made widely available it will become less pernicious, since its inflated reputation will thus be destroyed. He admits that Soner argues 'subtly and ingeniously', and he therefore gives a refutation of Soner's thesis. This refutation is that

---

[1] Petersen, *Uranias qua opera Dei magna omnibus retro seculis et oeconomiis transactis usque ad apocatastasin seculorum omnium per spiritum primogeniti gloriosissime consumanda carmine heroico celebrantur . . .*, Francofurti et Lipsiae, 1720. There is a copy of this extremely rare book in the library of the Harvard Divinity School.

[2] Leibniz, *Op. Omn.*, 1768, T. V, p. 301.

[3] V. supra, pp. 7–8.

eternal torment is justified by the eternal sinning of the damned, an argument which, as we have seen, assumes an unorthodox dynamic afterlife with its attendant dangers.[1] If this was the best that Leibniz could do against Soner, it is not surprising that he did not publish the treatise.

Lessing, having quoted Leibniz's preface, goes on to discuss his views on hell. A contemporary advocate of universal salvation, Eberhard, had asserted, in his *Apologie des Sokrates*, that Leibniz really disbelieved in eternal torment and that the defences of it in the *Théodicée* were therefore insincere. Lessing admits that in the *Théodicée* Leibniz's treatment of hell is 'very exoteric', and that esoterically he would have written about it quite differently. But he thinks that Leibniz did truly believe in eternal torment precisely because his esoteric philosophy demanded it.[2] Since the whole of its past and future is always logically implied by any given state of a monad, none of a man's actions, good or bad, can ever be wiped out, and hence, as there is a preestablished harmony between sin and suffering, each sin will have endless painful consequences. Lessing then proposes a kind of dynamic afterlife, which may well be very near Leibniz's esoteric views: there is no gap between heaven and hell—'everyone must still find his hell in heaven, and his heaven in hell',[3] and each soul, though eternally suffering the 'natural' punishment of its sins, may endlessly become better—Dives may make continual moral progress, but Lazarus will always be so many steps ahead.[4] Since Lessing assumed that all punishment must be curative, the moral evolution must always eventually be upwards;[5] since Leibniz accepted purely vindictive punishment, his afterlife would presumably have included some souls which evolved morally downwards.

---

[1] Lessing, *Zur Geschichte und Litteratur Aus den Schätzen der Herzoglichen Bibliothek zu Wolfenbüttel Erster Beytrag*, Braunschweig, 1773, in Lessing, *Sämtliche Schriften*, ed. K. Lachmann, 3rd ed., Stuttgart, 1895, Bd. XI, pp. 461–466.

[2] Lessing, ibid., pp. 469 seq.

[3] Ibid., p. 483: 'ein jeder muss seine Hölle noch im Himmel, und seinen Himmel noch in der Hölle finden.'

[4] Ibid., pp. 479 seq. Cf. Karl Aner, *Die Theologie der Lessingzeit*, Halle/Saale, 1929, pp. 276–85.

[5] Lessing, ibid., p. 479; for Lessing the punishment is presumably also vindictive, since he quotes (ibid., p. 472) with approval Leibniz's defence of vindictive justice (cf. supra, p. 208).

Chapter XIII

ENGLISH PHILADELPHIANS

(1) Mrs Lead

T HE Philadelphian Society was a small group of chiliastic mystics led by an elderly widow, Mrs Jane Lead. The name 'Philadelphian' derives from the sixth of the seven Churches of Asia to which Christ, at the beginning of the Apocalypse, sends messages. It is clear from the text, if one reads it as a prophecy of successive ages of the Church, that the Philadelphian Church is to be the one which has preserved the true spirit of Christ, and which will be there at His second coming. In consequence, chiliasts have always been inclined to call themselves Philadelphians, as did, for example, Joachim of Flora.[1] This movement also made use of the meaning of the word in Greek: brotherly love.

In about 1674 Mrs Lead, then aged fifty, became closely asociated with Dr John Pordage and his wife, visionary mystics who were deeply influenced by Jakob Boehme.[2] In 1654 Pordage had been turned out of his living on the charge of having commerce with spirits. He himself admitted to being molested by evil spirits, and claimed that from 1653 to 1658 he

---

[1] See Ernst Benz, *Ecclesia Spiritualis*, Stuttgart, 1934, p. 298.

[2] Mrs Lead first knew Pordage in 1663; see her preface to Pordage's *Theologia Mystica*, London, 1683, p. 2. Cf. Nils Thune, *The Behmenists and the Philadelphians*, Uppsala, 1948, pp. 60–2.

had had direct experience of the torments of hell.[1] He trans-
mitted to Mrs Lead his simplified version of Boehmenism,
which we know about from his posthumously published
Theologia Mystica (1684) and from works later translated into
German by another Boehmenist and Philadelphian, Loth
Fischer of Utrecht.[2]

From 1681 Mrs Lead published a series of visions or revelations,[3] and, on Pordage's death in that year, she became the
accepted leader of the movement. In 1694 appeared her
Enochian Walks with God, in which she first expounded the
doctrine of universal salvation, revealed to her several years
before.[4] In the same year Loth Fischer published a German
translation of her *The Heavenly Cloud now Breaking* (1681),
and this led to a correspondence between Mrs Lead and Baron
Freiherr von Knyphausen, a highly placed administrator at the
court of Frederick III Elector of Brandenburg.[5] Knyphausen,
already a patron of the Petersens,[6] gave her financial support
and paid Fischer a salary to translate all her works, which, from
1694 onwards, were published in German in Amsterdam usually
in the same year as the English edition. At this time she was
joined by two new followers, both Fellows of St John's College
Oxford: Francis Lee and Richard Roach.

Francis Lee, who had studied medicine at Leiden and Padua
and was a good Hebrew scholar, was a non-juror, and therefore,
though in orders, was unable to hold a living or a post at the

---

[1] See Pordage, *Göttliche und Wahre Metaphysica*, Frankfurt and Leipzig,
1715, Bd. III, p. 10: 'kam zu mir von dem Geist der Ewigkeit folgendes Wort
mit grosser Krafft und Gewalt: Werffet diesen unnützen knecht hinaus in die
äusserste Finsternüsz / alwo ist Weinen / Heulen und Zähnklappen. Sobald
dieses Wort gesprochen / ward ich in das finstere Centrum eingenommen /
darinn ich fünf gantzer Jahre lang herum zirkulirte / ehe ich daraus erlöset
wurde'; cf. ibid., Bd. II, Einleitung, c. 7, and Francis Lee's correspondence in
Christopher Walton, *Notes and Materials for an adequate Biography of the
celebrated Divine and Theosopher, William Law*, London, 1854, pp. 192, 204.

[2] See Thune, op. cit., p. 99.

[3] Beginning with *The Heavenly Cloud now Breaking*; cf. Thune, op. cit., pp.
79 seq.

[4] Jane Lead, *The Enochian Walks with God*, London, 1694, Introduction and
pp. 17–9, 35–7; she states, in *Eine Offenbarung der Bottschafft des Ewigen
Evangelii*, Amsterdam, 1697, p. 27, that she waited several years before publishing the doctrine.

[5] See Thune, op. cit., p. 81.

[6] V. infra, p. 232.

University. On his way back from his continental studies, in 1694, he heard tell of Mrs Lead in Holland, where Fischer's translation of her treatise had already aroused interest. He called on her in London and soon became her devoted disciple.[1] In 1695 Mrs Lead went completely blind, and Lee acted as her secretary, dealing with the now heavy religious correspondence from Holland and Germany, editing her writings and providing prefaces for them.[2] In the next year Mrs Lead had a revelation that it was God's will that Lee should marry her widowed daughter, Mrs Barbara Walton, a proposal which Baron Knyphausen also seconded vigorously. After anxious consideration Lee was convinced that this was indeed the will of God, they were married, and all three settled in a house in Hoxton Square, rented by Mrs Lead at Knyphausen's expense.[3]

Richard Roach had been a friend of Lee's since their school-days together at Merchant Taylor's,[4] and Lee must quite soon have introduced him to Mrs Lead; for in 1695 she wrote to him at St John's to inform him that he had been designated by the Virgin Wisdom as a 'priest in her orb'—Mrs Lead had been[5]

> commanded to lead you up with some others to the High Court of the Princely Majesty who sealed you a commission to go forth in the Power of a Holy-Ghostly Ministration.

Roach did in fact become a very active member of the Philadelphians, and led the movement after Mrs Lead's death in 1704.[6] In the late 1720's he was still faithfully expounding the Philadelphian message. From his ordination in 1690 until his death in 1730 he was Rector of St Augustine's in Hackney.[7] This fact testifies to the remarkable tolerance of the Church of England.

Until 1697 the Philadelphians were a small, informal society, holding regular private meetings at Mrs Lead's house in Hoxton Square or at the home of Mrs Openbridge and Mrs

[1] See Thune, op. cit., pp. 82–3; C. Walton, op. cit., pp. 141, 508.
[2] See Thune, op. cit., p. 85; C. Walton, op. cit., pp. 233 seq. Several of the prefaces are signed 'Timotheus'.
[3] See Thune, op. cit., pp. 85–6; C. Walton, op. cit., pp. 226–7, 508.
[4] See *Dict. Nat. Biogr.*, art. 'Roach'.
[5] Bodleian, Rawlinson MS., D 832, fo 51; the letter is undated, but in it Mrs Lead speaks of 1696 as next year.
[6] See Thune, op. cit., p. 135; cf. infra, p. 253.
[7] Ibid., p. 87.

Bathurst in Baldwin Gardens.[1] Their meetings were conducted
in a manner similar to the Quakers', that is to say, there were no
set rules of procedure and everyone waited in silence until the
spirit moved someone to speak.[2] Although Dr Pordage had had
a violent anti-Quaker revelation in 1675,[3] the Philadelphians
recognized the similarity between the two movements, but also
pointed out the few but important differences: the Philadelphians set no store by simplicity of dress and forms of speech,
they were anxious not to be sectarian and remained practising
members of the established Church, they believed in the
imminence of the millennium, and their leader, and some but
not all of their members, believed in universal salvation.[4]
Although Boehmenism was certainly the most important single
influence on their religious outlook, it was not the only one.
The Philadelphians felt themselves close to contemporary continental mystics—German Pietists, Antoinette Bourignon
(another *protégée* of Knyphausen's) and Pierre Poiret, French
Quietists, Christian Cabalists, and may well have absorbed
some of their views.[5] In principle, of course, the main source of
their religion was direct inspiration and revelation by God; but,
unless we accept that God and the whole invisible world are in
fact as Boehme, Pordage and Mrs Lead described them, we
may leave this source out of account.

Mrs Lead's visions derive unmistakably from Pordage's
Boehmenism, and Boehme may well be the main source of the
Philadelphians' chiliasm, which looked for the preparation of
the millennium in the gradual purification and unification of the
Protestant churches, rather than in the sudden and violent

[1] See Roach, Rawlinson MS., D 833, fos 56 vo–57; Roach, *The Great Crisis*,
London, 1725 (1727), p. 99; Thune, op. cit., p. 86. Mrs Bathurst's mystical
writings are preserved in Rawlinson MSS., D 1262, 1263.

[2] See *Theosophical Transactions by the Philadelphian Society*, London, 1697,
pp. 221–2. The meetings were opened by the reading of a portion of the Scriptures.

[3] Pordage, *Sophia: das ist | Die Holdseelige ewige Jungfrau der Göttlichen
Weisheit*, Amsterdam, 1699, pp. 143, 160.

[4] See Roach, *The Great Crisis*, pp. 42–4; Roach, Rawlinson MS., D 833, fos
54 vo–55; cf. Thune, op. cit., pp. 64–5, 91–3.

[5] See Roach, *The Great Crisis*, pp. 9, 97, 105–7; *Theosophical Transactions*,
pp. 155–7, 160, 269 seq. Roach was in correspondence with Poiret, who in 1704
wrote him a letter about Mrs Lead's death (Rawlinson MS., D 832, fo 33).

destruction of the forces of Antichrist.[1] When Mrs Lead tells us that it is by direct mystical experience that she knows about the still sphere of eternity, which 'there is no way possible for anyone to describe, or give account of, but by being taken up into it', and then gives us a picture of its contents, the Trinity, the Virgin Wisdom, the seven superplanetary spirits, and so forth, we cannot help thinking that she could quite as easily have read it all in Pordage's *Theologia Mystica*, for which she wrote a preface.[2] But some of her visions have a more genuine ring. On the 17th of October 1695, for example, she was watching the progress of a recently deceased friend, and noticed that she had passed through the elementary regions:

> Then Paradise being open'd. I searched for her, and after about two hours, I found her in the Third Degree of this Heavenly World. . . . As soon as I had met her, I congratulated her, and said, I have been a long while seeking to find you. To which she Answer'd, very well you might; for I have been so taken up with the Variety of the Pleasures of this Place, that I had forgot all my Mortal Friends.

Mrs Lead reminded her that she, Mrs Lead, had often assured her that death would lead to great joys;[3]

> Upon which she smilingly said, Now I find it so to be. And so seeming to be unwilling to entertain any further Discourse with me, as if thereby she was held from a better Enjoyment, she left me.

Another revelation which Mrs Lead certainly did not get from Boehmenism was that of universal salvation. Indeed Boehmenism is the main obstacle to her working out a satisfactory theology to support this doctrine. One of the salient features of Boehme's philosophy is the attempt to solve the problem of evil by putting the origin of evil, the dark fiery principle, into the godhead, where, before creation, it was harmlessly harmonized with its opposite, the principle of light. In

---

[1] See E. Benz, 'Verheissung und Erfüllung', in *Zeitschrift für Kirchengeschichte*, Stuttgart, 1935, Bd. LIV, pp. 488 seq.

[2] J. Lead, *The Wonders of God's Creation Manifested, In the Variety of Eight Worlds*, London, n.d. (circa 1695), pp. 39 seq.; cf. Pordage, *Theologia Mystica*, pp. 16 seq.

[3] Lead, ibid., pp. 72–4.

the creation the dark fire comes forth as sin in fallen angels and men, and as avenging anger in God.[1] Sin and punishment thus have eternal roots, and the eternity of hell has a strong metaphysical basis. Already in Pordage's *Theologia Mystica* there is an effort to tone down the dualism of Boehme's God by emphasizing that the fiery principle was wholly good until abused by the free will of angels and men.[2] But the dualism still persists in Mrs Lead and involves her in obvious inconsistencies when she is arguing in favour of universal salvation.

One of her main arguments, which we have already met in Jeremiah White, is that sin begins in time and therefore cannot be eternal. In the *Enochian Walks* we read:[3]

> Behold, saith the Lord, 'I will make all things new, the End shall return to its Original-Primary-Being . . . for as there was neither Sin, nor Center to it, so it must be again . . .

Yet in the same work, when dealing with the origin of evil, she states that before the creation God[4]

> had all Principles and Centres, both of Light and Darkness in Himself; with Good and Evil, Death and Life. But all of These (tho seeming contrary) were bounded in Unity and Harmony.

Mrs Lead herself realized that universal salvation went against Boehmenist principles and against his express assertion of the eternity of hell; but she made no attempt to resolve the conflict, merely remarking that in Boehme's day the time was not yet ripe for this revelation.[5]

Francis Lee, in his apologia for Mrs Lead's theology sent to Henry Dodwell in 1699, states the conflict clearly and resolves it by denying the dualism.[6] The 'finiteness of hell torments', he says,

> is absolutely inconsistent with the origin of good and evil from

---

[1] See A. Koyré, *La Philosophie de Jacob Boehme*, Paris, 1929. Petersen (*Mysterion*, T. I, Gespräch III, p. 109) quotes from Boehme a clear affirmation of the eternity of hell.

[2] Pordage, *Theologia Mystica*, pp. 127, 135, 137, 148.

[3] Lead, *Enochian Walks*, p. 18.

[4] Ibid., p. 35.

[5] Lead, *Eine Offenbarung der Bottschafft des Ewigen Evangelii*, Amsterdam, 1697, pp. 35–6. I have not been able to find a copy of the English original of this (*A Revelation of the Everlasting Gospel-message*, London, 1697).

[6] In C. Walton, *Notes and Materials . . . William Law*, p. 213.

two co-eternal principles, in the Deity. For if they are co-eternal *a parte ante,* they must necessarily be co-eternal *a parte post,* and consequently the torments of hell must be as infinite as the joys of heaven . . .

Conversely, the doctrine of eternal torment necessarily implies a Manichaean God, 'an eternal principle of evil, as well as of good, that is, an eternal root and cause of hell in the Deity'. He then argues that, since universal salvation and dualism are quite incompatible, and since Mrs Lead has 'so professedly expressed herself in favour of the former, and never professedly in favour of the latter', she must be absolved from the charge of Boehmenist dualism. This argument is valid only on the extremely doubtful assumption that Mrs Lead was incapable of holding two logically incompatible beliefs.

Although Mrs Lead cannot have derived the doctrine of universal salvation from Boehme, the setting of the vision in which this doctrine was revealed to her is still clearly Boehmenist. She saw first an innumerable multitude of the dead, who were imprisoned in 'dark Centres' and were bewailing their failure, while on earth, to profit by the redeeming love of Christ. She was then led into a 'Light-World', where she saw Christ interceding with God the Father, and also Adam and Eve. She noticed many spirits, like bright flames, flying rapidly into this light-world, and asked who they were. Christ answered

> These are they for whom my blood was shed, although they have lain long swallowed up and imprisoned in the second death, and have passed through many bitter struggles and deathly fears; but now behold! how, set at liberty, they come here so that they may be clothed with new bright bodies.

Thereupon she saw Adam and Eve stand up with great jubilation and heard them say:

> In this wise shall the whole race of our descendants be restored, and one after another come in here to us.

Mrs Lead went up to Adam and asked him how it could be possible for all these wicked souls to be saved; he replied,

> The second Adam, the Lord of heaven, is more than sufficient to heal the breach that was made through me.

As she was still not quite convinced, Christ drew her spirit near to Him and said:

> If thou art amazed at this full and complete redemption of my human creatures, what wilt thou then say when the love of the immeasurable godhead reveals itself yet more wonderfully and deeply. . . .

And He went on to reveal to her the eventual restoration of Satan and his angels.[1] We may reasonably assume that this vision had human as well as divine sources; indeed, just before recounting it, Mrs Lead states that she had already heard of the doctrine and had rejected it.[2] Since a Boehmenist source is ruled out, we have the following probable sources, from any or all of which she may have heard of universal salvation. Rust's defence of Origen is cited in Lee's preface to the *Revelation of the Everlasting Gospel-Message*,[3] in which the above vision appears, and it is quoted at length in Roach's preface to White's *Restoration*.[4] But perhaps more likely are Lady Conway and Van Helmont, whose religious outlook, combining Quakerism and Cabalism, had close affinities with the Philadelphians' mysticism and chiliasm. In their short-lived periodical, *Theosophical Transactions by the Philadelphian Society* (1697), one of the very few books advertised, apart from Mrs Lead's publications, is Lady Conway's *Principles of the most Antient and Modern Philosophy*.[5] In the last number of the *Transactions* appeared '*A* Theosophical *Epistle from a Learned Gentleman Living very Remote from* London, *to One of the Undertakers of these* Transactions, *upon the Receiving the first of them*'.[6] The author of this letter is a Lurianic Cabalist, he quotes from the *Kabbala Denudata*, and he advocates universal salvation; I think it more than likely that he is Van Helmont.

Whatever Mrs Lead's sources may have been, if any, she certainly set her own stamp on the doctrine of universal salvation by making it part of her chiliastic programme. In defence

---

[1] Lead, *Eine Offenbarung*, pp. 17–18.
[2] Lead, *Eine Offenbarung*, pp. 16–17, cf. p. 27.
[3] Ibid., p. 11.
[4] White, *Restoration*, sig. a3 vo–a7.
[5] *Theosoph. Trans.*, p. 98.
[6] Ibid., pp. 269 seq.

of this doctrine she was able to exploit an element already present in chiliastic tradition,[1] namely, the belief that in the Last Days there will be a new revelation of religious truth, that the 'Everlasting Gospel', which the angel in the Apocalypse is to preach to all nations (Rev. XIV, 6), is not identical with the New Testament, but something new and surprising added to it or discovered in it. This new truth, the salvation of all men and all angels, is both a sign of the nearness of the Parousia and a means of bringing it about. The preaching of this new revelation of the infinite extent of God's love will produce such a wave of true repentance and regeneration that there will soon be a sufficient body of purified souls for Christ to begin His millennial reign; the bride will be ready and the bridegroom will not tarry, the temple will be built and its High Priest will come soon to sanctify it,[2]

> For the day has now broken and the blessèd year has come, when by the casting of this golden Love-Net such an innumerable multitude of souls will be caught, such a draught landed, that they will complete the structure of the spiritual Temple-Body.

In spite of this optimistic faith in the happy consequences of preaching universal salvation, Mrs Lead, and those of the Philadelphians who accepted the doctrine, were well aware that it was generally considered that such preaching would have disastrous moral results. Henry Dodwell, in the letter of 1698 which called forth Lee's apologia, wrote, after an account of Mrs Lead's heresies:[3]

> But in this age of licentiousness, there is hardly any doctrine of hers of more pernicious consequence than that of her pretending Divine revelation for her doctrine concerning *the finiteness of hell torments.*

Lee replied that other Christian truths are liable to abuse—he gives no examples, but we may suppose that he was thinking on the same lines as Camphuysen. He also argued that, from the lateness of Origen's condemnation, one might presume that

[1] Cf. Benz, *Ecclesia Spiritualis*, pp. 13 seq., 36, 244–9.
[2] Lead, *Eine Offenbarung*, pp. 43–5; cf. Lead, *The Wonders of God's Creation*, pp. 51–3; Lee in Walton, *Notes and Materials*, pp. 195, 197.
[3] Walton, *Notes and Materials*, p. 193.

universal salvation was an orthodox doctrine in the first three
centuries,[1]

> or if it were not then publicly known as a general doctrine, but
> reserved only, among some few that were initiated into the
> mysteries, it doth not thence appear that it ought not to be
> published now; or that it is unsound, because *unfit for every age.*

We have here a variant of Mrs Lead's connection between
chiliasm and universal salvation: the Everlasting Gospel is not
a new revelation, but an esoteric truth which now, in these
Last Days, is to replace the exoteric doctrine.

Mrs Lead herself returns constantly to this all-important
objection to universal salvation. Her main defence is to
emphasize the duration and severity of hell-torments, in
particular the bitter regret of the wicked who, for want of a
little effort in this short life, have missed the millennium and
perhaps whole Ages of heavenly bliss. For unexplained reasons,
moral progress in the afterlife is much slower than in this life;
it is therefore very much in our interest to achieve salvation here
and now. Mrs Lead addresses thus the sinners whom Christ
will cast into outer darkness:[2]

> Admit there should be a Delivery, out Here, at the End of all
> Generations, and Ages; Yet how numerous years may you abide
> in These Purging and Trying Furnaces; one Day (Here, while
> in the Body) would have set forward your work more, than
> Years in those Centers, where you are to be confined . . .

These punishments are of course appropriately graded. Totally
unregenerated souls, who have been deeply infected by 'all that
is Diabolical', go to the 'Dark Hellish World',

> with all those Punishments, that the Evil Angels will delight to
> inflict upon them.

Less wicked ones go to less painful worlds, watery or aerial.[3]
It is not quite clear whether the torments will be only mental;
it is certainly on these that she lays most weight, but the descriptions just quoted suggest physical pain as well.

[1] Ibid., p. 214.
[2] Lead, *The Enochian Walks*, p. 16, cf. pp. 21–2, 37 and Introduction; cf.
Lead, *Eine Offenbarung*, pp. 23, 25.
[3] Lead, *The Wonders*, pp. 12–15.

Mrs Lead's afterlife is intensely dynamic. The blessèd as well as the damned move up through successively higher and happier worlds, and this progress has no end, even for those who have reached the highest world; for God

> does multiply amongst them most Amazing, and renewed Wonders, which gives perpetual Matter to renew Love-Admirations.

These saints and angels are also occupied with helping less fortunate souls to rise in the hierarchy. Even during this life angels sometimes draw up our souls into heaven,[1]

> being very affable and friendly to shew their Princely Thrones, and their delightful solaces and enjoyments they have from the perpetual motion of the Triune Deity.

The greatest saving work done by angels will be among their fallen fellows. When the last human souls have been freed from hell by the redeeming power of Christ's sacrifice, Satan and his angels will find themselves 'bereft of all their fierce fiery power', with no more subjects to rule and torment;

> This will powerfully abase their pride and arrogance, and effect an inconceivable softening of their fierce obstinacy.

God will then dispatch the good angels to convert their now humbled former companions, assisted by the ubiquitous Virgin Wisdom, who, as the mother of all spirits, retains 'a maternally kind heart' towards even her diabolic progeny.[2]

As for all Origenists, this salvation of devils was for Mrs Lead a troublesome part of the doctrine. She could find no scriptural evidence for it, and it cost her the support of Johann Georg Gichtel, one of the leading German Boehmenists of this period, who, up to this time, was a friend of Loth Fischer, Mrs Lead's translator. According to Gichtel, Mrs Lead had at first believed that the devils, like men, were to be saved by the sacrifice of Christ, and had written a letter to this effect to the Petersens. Gichtel thereupon sent to her objections to this doctrine and these led her to alter it in favour of the mode of salvation described in the *Revelation of the Everlasting Gospel-Message*

---

[1] Lead, *The Enochian Walks*, pp. 23–4.
[2] Lead, *Eine Offenbarung*, pp. 28–30, cf. pp. 18, 31, 33.

and outlined above.[1] These objections were as follows. First, the salvation of devils is incompatible with the true Boehmenist doctrine of the eternity of the fire-anger principle in God;[2] Gichtel implies that universal human salvation would not be incompatible, though he never overtly maintains this doctrine. Second, in order to redeem devils, Christ would have to be incarnated into a snakelike body; the angelic bodies of Satan and his angels had been changed at their Fall into monstrous, writhing bodies made of worms, which Gichtel himself had seen in a vision.[3] The first objection was valid, and, as we have seen, Mrs Lead could only evade it by inconsistencies. The second objection she dealt with by saving the devils through God the Father, using the angels as instruments. This solution Gichtel rejected on the grounds that, if no incarnation were necessary to save angels, none was necessary to save men.[4] In any case, the fact that Mrs Lead's revelations were thus shown to be variable, adjustable to criticism, proved for him that they were not genuine.[5]

Apart from her unconvincing account of the salvation of devils, and her Boehmenist dualism, Mrs Lead had other defects as a propagandist of universal salvation. Her style, with its oddly Germanic word-order, is unnatural, ungrammatical and often obscure. The various Boehmenist entities, especially the Virgin Wisdom,[6] who is dangerously near to pushing her way into the Trinity, make her theology untidy and unnecessarily unorthodox. But more important still, the chances of her Origenist and chiliastic messages being received by Protestants must have been gravely diminished by her Quaker-like reliance on the direct inspiration of the Spirit and consequently casual attitude to scriptural authority. In her treatise, *The Wonders of God's Creation Manifested in the Variety of Eight Worlds, as they were made known experimentally to the Author* (1695), she deals with the objection, that none of these worlds is mentioned in the

[1] Gichtel, *Theosophia Practica*, 3rd ed., Leyden, 1722, Bd. V, pp. 3649–3650, 3707, 3734.
[2] Gichtel, ibid., Bd. I, pp. 229–30, 326, Bd. V, pp. 3121–4, Bd. VI, p. 1463.
[3] Ibid., Bd. I, pp, 223, 228, Bd. II, p. 1270.
[4] Gichtel, *Theosoph. Pr.*, Bd. III, pp. 2437–8, 2446.
[5] Ibid., Bd. III, pp. 2403, 2412.
[6] On the origins of Boehme's Wisdom, see A. Koyré, *La Phil. de J. Boehme*, p. 213.

Bible, by putting forward a Joachimite division of ages of revelation: the Father inspired the Old Testament, the Son the
New, and now it is the turn of the Holy Ghost,[1]

> which will excel all before it, to Unseal and Reveal what yet
> never was known or understood, that will be communicated to
> and by such as are in an extraordinary manner sanctified and set
> apart for this Holy Function,

that is, to and by such as Mrs Lead. Two years later, in the
Everlasting Gospel-Message, she does attempt to give scriptural
support to her revelation, and is seriously worried by the lack of
it for the salvation of devils.[2] But by that time the conversion
of the Petersens had occurred and she must have known that
her failure to provide scriptural evidence nearly prevented their
accepting universal salvation.

[1] Lead, *The Wonders*, p. 8.
[2] Lead, *Eine Offenbarung*, pp. 18–19; cf. Lead, *A Living Funeral Testimony*,
London, 1702, pp. 20–2.

Chapter XIV

❖⟡❖⟡❖⟡❖⟡❖⟡❖⟡❖⟡❖⟡❖⟡❖⟡❖⟡❖⟡❖⟡❖⟡❖⟡❖⟡❖⟡❖⟡❖⟡❖

GERMAN PHILADELPHIANS
The Petersens

❖⟡❖

THE life of Johann Wilhelm Petersen was marked throughout by more or less miraculous, but always favourable, interventions of Providence. These greatly strengthened his belief in his own revelations and encouraged him to propagate them. Soon after his birth in 1649 he fell from a window high up in a house in Lübeck, and landed unhurt in a gutter, which happened to be full of sand.[1]

He studied at the Universities of Giessen and Rostock, at the latter of which he took his doctorate of theology in 1686. About ten years before, he had got to know the great Pietist theologian Philipp Jakob Spener, who taught him the spiritual understanding of the Scriptures, and who remained a life-long friend.[2]

In 1680 he married Johanna Eleonora von und zu Merlau. Her father was opposed to the marriage; but, owing to Petersen's prayers and Providence, he felt unaccountably frightened whenever he contemplated refusal, and so eventually gave his consent.[3] Frau Petersen had begun to have 'divine dreams' at the age of seventeen, as she tells us in her autobiography, and from her earliest youth had been deeply troubled by the difficulty of reconciling God as love with the eternal torment of all unbelievers, especially of 'the poor children of the heathen, who

---

[1] J. W. Petersen, *Lebens-Beschreibung*, 2nd ed., n.p., 1719, p. 5.
[2] Ibid., pp. 10, 17–18.
[3] Ibid., pp. 49–50.

231

had never had the opportunity of knowing God'.[1] In 1662, at the age of eighteen, she dreamt that she saw the date 1685 written in the sky in large gold letters, and that a man near by told her that in that year great things would happen and that something would be revealed to her. What happened was the revocation of the Edict of Nantes, and what was revealed was the meaning of the Apocalypse and the imminence of the millennium.[2] Before this year neither she nor her husband had studied the Apocalypse. She made a list of *loci* to support her interpretation and took it to show to her husband. He had written the same list, and the ink was still wet. This story is corroborated by Petersen's autobiography.[3] From this time forth they were both convinced chiliasts, though for a few years they did not preach their message.

In 1688 Petersen took up the post of Superintendent at Lüneburg. The next year, while going by boat to Hamburg, he was in great danger from broken ice; he made a vow that, if he survived, he would publicly preach the nearness of the millennium.[4] He fulfilled his vow and was eventually, in 1692, dismissed from his post for persistently preaching this doctrine, which had been condemned in the Augsburg Confession, in the same article as that condemning Origenism.[5] He had also come under suspicion through his acceptance of the prophetic visions of a young noblewoman, Fräulein Rosamunde von Asseburg, in defence of which he published a letter in 1691.[6]

Baron von Knyphausen read this defence and was convinced

---

[1] *Leben Frauen Johannä Eleonorä Petersen, Gebohrner von und zu Merlau, Herrn D. Joh. Wilh. Petersens Ehe-Liebsten, von Ihr selbst mit eigner Hand aufgesetzt und vieler erbaulichen Merckwürdigkeiten wegen zum Druck übergeben* . . ., 2nd ed., n.p., 1719, pp. 21, 49–51. She then came to believe that when Christ descended into hell (I Peter, III, 19–20, IV, 6) He released everyone there except devils and sinners against the Holy Ghost. Another incident bearing on hell occurred soon after the Petersens' marriage. A young man used to be visited, while he was ploughing, by a raven which turned into a black horse, on which he went to see the dead, 'wie ihre Leichnam von den bösen Geistern am Spiesz gebraten, und mit Salz besprenget wurden'. Petersen investigated the case and found it genuine. (J. W. Petersen, *Lebens-Beschreibung*, p. 62).

[2] J. E. Petersen, *Leben*, p. 57.

[3] J. E. Petersen, *Leben*, pp. 55–6; J. W. Petersen, *Lebens-Beschreibung*, p. 70.

[4] J. W. Petersen, *Lebens-Beschreibung*, pp. 81–2, 133.

[5] Ibid., pp. 79, 158–218; cf. supra, p. 22.

[6] Ibid., pp. 153 seq.; Petersen, *Mysterion*, T. III, Apologia . . . contra . . . Fechtium, p. 16; cf. infra, p. 235.

by it. He wrote to Petersen, offering him a pension of 700 thaler, to be paid by the Elector Frederick III. Petersen accepted, bought an estate, Niederdodleben near Magdeburg, and devoted himself, now free of other duties, to gaining converts to his chiliasm.[1] Through Knyphausen's patronage, he seems to have enjoyed considerable favour at court and was quite often in Berlin. He gives a list of his converts at this time; they are mostly female, and many of them noble.[2]

In 1691 or 1692 Petersen had a prophetic dream. He was standing in front of a Superintendent's residence, near the door, talking to a gentleman and a nobleman. Twelve huge black slaves were carrying into the house an idol on a bier; at the front of the coffin, where the feet should have been, the idol was sticking its head out, moving it in a horrible way and champing with its great jaws. As they passed, one of the slaves sprang out at Petersen, stamped with his feet, bared his long teeth, and said: 'The Devil is greater than God; therefore I serve the Devil.' Petersen answered: 'The seed of woman shall bruise the serpent's head.' The gentleman then told Petersen that it was customary to tip the bearers, as the nobleman was doing. He gave Petersen twelve pieces of gold, of which Petersen gave six to the slaves and handed the other six back. The same slave then said the same words again, and Petersen answered that Christ was stronger than the Devil and his angels, and would cast them into the pit and bind them with chains. The bearers carried the idol into the house and came out again with the empty bier. The same bearer came up to Petersen for the third time and showed him a black book in-4°, which contained the 'Acta' of the Devil—what a greaty booty of human souls he had captured from the creation until now; and he asked why, if Christ loved men and was powerful enough to save them, he allowed the Devil to land the greatest catch of souls. Petersen, very angry, replied: 'The robber's booty shall be taken from him.' At the time he did not understand the 'great depth' in these words. The slave said no more, turned into a helpless old woman, and disappeared.[3]

[1] Petersen, *Lebens-Beschreibung*, pp. 219, 226–7.
[2] Ibid., p. 236.
[3] Petersen, *Mysterion*, T. I, Vorrede, pp. xxii–xxv; cf. ibid., Gespräch I, pp. 1–2. Benz ('Der Mensch und die Sympathie aller Dinge', *Eranos-Jahrbuch*, Bd. XXIV, 1955, pp. 168–9) recounts this dream, but gives a false reference.

Petersen interpreted this dream as an assurance that he would triumph over his enemies, namely, the members of the established Church, represented by the Superintendent's residence, who were doing the Devil's work by refusing Petersen's chiliastic message and persecuting him. It was not until a few years later that he understood, thanks to Mrs Lead, the 'great depth' of his own reply to the black slave.

Knyphausen sent the Petersens a manuscript of Mrs Lead's *Eight Worlds* in 1694 or 1695, and asked for their opinion of it. They noticed that the doctrine of universal salvation was not proved from Scripture, but just flatly founded on personal revelation ('nur platt auf die Offenbarung gegründet'); so, after a short prayer, they sat down to refute it from Revelations XIV, XX, Matthew XXV, etc., intending to send this report on the work to Knyphausen. But suddenly there was a stillness in both their spirits, as if someone had interrupted them ('als wenn uns einer in die Rede fiele'), and there came into their minds the words spoken by Him who sat on the throne (Rev. XXI, 5): 'Behold, I make all things new.' This led rapidly to other similar texts, and they were overjoyed to find that they need not refute their dear friend and her very probable opinion ('die so geliebte Freundin und ihre sehr probable Meynung').[1] They accepted the doctrine, Petersen says very firmly,[2]

> not because the illuminated Mrs Lead, to whom we were much attached, had received it in a vision from God, but because we discovered it to be founded on scripture and the Lord had unsealed it to us out of scripture.

They sent a favourable report to Knyphausen, who sent it on to the English Philadelphians. These, says Petersen, were much strengthened in their belief in universal salvation when they realized, from the texts supplied by the Petersens, how firmly it was grounded in Scripture.[3]

From this time onwards there were quite close connections between the Petersens and Mrs Lead's group. In 1695 Francis Lee published an English translation of Petersen's defence of

---

[1] Petersen, *Lebens-Beschreibung*, pp. 297–9; J. E. Petersen, *Leben*, pp. 57–62; cf. Petersen, *Mysterion*, Gespräch, III, p. 74.
[2] Petersen, *Lebens-Beschreibung*, p. 299.
[3] Petersen, *Lebens-Beschreibung*, pp. 299–300.

Fräulein von Asseburg,[1] and in 1697 both the Petersens contri-
buted pieces to the Philadelphian *Transactions*.[2] But it was not
until three or four years after their conversion to universal salvation that the Petersens published anything in defence of the
doctrine. In 1698 appeared Frau Petersen's *Das Ewige Evangelium Der Allgemeinen Wiederbringung Aller Creaturen. . . . Von
einem Mitgliede D[er]. Ph[iladelphischen]. G[emeinde].*,[3] and
between 1700 and 1710 her husband published his massive
work, in three volumes: Μυστηριον Αποκαταστασεως Παντων
Das ist: Das Geheimnisz Der Wiederbringung aller Dinge.[4] The
reason why they did not publish sooner was that their friend
Spener, who had officiated at their wedding, had begged them
not to—they had already caused enough trouble with their
chiliasm. When finally they felt forced to publish so great a
truth, he was deeply worried about the harm it would do to the
cause of Pietism ('von Grund der Seele darüber erschrocken').
But Spener rejected the doctrine *only* because he thought it
incompatible with Scripture; he never wrote against it and
remained on very good terms with the Petersens.[5]

Petersen, quite as much as Mrs Lead, connected the doctrine

[1] *A Letter to some Divines, Concerning the Question, Whether GOD since Christ's Ascension, doth any more Reveal himself to Mankind by means of Divine Apparitions? With an Exact Account of what God hath bestowed upon a Noble Maid, from her Seventh Year, until Now, MDCXCI. Written originally in High-Dutch, and now set forth in English by the Editor* [i.e. Francis Lee] *of the LAWS OF PARADISE* [by Jane Lead], London, 1695. Roach reprinted a long extract from this letter in his *The Imperial Standard of Messiah Triumphant*, London, n.d. (circa 1727), pp. 205–17.

[2] *Theosophical Transactions*, pp. 46 seq., 83 (an account by 'a Member of this Society in Niederdoddeleben' (i.e. Petersen) of a youth who had become con-
vinced that a certain baby in Gutenburg was the new Christ), pp. 142 seq. (an extract from Frau Petersen's *Anleitung zu gründlicher Verständnisz der Heiligen Offenbahrung Jesu Christi*, Franckfurt & Leipzig, 1696, a chiliastic treatise). Mrs Lead later recommended Petersen's *Mysterion* (J. Lead, *A Living Funeral Testimony*, London, 1702, p. 30).

[3] I have not been able to find a copy of this edition; it is reprinted in T. I of Petersen's *Mysterion*.

[4] The first two volumes (1700, in some copies 1701, and 1703) are anonymous. On this work, see Joannes Fabricius, *Historia Bibliothecae Fabricianae*, Pars II, Wolffenbuttelii, 1718, pp. 198–202; Kurt Lüthi, 'Die Erörterung der Allver-
söhnungslehre durch das pietistische Ehepaar Johann Wilhelm und Johanna Eleonora Petersen', in *Theologische Zeitschrift*, 12. Jhg., Basel, 1956, pp. 363–77.

[5] Philipp Jacob Spener, *Letzte Theologische Bedencken*, Halle, 1711, Theil III, pp. 665–8; cf. Paul Grünberg, *Philipp Jakob Spener*, Göttingen, 1893–1906, Bd. I, pp. 173, 184, 271, 350 seq.; Petersen, *Lebens-Beschreibung*, pp. 330–1.

of universal salvation with chiliasm. This doctrine was also for him the Everlasting Gospel, a sign of the Last Days and a means of bringing them about. But, unlike her, he thought that this new revelation must be, and was, latent in Scripture. Just as the Jews had failed to see the Christian truths in the prophecies and types of the Old Testament, so the Christians until now had failed to see in both Testaments this revelation of God's infinite love and mercy. The doctrine was always there to be found, and, from Origen onwards, a few Christians had seen it. But they had expounded it in an obscure or esoteric way, and had made no converts; in this they were guided by Providence, since the time was not yet ripe and this culminating revelation was to be reserved until the period of the Philadelphian Church, now beginning.[1]

Petersen was a highly trained and very erudite theologian, and this stood him in good stead in his mainly scriptural defence of universal salvation. In the polemical works against specific attacks which form so large a part of the *Mysterion* he defends this doctrine with expert and, given the weakness of his case, convincing exegesis. His erudition also enabled him to build up a remarkably complete list of earlier and contemporary writers who had also, more or less clearly, seen this doctrine in the Scriptures. He quotes Origen at great length, together with Pico and Huet on him,[2] and can find even earlier, though more doubtful witnesses in Hermes Trismegistus and Pseudo-Dionysius.[3] The Middle Ages, except for Scotus Erigena, first printed at Oxford in 1681,[4] are a little thin; but he does his best with Joachim of Flora, Ruysbroek and Tauler.[5] The 16th century provides a richer harvest: Johann Denck, Francesco Giorgi, Guillaume Postel, Curione, David Joris, and Campanella.[6] He makes great efforts to bring Luther into his camp, and

[1] Petersen, *Mysterion*, T .I, Vorrede, pp. xv–xvi, Gespräch I, pp. 78–9, 88–90, 271, Gespräch III, p. 4; T. II, Auffgelösete Dubia, p. 44; T. III, Halljahrsposaune, pp. 23–4, Apologia . . . contra . . . Fecht., pp. 48–51.

[2] Ibid., T. I, Gespräch I, pp. 39, 42–3, 53, 63–9, 271, Gespräch II, pp. 68, 88; T. III, Halljahrsposaune, pp. 19, 34–9.

[3] Ibid., T. II, Einige Zeugnisse, p. 61; T. III, Halljahrsposaune, pp. 8–9.

[4] Ibid., T. III, Halljahrsposaune, pp. 13–17.

[5] Ibid., (Joachim:) T. I, Gespräch II, pp. 29–43, T. II, Auffgelösete Dubia, pp. 74–5, T. III, Halljahrsposaune, p. 16; (Ruysbroek:) T. I, Gespräch I, p. 53; (Tauler:) T. I, Gespräch I, p. 80.

[6] Ibid., (Denck:) T. I, Gespräch I, pp. 83–4; (Giorgi:) T. I, Gespräch I, pp. 5,

is able at least to show that Luther believed in the possibility of gaining faith after death.[1] Nearer his own time, he cites, usually with very long quotations, Soner, Hobbes, Episcopius, Petrus Serarius, F. M. Van Helmont and Lady Conway, Pierre Poiret, Thomas Burnet (without being able to know of the *De Statu Mortuorum*), and of course Mrs Lead.[2]

Petersen's kindly protective attitude to the more outrageously heretical among these witnesses is very like that of Gottfried Arnold, to whom perhaps he owed the discovery of some of them. Arnold's *Unparteyische Kirchen- und Ketzer-Historie* began to come out in 1699, and at this time he was a believer in universal salvation, as appears from a short passage at the end of its Second Part.[3] He was also a Boehmenist, as his *Geheimnisz der Göttlichen Sophia* (1700) clearly shows.[4] Petersen praised Arnold, and his adversaries blamed him, for being in his history especially favourable to the advocates of the Restoration of All Things.[5] This is in fact not so. Arnold is extremely favourable to all heretics; but he deals at length with, for example, Camphuysen, F. M. Van Helmont, and Mrs Lead without mentioning universal salvation at all,[6] and in expounding Origen's doctrine makes no comment on it.[7] Petersen certainly approved of his

[1] Ibid., T. I, Ewiges Evang., pp. 25–32, Gespräch II, p. 24, T. II, Vorrede, pp. (18–20), (26). Cf. supra, p. 60.

[2] Ibid., (Soner:) T. I, Gespräch I, pp. 101–2; (Hobbes:) T. I, Gespräch I, p. 173, Gespräch II, p. 5, T. III, Antwort auff . . . Pfaffen, p. 200; (Episcopius:) T. III, Untersuchung . . . Schwerdtner, pp. 292–3; (Serarius:) T. I, Vorrede, pp. iii–iv, Gespräch I, p. 87; (Van Helmont and Lady Conway:) T. I, pp. 84–6, T. II, Einige Zeugnisse, pp. 39–43; (Poiret:) T. III, Fundamentum Restitutionis, p. 537; (Burnet:) T. I, Gespräch I, pp. 87, 156–7; (Mrs Lead:) T. I, Gespräch I, pp. 92–100, 278–84.

[3] Arnold, *Unparteyische Kirchen- und Ketzer-Historie*, Franckfurt, 1700, p. 695; quoted by Erich Seeberg, *Gottfried Arnold*, Meerane i., Sa., 1923, p. 173.

[4] Leipzig, 1700. On p. 167 he recommends Pordage's *Sophia*.

[5] Petersen, *Mysterion*, T. I, Gespräch II, p. 5; E. S. Cyprian, *Allgemeine Anmerckungen*, in Arnold, *Unp. K. & K. H.*, Schaffhausen, 1742, Bd. III, Abschnitt I, pp. 79–80.

[6] Arnold, *Fortsetzung und Erläuterung Oder Dritter und Vierdter Theil der Unparteyischen Kirchen- und Ketzer-Historie*, Frankfurt, 1715, (Camphuysen:) p. 1035, (Van Helmont:) p. 78, (Mrs Lead:) pp. 199 seq., 298 seq.

[7] Ibid., p. 345.

81–3, T. II, Einige Zeugnisse, pp. 15–17; (Postel:) T. I, Vorrede, pp. iv–v, Gespräch I, pp. 86–7, T. II, Einige Zeugnisse, pp. 18–19; (Curione:) T. I, verso of dedication, Gespräch I, pp. 200–3, T. II, Auffgelösete Dubia, pp. 47–8; (David Joris:) T. I, Gespräch I, p. 35, Gespräch II, p. 33; (Campanella:) T. II, Auffgelösete Dubia, p. 45.

history and was a friend of his; in 1701 he published a polemical treatise against Johannes Andreas Corvinus, who had accused Arnold of deliberately falsifying historical evidence in favour of the Arians.[1] But Arnold must have been an unreliable ally; in 1701 he publicly and angrily denied that he, or Petersen, had anything whatever to do with the Philadelphians.[2]

Corvinus, in his *Corpus Doctrinae* (1701), had also accused Petersen and Arnold of being revolutionary heretics, like John of Leiden, the bloodthirsty and polygamous Anabaptist tyrant of Münster in 1534, who, he claimed, also had believed in universal salvation.[3] They complained to Frederick III, now King of Prussia, as Petersen had prophesied in an *heroicum carmen* in 1691,[4] and Corvinus was obliged to retract.[5] Petersen denied, probably rightly, that the Münster Anabaptists held that doctrine. While Petersen was in Berlin for this affair, God so arranged it that he met at court a Secret Councillor, Von Fuchs, who, while talking about the afterlife, said to the Queen that he had never believed in eternal torment.[6] Petersen thereupon told him about the *Mysterion*; he was most encouraging, and in consequence Petersen's book was on sale in every bookshop in Berlin—this was[7]

> certainly a great example of God's Providence, which knows well how to find means that His truth, although it is being suppressed by enemies, shall come forth yet more gloriously.

Corvinus was by no means the only enemy of the Petersens' new doctrine. They had many shocked and angry adversaries, and from the time of Frau Petersen's *Ewiges Evangelium* there was a flood of polemical literature directed against them, nearly all of which Petersen tirelessly refuted. Some of these attacks were extremely violent. Fischlinus, for example, published in 1708 a *Theatrum Mysterij* ἀποκαταστάσεως πάντων *denudatum*

[1] Reprinted in Arnold, *Unp. K. & K. H.*, 1742, Bd. III, Abs. I, pp. 345 seq.
[2] Arnold, *Endliche Vorstellung seiner Lehre*, in *Unp. K. & K. H.*, 1742, Bd. III, Abs. I, p. 493.
[3] Petersen, *Lebens-Beschreibung*, pp. 294–5.
[4] Ibid., p. 280.
[5] Ibid., pp. 295–6.
[6] Ibid., p. 296.
[7] Ibid., p. 297: 'welches gewiss ein grosses Exempel der Providence GOTTES ist, die da wohl weiss Bahn zu machen, dass seine Warheit, ob sie gleich von den Feinden untergedrucket wird, darauf desto herrlicher hervor komme.'

& destructum, in which he asserted that the preachers of the Everlasting Gospel were 'Patrons of the hellish Gospel', were inspired by the Devil, and, like him, 'left a great stink behind them'; that the doctrine of the salvation of Satan induced people to make pacts with the Devil; and that the denial of eternal torment had led vicious criminals to go on happily sinning and join the Philadelphian Society.[1]

On the other hand, the Petersens also made many converts, including some Socinians and even some Catholics. In 1710 Petersen claimed that 'many hundreds' had been convinced by his propaganda; they told him that they had long been secretly wishing to believe in universal salvation, but had been held back by respect for the Bible—Petersen's exegesis had removed this barrier.[2] Some of these converts became active helpers, such as Georg Klein-Nikolai, one of whose treatises Petersen printed in the first volume of the *Mysterion*.[3] Others continued to spread the doctrine after Petersen's death in 1727, such as Ludwig Gerhard, whose *Systema* ἀποκαταστάσεως appeared in that year,[4] and later still Friedrich Christian Oettinger.[5]

The Petersens' eschatology is fully worked out and based almost exclusively on the Apocalypse. At death there is no immediate judgment of souls, but only a kind of preliminary sorting into two main classes: the very few elect go to a peaceful place, where they happily await the millennium, for which they, and they alone, will resurrect (Rev. XX, 5, 6); all the others go to places of curative torment, of which there are three: sea, hell and death, each guarded by a punishing devil (Rev. XX, 13–15). At the end of the millennium the non-elect will resurrect and be judged by Christ and the elect. Those who have been reformed and are found to be inscribed in the Book of Life will join the elect for eternal bliss; those not in the Book will be cast into the lake of fire and brimstone, together with Satan and

---

[1] Petersen, *Mysterion*, T. III, Völliger Beweisz ... gegen ... M.L.M.F.D.S., p. 306 (cf. Fabricius, *Hist. Bibl.*, II, 199).
[2] Petersen, ibid., T. III, Gründliche Antwort, p. 207; *Lebens-Beschreibung*, pp. 304–5, 307, 329.
[3] Georg Paul Siegvolck (i.e. Klein-Nikolai), *Das von Jesu Christo . . . Allen Creaturen zu predigen . . . befohlene Evangelium . . .*, last item in T. I of the *Mysterion*.
[4] See J. G. Walch, *Hist. und Theol. Einleitung in die Religions-Streitigkeiten der Evang.-Luth. Kirchen*, 2nd ed., 1733–9, III, 259–533.
[5] See Benz in Eranos-Jahrbuch, Bd. XXIV, pp. 158, 170 seq.

his angels (Rev. XX, 10). There they remain for thousands of years.[1] Petersen, I think, takes the lake of fire literally; it burns, he warns sinners,[2]

> with sulphur and pitch . . . moths will be your beds and worms your blankets. You will lie, bound as it were hand and foot, in the darkness where there will be weeping and gnashing of teeth.

The effect of this punishment is to humble the sinner, to crush his perverse will. The expression Petersen always uses for this humbling process is 'to soften up (mürbe machen)'—[3]

> God has fire enough, he can make one soft enough.

When the sinner is sufficiently softened, he receives the gift of faith and is saved by the merits of Christ. Petersen is very concerned to preserve a pure Lutheran doctrine of justification, and to prevent the sinner playing more than a negative and passive part in his own salvation.[4] Even Satan will eventually respond to this treatment. Frau Petersen was worried that Mrs Lead gave him only 8000 years of torment, whereas the correct figure was 50,000.[5] The Petersens agreed with Mrs Lead that the last straw which breaks his back is the realization that everyone else has been saved, and that he is left alone with no one to torment.[6]

Though Petersen had read Boehme, and though the *Mysterion* is prefaced by a Boehmenist dedication to the Philadelphian Society, addressed to the Virgin Wisdom,[7] he was not a Boehmenist, and he realized that universal salvation was incompatible with Boehmenist dualism.[8] In consequence, unlike the

[1] Petersen, *Mysterion*, T. I, Vorrede, pp. (xi)–(xv), *Ewiges Evangelium*, pp. 4–7, Gespräch I, pp. 11–13, 106–7, Gespräch II, pp. 76–7.
[2] Ibid., T. III, Anmerkungen against Mercker, p. 380: 'der feurige Pfuhl, der mit Schwefel und Pech brennet . . . Motten werden euer Bette seyn / und Würmer eure Decke. Ihr sollet / als an Händen und Füssen gebunden / im Finsternisz liegen / da Heulen und Zähnklappen seyn wird.'
[3] Ibid., T. I, Gespräch I, p. 52: 'Gott hat Feuer genug / er kan einen mürbe genug machen . . . Wer sollte sich nicht fürchten für solchem Gott / dessen Odem das Feuer anzündet / und die Wiederwärtigen unter solchen erschrecklichen Leiden verzehret?'
[4] Ibid., T. I, *Ewiges Evangelium*, p. 4, Gespräch I, p. 21, T. III, *Apol. contra Fecht*, p. 19.
[5] J. E. Petersen, *Leben*, pp. 57–62.
[6] Petersen, *Mysterion*, T. I, Gespräch I, pp. 13, 31.
[7] 'Die ewige unbefleckte Weisheit.'
[8] Petersen, *Mysterion*, T. I, Gespräch III, p. 109.

English Philadelphians, he was able to argue without impediments that sin and punishment, evil, and vengeance, have no eternal roots in God and must therefore have an end;[1] and he does quite often assert the absolute supremacy of God's love over His justice and the curative intention behind all divine punishments, in this world or the next.[2] No one, says Petersen, has described the deity better than the Holy Ghost, according to Whom God is: a Spirit (John, IV, 24), a light without darkness (I John, I, 5), a consuming fire (Hebrews, XII, 29), love (I John, IV, 16);[3]

> from this it follows undeniably that everything, everything, with no exception, that God does, however frightful it may be, comes from love . . . because God and love are one and the same.

Nevertheless, like the English, and even more so, he was very preoccupied with the moral and social dangers that the doctrine of universal salvation might be thought to produce.[4] Hence he constantly emphasizes the severity and duration of God's punishments.[5] He argues, like Pordage, whom he cites, that, though God in Himself is pure love, God in nature, i.e. in the creation containing sin, is angry and avenging:[6]

> There is no one who would wish to deny our God His avenging and angry justice.

Even though he is eventually to be saved, the unrepentant sinner must look forward to several thousand years' torment in 'our dear God's hard reformatory, the hot-cold and cold-hot furnace (*Schmeltz-Ofen*)'.[7]

[1] Petersen, *Mysterion*, T. I, Gespräch I, pp. 25, 102, 154, 252, Gespräch II, p. 16.

[2] E.g. ibid., T. I, (God as Love:) Vorrede, p. (xvi), Gespräch I, pp. 105, 222, 273–4, Gespräch III, p. 14, (curative justice:) Gespräch I, pp. 196–7, Gespräch II, p. 112, Gespräch III, pp. 8–9.

[3] Ibid., T. I, Gespräch II, p. 14: 'hierausz folget unwidersprechlich / dasz alles / alles / nichts auszgenommen / was Gott thut / es sey auch so erschröcklich / als es immer wolle / von der Liebe herrühret . . . weil Gott und liebe eins ist'; cf. Klein-Nikolai's *Das . . . befohlene Evangelium*, ibid., T. I, p. 4.

[4] Ibid., T. I, Vorrede, p. (xxi), *Ewiges Ev.*, pp. 4, 10, Gespräch I, p. 111, Gespräch III, p. 26.

[5] Ibid., T. I, *Ewiges Ev.*, p. 9, Gespräch I, pp. 106–7, 152.

[6] Ibid., T. I, Gespräch I, pp. 103–4: 'Niemand ist / der unserm Gott seine Rach- und Zorn-Gerechtigkeit disputieren wolle.'

[7] Ibid., T. I, Vorrede, p. (xiii): 'des lieben Gottes hartes Zucht-hausz / der heisz-kalte / und kalt-heisse Schmeltz-Ofen.'

God's punishments in this world are also violent and not noticeably curative and loving. After Petersen had been dismissed from his post at Lüneburg, the chief theologian who had attacked him and two of his colleagues died, a year later on the same day and month as the dismissal. Petersen writes about this:[1]

> That my enemies were not pleasing to God His vengeance on them showed clearly enough.

Some other enemies were punished a little more mildly; one became blind in the right eye, and another had his right hand paralysed, so that he was unable to administer the sacrament.[2] Some time later three doctors of theology made a pact to attack Petersen's chiliasm and also, if any one of them should die, to help his widow.[3]

> But [says Petersen] divine Nemesis, all three men having died within a month, made all the wives widows; and, this malignant trio being broken up, there was no one left to help the widows.

One of these, Dr Pfeiffer, had made his son promise not to become a Pietist; the son later stabbed a young man from Hamburg and became a fugitive from Justice,[4]

and thus showed conspicuously enough that he was no Pietist.

Petersen triumphantly concludes:[5]

> There are now none of my adversaries living, not one, but all stand before the Judge, whose is the Kingdom . . .

---

[1] Ibid., T. III, Apologia contra Fecht, p. 17: 'Punit etiam illos vel in hoc mundo Deus, qui suos laeserunt . . . Non placuisse illi hostes meos, vindicta ejus in illos satis docuit: illo ipso enim mense & die, Sandhagenius, fax & tuba persecutionis, duoque alii collegae, post annum morte abrepti sunt'; cf. Petersen, *Lebens-Beschreibung*, pp. 230 seq.

[2] Petersen, *Mysterion*, T. III, Apologia contra Fecht, p. 17: 'Alii collegae alia poena visibili à Deo plectebantur, cum manus dextera uni rigoret, ut hostias populo porrigere amplius non posset: alteri dexter oculus laederetur, caecusque maneret.'

[3] Ibid.: 'Sed divina Nemesis omnibus hisce tribus viris per mortem intra mensem ablatis uxores viduas fecit omnes: Discissâque illa malignantium trigâ, nemo fuit, qui viduis succurreret.'

[4] Petersen, *Lebens-Beschreibung*, p. 232: 'und sich damit gnugsam signalisirte, dasz er kein Pietist wäre.'

[5] Ibid.: 'Es ist jetzunder auch keiner von meinen Widersachern mehr am Leben, ohne einer, sondern sind nun alle schon vor dem Richter, dessen das Reich ist . . .'

One can see that, in spite of the pull towards love and pity exerted by the doctrine of universal salvation, Petersen's God retains a considerable amount of anger and vengeance, and that he himself is still able frankly to enjoy the suffering of his enemies, and even that of their widows and sons.

Petersen was very seriously worried by the moral dangers of his doctrine. Apart from harping on the anger of God and His dreadful punishments, he provides other, less crude arguments to show that a belief in universal salvation ought not to produce a false sense of security (*Sicherheit*), and hence vicious conduct. He admits that some of the really wicked will abuse the doctrine by saying to themselves:[1]

> since such mercy is finally to be mine, I will enjoy the pleasures of this world a little longer; I'll risk it, since anyway I shall be saved sometime or other.

This will turn to their greater damnation, and they will find themselves in the lake of fire (*der feurige Pfuhl*). But those not thoroughly depraved will respond to God's infinite love and will make every effort to be one of the tiny minority of the elect, who alone will enjoy the millennium and be judges, not judged, at the Last Judgment.[2]

He also suggests that it is the orthodox doctrine which in most cases is likely to produce false security and hence moral and religious laziness. The average, morally mediocre Christian knows that he is not wicked enough to deserve eternal torment, and hence, confident of salvation, makes no efforts towards self-improvement. It is as if there were a system of laws which inflicted only capital punishment and only for major crimes; people would be encouraged to commit minor misdemeanours.[3]

Moreover, the doctrine of eternal torment often leads to atheism—[4]

---

[1] Petersen, *Mysterion*, T. I, Vorrede, p. (xxi): 'Wo noch eine solche Gnade zu letzt vor mich behalten ist / so will ich eine weile die Lust dieser Welt geniessen / und es darauffhin wagen / ich werde einmahl selig werden.'

[2] Petersen, *Mysterion*, T. I, Vorrede, p. (xxii), *Ewiges Ev.*, p. 4, Gespräch I, p. 154.

[3] Ibid., T. I, *Ewiges Ev.*, pp. 10–11.

[4] Ibid., T. I, Gespräch III, p. 26: 'Was hat doch die Lehre von der unauffhörlichen Verdamnisz biszher gefruchtet? Sind die Menschen dadurch frömmer

What fruit has the doctrine of eternal damnation born up till now? Has it made men more pious? On the contrary, when they have properly considered the cruel, frightful disproportion between the punishments and their own finite sins, they have begun to believe nothing at all, and have thought that these books of Holy Scripture have just been compiled by the priests, who made up such threats for the common people as they thought fit, in order to keep them in check.

Petersen once heard an atheist talk in this way; when he explained to him the Restoration of All Things,[1]

he opened his eyes and sighed, as if awakened from a deep sleep, and confessed to me that this stone had long lain upon his heart, but had now been rolled off it.

It is interesting that, by thinking about hell, Petersen was led to ask awkward questions about human deterrent punishment. Are sorcerers encouraged by being threatened with only a few minutes' burning? ought we to punish them in 'the most frightful and long-drawn out manner?'[2]

---

[1] Ibid., T. I, Gespräch I, p. 222: 'da bekam er Augen / und erseufzete / als einer / der ausz einem tiefen Schlaff erwachete / und hat mir darauff bekant / wie ihm solcher Stein lange auff seinem Hertzen gelegen / nun aber abgewältzet wäre . . .'

[2] Ibid., T. II, Gegen-Anmerckungen, p. 14.

---

worden? Vielmehr haben sie / wenn sie der Sachen recht nachgedacht / aus der grausamen erschrecklichen disproportion der Straffen / und ihrer endlichen Sünden / gar nichts anfangen zu glauben / und haben gedacht / es wären solche Bücher der Heil. Schrifft nur von den Pfaffen zusammen getragen / die nach Gutbefinden solche Dräuungen für dem gemeinen Volck hätten angesetzt / dasz sie dadurch im Zaum möchten gehalten werden.'

Chapter XV

◈◈◈

ENGLISH PHILADELPHIANS
(2) Roach and the Camisards

◈◈◈

(i) THE PUBLIC TESTIMONY

1697 was the great year of the English Philadelphians' 'public testimony' to the approaching millennium. In that year their meetings, which had hitherto been small private gatherings, became larger and more public, and were transferred from Mrs Lead's and Mrs Bathurst's homes to Westmoreland House.[1] On August 31st of that year Mrs Lead wrote to Richard Roach of the first meeting:[2]

> there was a very great concourse of people on Sunday. And though there was some molestation from Boys and some rude fellows, yet there was a sober sort of company very attentive and inquisitive.

A few days earlier, on August 23rd,[3] Roach had presented to the Archbishop of Canterbury, Thomas Tenison, a declaration

---

[1] They also had public meetings at Hungerford Market, and later at Lorimer's Hall; see Roach, Rawlinson MS., D 833, fos 65 vo–66; Roach, *Great Crisis*, p. 99; Thune, *The Behmenists*, pp. 90, 96.

[2] Rawlinson MS., D 832, fo 53.

[3] Thomas Beverly had calculated that the Last Days would begin on this date; see Roach, *Imperial Standard*, p. xix, and Rawlinson MS., D 833, fo 83.

of the aims of the Philadelphian Society.[1] The Archbishop remained unconvinced, but assured Roach that he would not allow the Society to be persecuted.

In March 1697 the Philadelphians began to publish a monthly periodical, *Theosophical Transactions by the Philadelphian Society*, of which only five numbers appeared, ranging in price from 6d. to 1s. 3d., according to size. The title-page of the first number bore the slightly altered text from Daniel XII, 4: 'many shall run to and fro, and Theosophy [originally: knowledge] shall be increased'—the whole verse is one of the main texts for the assertion that in the Last Days there will be a new revelation: 'But thou, O Daniel, shut up the words, and seal the book, even to the time of the end.' Its contents, at first sight, are rather puzzling. There are a few statements of the aims of the Society; but there is not very much about the approaching millennium, and almost nothing overt and explicit about universal salvation. On the other hand there is quite a lot of Sunday paper news—stories of ghosts recently seen, 'a Relation out of France, concerning a Black Bituminous vapour that arose out of the earth, and did considerable Mischief', an account, in a letter from 'a Member of this Society in *Niederdoddeleben*' (i.e. Petersen), of a young man who was deluded into thinking that a certain baby in Gutenburg was a new Christ, and so forth.[2] There are several pages of vocal music, together with two discourses on a new expressive kind of 'Natural Recitative'.[3] The songs are mostly very florid recitative, with an unfigured bass, which either contains a great many misprints or was composed by someone ignorant of the elementary rules of harmony;

[1] Rawlinson MS., D 833, fo 83 vo; Tension dismissed Roach, saying: 'I perceive you are rooted in your Opinions; however I will not be a persecutor, nor give you or your Friends any disturbance.' Cf. Thune, op. cit., p. 87.

Mrs Lead's letter of August 31 1697 (v. supra, note (2)) ends with a mysterious postscript by Francis Lee, in which he tells Roach to be very cautious because something may have come to the Archbishop's ear; he continues: 'The Spies are many and of various kinds. Let all that is possible of civility be shewn to this gentleman, the Baron of Knyphausen, who comes to you by tomorrows coach: He is of a very good Disposition, but a stranger to all our Affairs.' I can find no other evidence of Knyphausen's having visited England.

[2] *Theosophical Transactions*, p. 43 ('A Relation of the Apparition of a Spirit, keeping the Treasures of the Earth; and of his Delivery of the Key of a certain Mountain in Germany to a Considerable Person; and what thereupon ensued'), 45 ('A Relation out of France'), 46, 83 (Petersen).

[3] Ibid., pp. 66, 100–2 (songs), 60 seq., 174 seq., 197–9 (writings on music).

the texts are chiliastic—one, for example, is part of a poem prefixed to Mrs Lead's *A Fountain of Gardens*; it begins:[1]

The Glorious Aera NOW, NOW, NOW begins.
NOW, NOW the great Angelick Trumpet sings:
   And in ev'ry Blast
   Love's EVERLASTING GOSPEL rings.

In some of the contributions on religious matters there is an oddly jocular, frivolous tone.[2]

The lack of overt propaganda for universal salvation is probably due to the fact that, as we know from Lee, not all the Philadelphians held this doctrine.[3] This lack, and the paucity of chiliastic propaganda, can also be explained by deliberately esoteric intentions. The aim of publishing the periodical was certainly to gain adherents, to build up the true Philadelphian Church ready for the Second Coming; but the message must reach only suitable ears—the true church must be built of sound material. In their *Reasons for the Foundation and Promotion of our Society*, published in this periodical,[4] the Philadelphians, with endearing modesty, admit that only a few of their members are saints and that most are like rough-hewn stones, 'with great Unevenness and some Rubbish', which must be cleaned and polished before they can become the foundation of the temple of the Lord. They naturally did not want to attract a lot more rubbishy members. At the end of the cabalistic letter already mentioned,[5] which contains suggestions of universal salvation, there is an editorial comment, explaining its obscurity by the ancient theory that religious truths must always be veiled from the vulgar in 'Hieroglyphical and Parabolical Terms, as *none of the Wicked shall understand, but the Wise shall understand.*'[6]

---

[1] Ibid., pp. 100–2; Walton (*Notes and Materials*, pp. 252–7) reprints most of the poem, ascribing it to Lee; it is more probably by Roach.

[2] E.g. ibid., pp. 6 seq. ('Occasional Thought upon Rev. xxi. 18.'), verso of title to No. 1 ('A Safe Guide').

[3] Lee in Walton, op. cit., p. 219; cf. Lee's preface to Mrs Lead's *Eine Offenbarung*, p. 6.

[4] *Theosoph. Trans.*, pp. 195–7.

[5] V, supra p. 225.

[6] *Theosoph. Trans.*, pp. 292–3; cf. the announcement at the beginning of the *Transactions*, in which the hope is expressed that they will conduce to the

The explanation of the music, the strange events, apparitions, etc., and of the jocularity, is to be found in the writings, printed and manuscript, of Richard Roach. From these it is clear that the approach of the millennium is a gradual process, already far advanced, and that it is concentrated on the English, the chosen nation, through which all the others will eventually be brought into one fold. London will be the new Jerusalem.[1] In his *The Great Crisis* (1725–7), he tells us in great detail what life in the millennium will be like.[2] It will be a time of great religious progress, everyone being spiritually educated for the eternal bliss to come. But there will also be '*Outward* and *Temporal* Blessings': great advances in the natural sciences, and in all the arts of pleasure, which, at present so often abused, will be employed to good ends. In the theatre, for example, there will be 'Sacred *Mysteries*' performed, far exceeding the magnificence of modern or ancient Roman stage-shows, and dancing 'in beautiful and *Mystic* Figures, Instructive also and Representative of *Divine* Truths, and Movements'.[3] But above all there will be music, 'compos'd and perform'd by Inspiration, and that with *New Instruments* invented'. Angelical hymns will be transported to earth, for use in church and in the

> *Love-Feasts* of God's children in their more Private Associations. Not is it to pass Unobserv'd, how particularly in the *Genius* of this Nation there appears at this Day a more than Ordinary *Inclination* to, and Delight in *Music* . . . together with the Great and General *Improvement* of this Art.

This occurred especially during the reign of William and Mary, who prefigured the reign of Christ and His Bride the Church— Roach was a great admirer of Purcell, and his new expressive recitative was based on Purcell's practice—

> since which has been brought in the Politeness of the *Italian* and Improvements of the *German* Music; all Preparing for and tending to the *Perfection* of it.

[1] Roach, *Great Crisis*, pp. 18, 44–5, 57; *Imperial Standard*, p. xvi.
[2] *Great Crisis*, pp. 181 seq. Cf. Burnet's millennium (supra, p. 158).
[3] Ibid., p. 184.

---

restoration of '*primitive* and *Apostolical Christianity*', 'though the whole Secret be not possible to be Discover'd by any, that are not yet Initiated into the most Holy Rites of *Wisdom's Disciplehood*' (ibid., p. 3).

The songs published in the *Transactions* were the first fruits of the music of the millennium. I wish he had lived to hear the *Messiah*.

Another of these temporal blessings will be a great improvement in wit,[1] which, being

> the Peculiar *Gift* of *Wisdom* [i.e. the Boehmenist Virgin Wisdom], will be *sanctified* and Display'd in its highest Degree, both in Delightful Conversations, and as in the case of Elijah's Mockery of the *Prophets* of *Baal*, in the *Sarcastic* Part also.

One of the main objects of this mockery will be the 'Baffles' of Satan, at 'his last Shifts, and as at a Loss for New Projects; or at his Wits End, acting Wildly, Extravagantly, and Ridiculously'[2]—these last Shifts of Satan account for some of the strange events recorded in the *Transactions*. But this millennary wit will also appear in a far more extraordinary form:[3]

> the Appearances and Movements of the Judge Himself, towards his Chosen Ones, as under a *Mask* of Terror, and the *Love-wiles* as of Joseph to his brethren, trying and Exercising them in various manners before he Manifests Himself to 'em in his High Grace and Love, will afterwards have a Pleasant Remembrance, and be a Subject of their Innocent Mirth and Disport. And more generally the *Anger* and *Strict Justice* of God itself

will, as they give way to His mercy and love, seem like a game, a sport. The whole tragedy of Fall and Redemption, of sin and hell, of man's misery and Christ's agony and bloody sweat, is seen as one of God's grisly jokes, if I may borrow an expression from Professor Empson. This way of solving the problem of evil may derive from Sterry and White, where it appears in a more poetic and more convincing form. This millennary wit accounts for the jocularity of several contributions to the

---

[1] Roach, *Great Crisis*, p. 185.

[2] Ibid., p. 185; cf. pp. 27–32, a list of false prophets recently raised up by Satan (Muggleton, Naylor (the Quaker Messiah), Sabatai Zevi (the Jewish apostate Messiah), the English Arians, and '*Atheistical, Sodomitical*, and other *Hellish* Combinations and *Clubs*'). The Philadelphians announced that in the *Theosophical Transactions* they would unmask 'Satanical Spirits' appearing 'in these Last Times' as angels of light, as deceiving prophets.

[3] *Great Crisis*, p. 186; cf. *Imperial Standard*, pp. 89–90:

> 'Jesus *his Friends in* Mask *of Judgment proves*;
> *But Heavn'ly Grace* behind the Curtain *moves*:
> *I know that my Redeemer Lives and* Loves.'

Transactions, and we shall meet another surprising example of it in Roach's life.

The approach of the millennium is shown by two kinds of signs: first, signs of God's anger, His 'strict judgment work', that is, all kinds of disaster (storms, wars, earthquakes), and the last shifts of Satan (apparitions, false prophets);[1] secondly, signs of His love and mercy—great increase of mystics and true prophets (especially female ones, owing to the influence of the Virgin Wisdom: Mrs Lead, Antoinette Bourignon, Madame de Guyon), prosperity and scientific progress in England.[2] The general plan is that, after a period of divine judgment and punishment (the English Civil Wars, the plague and the fire of London), God's mercy is gradually overcoming His anger, the sun breaking through the clouds.[3] The first great culmination of His merciful work was the 'public testimony' of the Philadelphians in 1697 and the establishment of general peace in Europe in the same year.[4]

This theory of signs has the great advantage that absolutely any imaginable course of events can be interpreted as signs of the approaching millennium. A good example of this is the weather. In the preface to his *Great Crisis* Roach tells us he began the book the previous summer,[5]

> in such cold and winter weather; and the abounding Rains and Floods continued thro' the whole quarter, so contrary to the natural Course and Constitution thereof.

This was a clear sign of God's anger, but also of His mercy breaking through; for it was the beginning of a process of mixing up the seasons, which would end in a perpetual spring suitable for the millennium.[6] Some signs of God's anger, however, were less ambiguous: a woman in Scotland was[7]

> delivered of a terrible *Monster*, heard to Squeak and Cry in the Womb, and as it was coming forth shreiking so terribly, that all

[1] Roach, *Great Crisis*, pp. 6–8.
[2] Ibid., pp. 8–11, 96–8.
[3] Ibid., pp. 44–6, 49–52, 68–79; cf. *Imperial Standard*, pp. 28, 32–3, 70–1.
[4] *Great Crisis*, pp. 36, 79.
[5] Ibid., p. 3.
[6] Ibid., p. 13.
[7] Ibid., p. 48.

in the Room ran away affrighted. Afterward the Ministers and others coming in, a Creature was born all *Hairy*; with *Two Heads*, one above the other; and the Face of the Upper-most like a *Lyon*. It immediately ran up and down the House, crying, *Woe, Woe, Woe to the World*; till they knocked it on the Head.

The public testimony of the Philadelphians continued for six years, but with little success. On Easter Day 1699, at a public meeting, they read a *Declaration of the Philadelphian Society of England*, in which they complained that their millennary message had been contemptuously rejected. But the English continued to reject it, and, as Roach notes, God soon showed His anger by starting the War of the Spanish Succession in 1701.[1]

This turned the Philadelphians' thoughts to Germany and Holland, where Mrs Lead's writings were already well known through Fischer's translations and where the ground had already been prepared by the Petersens' propaganda. At the end of 1702 they drew up a detailed programme, in forty-four articles, for the formation of Philadelphian groups both in England and on the continent. These articles show that the projected movement, though claiming to be non-sectarian, was quite strictly organized; there are provisions for raising funds, and there is a descending hierarchy of travelling Inspectors, Regulators, Elders, Members, and Participants.[2] The Philadelphians also began to draw up a creed, which they never finished.[3] Early in 1703 they sent off their first missionary, Johann Dittmar of Saltzungen, who had come to England in the autumn of 1702. He took with him the articles, and was sent the creed in instalments. He travelled about Germany and Holland trying to collect money and adherents. At first he claimed to have had great success and to have gained over a hundred members. But in the *Catalogus amicorum in Germania* he compiled there are some very doubtful names:[4] Spener,

---

[1] Thune, *The Behmenists*, p. 96; Roach, *Great Crisis*, pp. 36–7.
[2] Thune, op. cit., pp. 115–16; C. W. H. Hochhut, 'Geschichte und Entwicklung der philadelphischen Gemeinden. I. Jane Leade und die philadelphische Gemeinde in England', in *Zeitschrift für die historische Theologie*, Gotha, 1865, pp. 229 seq. Both Thune and Hochhut use MSS. of E. S. Cryprian in the Herzogliche Bibliothek at Gotha, which I have not been able to consult.
[3] Printed in Hochhut, art. cit., pp. 257 seq.
[4] Thune, op. cit., pp. 114, 118–126; Hochhut, art. cit., pp. 224 seq.

who certainly did not appreciate Mrs Lead's writings,[1] and Arnold, who, as we know, had already denied any connection with the Philadelphians;[2] but it also contains some genuine adherents, such as the Petersens and Fräulein von Asseburg. Petersen found Dittmar overbearing and too uncompromisingly Boehmenist, and he wrote to Mrs Lead to object to this attempt to impose Boehmenism on the German Philadelphians.[3]

In Amsterdam Dittmar tried to gain the adherence of Gichtel, and ended by having a violent quarrel with him.[4] This is not surprising, since Gichtel, as we have seen, had already decided that Mrs Lead's visions were not genuine.[5] He had, moreover, broken with his former friend, Loth Fischer, because the latter, according to Gichtel, claimed that Mrs Lead was infallible and had tried to start a new sect based on her revelations.[6] Gichtel a little later asserted that Fischer had written to him suggesting that he too could have a pension from Knyphausen, if he would defend Mrs Lead and universal salvation.[7] Petersen indignantly denied this story, probably rightly, since Gichtel was exceptionally envious and spiteful.[8] Gichtel had once believed in universal salvation, as he himself admits.[9] According to Petersen, this revelation was withdrawn from him because, in an excess of zeal, he went too far and in his prayers addressed the Devil as his brother.[10]

Dittmar's mission was a failure, and by September 1703 he had abandoned the Philadelphians and was trying to find a job in Germany.[11] In England too the failure continued. Apart from

[1] Spener, *Letzte Theol. Bedencken*, Theil III, pp. 466–7 (letter of 1697, in which he says he cannot understand Mrs Lead's writings, and has been told they are incompatible with Scripture).

[2] V. supra, p. 238.

[3] Thune, op. cit., p. 133.

[4] Thune, op. cit., p. 129; Hochhut, art. cit., pp. 249 seq.

[5] V. supra, p. 229.

[6] Gichtel, *Theosoph. Pr.*, Bd. I, pp. 221–2, 226, 414, Bd. V, pp. 3741, 3787–8, Bd. VII, pp. 236, 390.

[7] Ibid., Bd. V, pp. 3540–1, 3650, Bd. VII, p. 328.

[8] Petersen, *Lebens-Beschreibung*, pp. 337–8. Seeberg's verdict on Gichtel is: 'Persönlich war der verschrobene Gichtel unfraglich ein unangenehmer Nörgler' (Seeberg, *Gottfried Arnold*, p. 366).

[9] Gichtel, *Theosoph, Pr.*, Bd. I, p. 229.

[10] Petersen, *Lebens-Beschreibung*, pp. 336–7. According to Petersen (ibid., p. 334), Gichtel in 1714 published a 'lästerliches Buch': *Entdeckter Atheismus aus der bekannten Lehre von der Wiederbringung aller Dinge und der gefallenen Engeln.*

[11] Thune, op. cit., p. 134.

public indifference or contempt, there were internal dissensions, and on Sunday, June the 12th, 1703 the Philadelphians read publicly a 'Protestation against the Degeneracy & Apostacy of the Christian Churches', and distributed printed copies of it. Then for a few years they retired into private meetings.[1]

In 1704 Mrs Lead died,[2] and shortly afterwards she appeared to Roach in a vision as

a small Globe beginning to descend from the Highest Region, which grew larger and larger as it came nearer to the Earth; not only large from its being near to the Eye, but as Dilating itself in its Descent. And I heard this word, the still Eternity displays it self.

This convinced Roach that 'the Mantle of that great Saint' had fallen upon him, and that he should henceforth lead the Society.[3]

(ii) THE CAMISARDS

The main chiliastic text, the Apocalypse, is a threatening, revengeful book. Vindictive justice, intense satisfaction in seeing the wicked punished, a justly angry God—these are ideas and emotions that one might expect to be prevalent in a chiliastic sect. Professor Cohn in his *Pursuit of the Millennium*[4] has shown that chiliasm often arises in groups which are living in a state of extreme misery, oppressed by tyrants whom they cannot rationally hope to throw off. The anger, the frustrated vengeance, find their outlet in the hope of a Messiah who will condemn and punish the wicked enemies, in the hope of the avenging wars and catastrophes that will precede and prepare his coming.

A typical example of this kind of chiliastic movement occurred in our period. After the revocation of the Edict of Nantes in 1685 Pierre Jurieu began to prophesy that the millennium would happen in a few years' time.[5] This event was of course

---

[1] Roach, Rawlinson MS., D. 833, fo 56 vo; *Great Crisis*, p. 36.
[2] Thune, op. cit., p. 135.
[3] Roach, Rawlinson MS., D 833, fos 57–57 vo.
[4] Norman Cohn, *The Pursuit of the Millennium*, London, 1957. Professor Cohn is of course fully aware that this is not the only type of chiliasm.
[5] See Delvolvé, *Religion . . . Bayle*, pp. 164–7; G. H. Dodge, *The Political Theory of the Huguenots of the Dispersion*, Columbia, 1947, pp. 35 seq.

to be preceded by the overthrow of the French monarchy and the re-establishment of Protestantism in that country. It was discovered long after his death that he did his best to make his prophecy come true by becoming a spy in the pay of the English.[1] This seed fell on fertile ground in the south-west of France, especially in the mountainous district of the Cévennes, where there was a large Protestant population. Together with enforced conversion, *dragonnades*, etc. it produced an extremely active chiliastic movement, expressing itself in deeds of armed violence and in an epidemic of prophets, many of them children, foretelling natural and supernatural disasters, judgments of God on their Catholic oppressors. In 1701, when the War of the Spanish Succession broke out, there was a large-scale armed revolt, supported not very effectually by English money and arms. It was serious enough to engage considerable forces of the French army; but in 1704 the leader of the Camisards, as they were called, signed a treaty with Maréchal de Villars, and only sporadic resistance continued.[2] By 1706 quite a number of Camisards had taken refuge in England, where they went on with their doom-laden, threatening prophecies; these were accompanied by spectacular bodily symptoms: convulsions, violent trembling, 'loud and terrifying hiccups', as one of their English converts says,[3] and were often delivered in the form of God speaking in the first person.

The Camisards soon began to foretell disasters about to overtake not France but London, since this city was rejecting their divine message. The reaction to these terrifying and blasphemous prophecies was strong, especially among the respectable Huguenots already established in London. Naturally enough, people did not want to be threatened with another Fire and Plague of London, and violence was met with violence. In 1707 the English authorities intervened by putting three of the prophets in the pillory,[4] one of them being Nicolas Fatio, an eminent mathematician and scientist of Genevan extraction and

---

[1] Dodge, op. cit., p. 104.

[2] See *Mémoires inédits d'Abraham Mazel et d'Elie Marion*, ed. C. Bost, Paris, 1931; G. Ascoli, 'L'Affaire des prophètes français à Londres', in *Revue du 18ᵉ siècle*, Paris, 1916; R. Knox, *Enthusiasm*, pp. 356 seq.

[3] Samuel Keimer, *A Brand pluck'd from the Burning*, London, 1718, p. 1.

[4] See Ascoli, art. cit., pp. 92–3.

a member of the Royal Society.[1] Nevertheless the Camisards made several English converts, the most active of which, John Lacy, a wealthy Justice of the Peace, we shall meet again. In December 1707 they prophesied that another convert, Dr Emes, then on his death-bed, would resurrect after five months,[2] and a certain Stephen Harefoot of Birmingham announced that he would die and resurrect within the year.[3] Dr Emes did not resurrect, and Mr Harefoot failed even to die. The Camisards were the occasion of Shaftesbury's *Letter Concerning Enthusiasm* (1708),[4] in which, perhaps not unreasonably, he advised that such religious movements should be dealt with by ridicule rather than force or persuasion.

If this is what chiliasts are like—violent, vindictive, worshipping a God of vengeance, it seems surprising that our chiliastic Philadelphians should preach universal salvation and the Johannine God of love. In explaining this apparent contradiction, the first point to notice is that, though many chiliastic movements may grow out of misery and oppression and hence be dominated by frustrated revenge, by no means all of them have this genesis. The English and German Philadelphians were all middle or upper class, well educated, comfortable people who, until they went in for chiliasm, enjoyed social and financial security. Even their chiliasm turned to their worldly advantage, through the agency of Baron Knyphausen. Roach insists on the high social standing of the Philadelphians; the public testimony was given[5]

not by *Obscure* Persons; but such as were of *Known Character*

---

[1] See G. A. Metzger, *Marie Huber*, pp. 14 seq.; cf. *Clavis Prophetica; or, a Key to the Prophecies of Mons. Marion, And the other Camisars With some Reflections on the Character of these New Envoys, and of Mons. F— their Chief Secretary*, London, 1707, in which the author argues that Fatio is too intelligent to be deceived by the Camisards and that he is using them to destroy the Church of England, in order to establish a new religion of his own.

[2] See, before the prophesied date of resurrection (May 25 1708): Richard Bulkeley, *An Answer to Several Treatises Lately publish'd on the Subject of the Prophets*, London, 1708, p. 87; John Lacy, *A Relation of the Dealings of God To his Unworthy Servant John Lacy*, London, 1708, pp. 29–31; after the date: Richard Bulkeley, *Warnings of the Eternal Spirit*, London, 1709, pp. 34 seq.; S. Keimer, *A Brand*, pp. 11 seq.

[3] See Francis Hutchinson, *A Short View of the Pretended Spirit of Prophecy*, London, 1708, p. 37.

[4] Shaftesbury, *The Life*, ed. Rand, p. xxv.

[5] Roach, *Great Crisis*, p. 36; cf. *Imperial Standard*, p. xix.

for Integrity, Probity and Learning; several *Fellows* of *Colleges*, and One a *Councellor* of one of the *Inns of Court*, being concerned therein.

We must also remember that the Philadelphians, as we have seen, did manage in their scheme of universal salvation to preserve much of the vindictive anger, divine and human, embedded in Christian and particularly chiliastic tradition.

In 1707 the Philadelphians came out of their retirement, and combined with the Camisards to announce once again in public that the Last Days had already begun.[1] This was a striking example of God's peculiar sense of humour. Roach regarded the Camisards partly as direct instruments of God's angry judgment work, prophesying disasters which did sometimes occur, and partly as false prophets, one of Satan's Last Shifts, but as such also a sign of the Last Days.[2] The basically jocular nature of God's anger was shown, according to Roach, by the comic contortions and hysterical laughter, the 'agitations', which accompanied their terrible prophecies.[3] We know from other sources that the Camisards' meetings did involve a lot of laughing. At one of them John Lacy and Sir Richard Bulkeley, another wealthy English convert, fell into a 'profuse Laughter' and claimed that this was 'extatick, proceeding from visionary Representations'. At another there was[4]

> Mr *Lacy's* Laughter, when he saw *Elizabeth Gray* rolling her eyes about in a distorted manner in her *Agitations*; who perceiving the Frowns of one in the Company upon him for so doing, He said, *I know not how it is; but when that Girl has Visions, I partake of the Joy of them.*

---

[1] Roach, Rawlinson MS., D 833, fos 31–2.

[2] Roach, *Great Crisis*, pp. 37–9; one of the disasters accurately prophesied was: 'Disappointment and Damp of Worldly Pleasures, as *Imbittering* the Harlots *Cup*, and in frequent *Vexation* of Spirit to the eager Pursuers of them'.

[3] Ibid., p. 186; the Camisards were as 'a sport, in Part at least, carry'd on by the Divine Justice thro' them . . . as the *Lamb*, to the Children of *Grace*, shall appear in the Throne, *smiling* thro' the *Judge*, and turning the Dispensation of Terror, tho' *Smart* indeed in the Preparation for and Ingredients of it, into a Jest or *Holy Sport* in the End'.

[4] Henry Nicholson, *The Falsehood of the New Prophets Manifested with their Corrupt Doctrines and Conversations*, London, 1708, pp. 21–2.

And according to another English convert, the French, but not the English, prophets[1]

> had Love Meetings commanded, where they would meet, *Kiss*, and *tickle* one another, *chucking* one another under the Chin, laughing and crying out, He, He, He, He, He, He, and using many lascivious Postures, which I shall not here mention.

The Philadelphians were delivering the opposite but complementary message of God's love and mercy breaking through, and eventually triumphing over His wrath. There is a manuscript account, probably written by Lacy, of meetings in the summer of 1710 at which these two messages clashed; the conflict between opposing divine attributes is acted out before our eyes.

The Philadelphians were represented by Roach and a young prophetess called Mrs Sarah Wilshere. In a letter of February 1711 Roach described the meetings thus:[2]

> This Person [sc. Mrs Wilshere] & I have been joynd in a Work together, to wrestle against the Ministration of Judgment in the Late Prophets [i.e. Camisards] & have had several Contests with them in their Publick Meetings, Power against Power, & Inspiration against Inspiration, exhibiting outwardly the emotions or Holy Contest of the Love & Anger, Grace & Strict Justice in the Mind of God. They thundering terrors & Judgments, & we Proclaiming the Mercies of God & Prophesying the Declension of their Ministration; & showing them the shortness & Defects of it.

From Lacy's accounts, it seems that God's justice decisively had the best of it. The Philadelphians had the disadvantage that, whilst preaching the loving God, they were obliged by their Boehmenist dualism, and by their natural liberalism, to accept the validity of their opponents' punishing God; whereas the Camisards could claim that there could not be two Gods, and had no doubt that their message alone was valid. The Camisards had the additional tactical advantage of frequently speaking in the person of God Himself.

[1] S. Keimer, *A Brand*, p. 71.
[2] Roach, Rawlinson MS., D 832, fo 77–77 vo.

The first of these meetings began thus:[1]

Mr Dutton had first an inspiration concerning Christ's coming to Destroy the Man of Sin or Antichrist,

and he ended by singing a hymn in praise of God's 'power in the Destruction of his Enemies'. Then

> Mr Richard Roach reads a Prayer of his own . . . & an Inspiration or two, as he call'd 'em, that were pronounced at Baldwin Gardens by Mrs Sarah Wilshere his copartner in the Philadelphian way; which were extolling the LOVE of God, and so as to Derogate from his equally glorious Attribute of JUSTICE. And because the spirit in the Prophets [Camisards] had condemn'd what she had [said] before at other times in their Assembly, Therefore he try'd again and offer'd these. Beginning to read, the Spirit came upon Mary Keimer, her eyes being shut, who standing up was made to lay hold of Mr R's left sleeve with her left hand; & all the time of speaking what follows shook as a Rod her Right Hand, & a Loud Voice.
> M.K. Who sent thee?
> R.R. The God of Love.
> M.K. By what dost thou know?
> R. By the witness of his Spirit with me, in his LOVE.
> K. Take thou care, lest a False Peace have possess'd thy Soul, & thou goest on believing thou art sent from God, when thou art not sent from Him . . . Take heed; God is the same . . . He can in no wise nor in any case contradict Himself . . .
> R. . . . Speakest thou by the eternal Love, or speakest thou in part from the eternal Justice?
> K. Consider thou O Man! I will confound thee, yea & bring thy Lofty thoughts down; I will lay thee even with the Dust. Who art thou O man that Exaltest thyself? Who art thou? *I am, I am*! How durst thou presume to speak unto me? I can this moment strike thee dead . . . *I am, I am, I am, I am, I am* . . . and ye shall know that I have spoken: for *quickly Judgments* shal be usher'd in. Then wilt thou know *who* has spoken, & who now does speak. 'Tis the God of Love . . .

There were other similar meetings: one at which a Camisard, under agitations, constantly interrupted poor Mrs Wilshere's inspiration by butting her with his head, and Mary Keimer was again the mouthpiece of the God of justice who was so angry

---

[1] Rawlinson MS., D 1318, fos 55–6; the accounts of these meetings are headed: 'POLEMICA SACRO-Prophetica Anti-ROACHiana-WILTSHIREiana.'

at not being recognized as being also the God of love;[1] another at which a Mrs Irwin seized a letter of Roach's, in which he justified his loving messages, and, while tearing it in pieces, said (also speaking as God):[2]

> As a sign . . . I have now torn in pieces that which is none of Mine; but a spirit deluding the simple . . .

It must have needed real courage to stand up to Mary Keimer. It had been prophesied that she should go to France and there speak to the King, 'who should upon his Disobedience be immediately struck dead by her mouth'.[3] And her brother later wrote:[4]

> I have seen my sister, who is a lusty young woman, fling another Prophetess on the Floor, and under Agitations tread upon her Breast, Belly, Legs etc. walking several Times backwards and forwards over her, and stamping upon her with violence. This was adjudg'd to be a sign of the Fall of the *Whore of Babylon*.

The next year Roach was able to take a little revenge on the thundering Camisards. Mr Lacy, having failed to convert his wife, left her and went to live with a prophesying actress, Elizabeth Gray, whom we have already briefly met; a 'Supernatural voice' threatened him with 'Hell-fire and eternal destruction', if he failed to do so.[5] Roach wrote a comic ballad for the occasion, entitled *Marriage a la Mode, or the Camisard Wedding*, in which he pokes quite kindly fun at the leading Camisards, refers to the meetings just described, and makes a few mildly obscene jokes about the so-called wedding. The actress, for example, is described thus:

> The Bride had all Graces a budding,
>   And seen too in Shaking Fit;
> O never was Quaking-Pudding,
>   So Butter'd, and sugar'd, and Sweet.[6]

---

[1] Rawlinson MS., D. 1318, fos 63 vo–64 vo. A similar, or perhaps the same, meeting is reported in S. Keimer, *A Brand*, p. 54.

[2] Rawlinson MS., D 1318, fo 65 (meeting on June 15th, 1712).

[3] S. Keimer, *A Brand*, p. 32.

[4] Ibid., p. 54.

[5] *A Letter from John Lacy, to Thomas Dutton, being Reason why the former left his wife, and took E. Gray a Prophetess to his Bed*, n.p., n.d., letter dated March 1711, bound with the British Museum copy of S. Keimer, *A Brand*.

[6] Roach, Rawlinson MS., D 832 fos 192 seq., 200 seq.

Samuel Keimer, Mary's brother, in his repentant autobiography, *A Brand pluck'd from the Burning* (1718), prints the ballad in full, 'tho' it is somewhat filthy'.[1] From a letter of Roach's about this ballad, we know that it was an example of millennary wit, written under the inspiration of the Virgin Wisdom, 'who has in various ways her sports and delights among the children of men'.[2]

The last meeting recorded consists of an inspiration Lacy had in November 1712. It was, he says,[3]

occasion'd upon the perusing of a book wrote by Mr Jer. White, concerning the Restoration of all things, including in it the Universal Salvation of Wicked Men & Devils also (according to Origen's Doctrine) To which book Mr Roach had put a Preface & to whom this Remonstrance of the Spirit was particularly directed.

The inspiration is made up of angry rhetorical questions, mostly asked by God, such as

Who is it presumes now to fill up that Book of Life with names of the abominable ? Nay, even without distinction, impose it on me ?

It is of great interest to know that it was Roach who published White's *Restoration* and wrote its long and well-informed preface.[4] White's book is certainly the most convincing defence of

[1] S. Keimer, *A Brand*, pp. 58–9; it was prophesied that, in order to confirm the rightness of Lacy's and Betty Gray's union, their first child should be a son 'and should work Miracles, as soon as born'; it was a daughter; the same thing happened with the next child.
[2] Roach, Rawlinson MS., D 832, fos 60–1. The Virgin Wisdom's inspiration took the form of a dream; at the end of the second copy of the Ballad (v. supra, note 4) Roach writes: 'The Author's Dream, long before, is here come out: which was that a Person of Great Authority brought Eliz. Gray before Him & turned up her Backside for Him to give her Correction: which he did by giving her one good spank on the Buttock.'
[3] Rawlinson MS., D 1318, fos 67–8, dated November 21st, 1712, headed: 'POLEMICA SACRO-PROPHETICA Anti-ROACHiana-WHITE-ORIGEN iana'.
[4] Roach also published an edition of White's *A Perswasive to Moderation and Forbearance in Love among the Divided Forms of Christians*, London, n.d. (1st ed. 1708), which he dedicated to John Tarrey, a Distiller, who was White's literary executor. Roach corresponded with Tarrey and a Mr Davis on the subject of objections to White's *Restoration* (Rawlinson MS., D 832, fos 83–90).

universal salvation among all those mentioned in the present study, and it asserts the priority in God of the attribute of love in its most absolute form.

In addition to transmitting White's admirable treatise and to setting off the Petersens' movement, the English Philadelphians are very probably the ultimate source of Rousseau's rejection of eternal torment in the *Confession de foi d'un Vicaire Savoyard*,[1] and this because of their imprudent association with the wild and violent Camisards. Nicolas Fatio de Duillier, the Camisard convert who was put in the pillory, was the great-uncle of a young Swiss girl, Marie Huber, who later became a very effective propagandist of universal salvation. She is the first person, to my knowledge, to assert that the happiness of the saved, far from being increased by their awareness of the torments of the damned, would be spoilt by it.[2] In 1719, at the age of twenty-two, she wrote to Fatio about this doctrine, which a previous letter of his had suggested.[3] Since he acted as scribe at the Camisard meetings, he would have heard Roach and Mrs Wilshere expound the doctrine. There is little doubt that Marie Huber's works were a major influence on Rousseau's religious ideas.[4] Roach's and Mrs Wilshere's painful contests with the Camisards were not quite in vain.

That some of the Camisards were influenced by the English Philadelphians at least to the point of being open to propaganda for universal salvation,[5] is suggested by Petersen's account of them. From June 1712, Fatio and three other Camisards travelled around Europe, still having inspirations.[6] They came

---

[1] Rousseau, *Collection Complete des Oeuvres*, Geneve, 1782, T. V. pp. 48–9.

[2] M. Huber, *The World Unmask'd*, London, 1736, p. 289: 'I am one of those who could not think themselves perfectly happy, did they know any Beings must be eternally miserable.' Cf. supra p. 41.

[3] G. A. Metzger, *Marie Huber*, p. 19.

[4] See P. M. Masson, *La Religion de J. J. Rousseau*, Paris, 1916, T. I, pp. 207 seq., cf. T. II, pp. 49, 72, 82.

[5] Richard Bulkeley writes at length on the Restoration of All Things, which he equates with the Everlasting Gospel (*An Answer to Several Treatises*, pp. 29–30, 59 seq.); but he does not, I think, mean universal salvation.

[6] Nicolas Fatio, Jean Allut, Elie Marion, Charles Portalés, *Plan de la Justice de Dieu sur la Terre, dans ces Derniers Jours*, Imprimé par les soins de N. F., n.p., 1714; Fatio, etc., *Quand vous aurez saccagé, vous serez saccagés*, n.p., 1714. These contain inspirations from December 1711 to December 1713. They were also published in Latin.

to Germany and met Petersen,[1] who, though he was not fully in agreement with their message, did not wish to reject them as false prophets. According to Petersen, two of them accepted the doctrine of universal salvation and thereafter preached the doctrine;[2] though others, he says, followed Gichtel's teaching and preached against it.

*   *   *

The religious movements and their leaders that I have described in these last three chapters were deluded, archaic and ridiculous, as much by the standards of their own time as by ours—perhaps more so. But they were one starting-point of a religious and ethical development which on the whole has been successful. Eternal torment is nowadays an unpopular doctrine among most kinds of Christians; the God of love has nearly driven out the God of vengeance; vindictive justice has had to take refuge among the advocates of hanging; and it is no longer considered repectable to enjoy the infliction of even the justest punishment. I am not asserting that we now behave or feel less cruelly, but only that we are more worried about the abominations we commit. It was the slightly crazy chiliasts—Mrs Lead, Richard Roach, the Petersens, F. M. Van Helmont, William Whiston—who publicly preached against the eternity of hell. The sane ones either spoke not at all, or anonymously, or posthumously, or dishonestly: Locke, Newton, Samuel Clarke, Thomas Burnet, Le Clerc, Sterry and White, George Rust, and probably many more disbelieved in eternal punishment, but none of them published against it in his lifetime and under his own name. The main reason for this caution or silence was certainly the general belief that society would collapse if the deterrent of eternal hell were removed. The chiliasts were aware of this danger, and made concessions to it; but they had

[1] They were in Germany (on their way from Stockholm to Constantinople) in May and June 1713 (Fatio, *Quand vous serez*, pp. 8, 78); but the meeting with Petersen may have taken place during later travels.

[2] Petersen, *Lebens-Beschreibung*, pp. 333–4. Petersen says of these two: 'Diese haben die Erkänntnisz von der Wiederbringung lauterlich eingesehen, und möchten wohl mit dem ersten à part davon zeugen, wie sie denn schreiben, dasz sie in Lesung meines Buchs von der Oeffnung des Geistes vollkommen wären überzeuget worden, dasz es aus dem Geist der Warheit geschrieben wäre.' This book of Petersen's was published in 1716.

the courage to speak out precisely because of their delusions. They had the certainty of direct inspiration from God; since they were living in the Last Days, they could risk the collapse of a society which was soon in any case to give way to a totally new one; since the Everlasting Gospel was to be a new revelation, they were able to accept the Restoration of All Things, and knew they must preach it to all nations.

INDEX

References in italics are to pages containing bibliographical indications.

INDEX

SECOND COMING, see PAROUSIA

SECRECY, 5–8, 48, 76–83, 91, 132, 144, 146, 158–62, 176–7, 182–3, 186–8, 193, 216–17, 227, 236, 247, 262

Seder Olam, *141*, 146

Serarius, Petrus, 237

Servet, Michel, 16, 74, *113*, 185

Shaftesbury, 10, 41–2, *49*, 54–5, 95, *167–8*, 169–77, 188, 255

Siegvolck, see Klein-Nikolai

Sinsart, *4*, 19, 34, 162, 164–5, 207

Slichting, Jonas, *79–80*

Smaltius, Valentin, *73*, 81–2, *84–5*

Smith, John, 105

SOCIAL EFFECTS OF HELL, see PUNISHMENT, INFERNAL, deterrent

Socini, Fausto, 73, *80–1*, *82–3*, *85*, 87

Socini, Lelio, *85*

SOCINIANISM, 4, 8–9, 16, 17, 22, 26–8, 5*i*, 67–8, 73–93, 180, 182, 184–5, 188, 190–1, 196–8, 239

Soner, Ernst, *43–4*, 66, 77, *84–5*, 86, 91–2, 216–17, 237

Spener, P. J., 231, *235*, 251

Spenser, Edmund, 115

Spinoza, 7, 41, 138, 159–60

SPIRITUAL BODY, 84, 94, 97, 100, 116, 135, 137, 161

STENCH, infernal (*see also* BRIMSTONE), 62, 136

diabolic, 239

Sterry, Peter, 9, 27, *47–8*, 53, 67, *104–5*, *106*–21, 148, 168, 196, 249, 262

STOICISM, 133–4, 137, 167, 174–6

SUFFERING

expiation by, 26–7

reformatory, 68, 139–40, 145

other people's, 30–2, 66–8, 101

as natural effect of virtue, 35, 69, 172

as natural effect of sin, 63–4, 68–9, 75, 113, 145

mental and physical (*see also* POENA DAMNI & SENSUS), 68–9

Swinden, Tobias, *39*–40, 61–2

Tarrey, John, 260

Tasso, Torquato, 115

Tauler, 236

Taylor, Jeremy, 125

Telesio, 138

Tenison, Thomas, 245–6

Tertullian, 29, *32*, 99

THEODICY, 36, 47, 53, 58, 62, 114–15, 117–19, 120, 130, 135, 146–55, 185–6, 188, 194–5, 202–13

Theosophical Transactions by the Philadelphian Society, 221, 225, 246–7, 249–50

Thomas Aquinas, *23*, 26, 29, 34, 44, 52, 61, 66

Tillotson, John, *6–7*, 94, 131, 156, 193

Titian, 115

TOLERANCE, religious, 4, 9, 78, 121, 167, 178, 183–5, 187, 220

TRANSUBSTANTIATION, 28, 100, 162

TRINITY (*see also* ARIANISM), 16–17, 26, 28, 75–6, 100, 179, 181–2, 184–5, 222, 229–30

UNIVERSAL SALVATION, 25, 33, 42, 67–70, 262–3

Arnold, 237

Conway, 8, 124, 140, 225

Coppin, 104

Gichtel, 252

Glanvill, 8, 137

Gregory of Nyssa, 20

Hallywell, 155

Helmont, 8, 124, 144, 146, 225

Huber, 261–2

Jurieu, 179

Lead, 11, 219, 222–30, 234

Le Clerc, 10, 190, 192–5

Leibniz 215–16

More, 127–8

Origen, 3, 13, 15, 18, 179, 185

Petersens, 11, 215–16, 234, 236–7, 243–4, 262

Philadelphians, 221, 246–7, 255

Roach, 260–1

Rousseau, 261–2

Rust, 9, 135

Sterry, 8, 106, 108–10, 114–15, 196

Winstanley, 104

White, 8, 50, 108–10, 114–15, 121, 260–1

Valdes, Juan de, 76

Vandyke, 115

Venice, Anabaptist Synod at, *73*–4

Virgil, 114–15

VIRTUE, disinterested, 41–2, 114, 168–77

Voidow, 78, 83–4

271